THE TRUCE

THE
TRUCE

Progressives, Centrists,
and the Future of
the Democratic Party

HUNTER WALKER
and **LUPPE B. LUPPEN**

W. W. NORTON & COMPANY
Independent Publishers Since 1923

For information about permission to reproduce selections from this book, write to Permissions, W. W. Norton & Company, Inc., 500 Fifth Avenue, New York, NY 10110

For information about special discounts for bulk purchases, please contact W. W. Norton Special Sales at specialsales@wwnorton.com or 800-233-4830

Manufacturing by Lake Book Manufacturing
Book design by Daniel Lagin
Production manager: Lauren Abbate

ISBN 978-1-324-02038-7

W. W. Norton & Company, Inc.
500 Fifth Avenue, New York, N.Y. 10110
www.wwnorton.com

W. W. Norton & Company Ltd.
15 Carlisle Street, London W1D 3BS

1 2 3 4 5 6 7 8 9 0

To Gloria, who made me the luckiest man on the face of the earth.

—H.W.

To Polly, who lights up the world.

—L.B.L.

CONTENTS

AUTHORS' NOTE

THIS BOOK IS BASED ON OVER TWO YEARS OF REPORTING AND CON-versations with key insiders at all levels of the Democratic Party, including past—and possibly future—presidential candidates, White House officials, senators, House members, local politicians, party officials, campaign consultants, and aides to all of the above. The bulk of our reporting consisted of hundreds of hours of interviews with hundreds of sources and subjects. These conversations were conducted in person, over the phone, and—with a pandemic having coincided with much of our reporting time—over Zoom. Whenever someone is quoted, unless the text says otherwise, we are quoting from original reporting based on public statements or our own interview with that person.

These conversations captured a major political party at a key turning point, facing an election that will decide whether the Democrats' victory in 2020 actually defeated the rise of Trump-fueled authoritarianism or merely managed to postpone it. Everyone we spoke to, whether they were upholding the party establishment or working against it, agreed that the stakes were immense. But despite controlling the White House and the Senate under the Biden administration,

Democrats had not settled on who will next lead them or how anyone besides the octogenarian Biden can unite the party.

Many political staffers (and even some of their bosses) were eager to share the truth, as they see it. Some were also terrified of losing their livelihoods and, as a result, reluctant to be candid on the record.

As one source who'd worked for Kamala Harris put it, "Obviously, she's the vice president, and I need to continue to work in this industry."

While we strove to push our sources to speak under their own names wherever possible, we granted requests for anonymity when we otherwise would not have been able to quote certain sources or obtain their most candid and honest assessments. Overall, we sought to learn as much as possible about the inner workings of the Democratic Party to help readers understand where it might go next.

THE TRUCE

PROLOGUE

JOE BIDEN HAS ALWAYS TRUSTED HIS GUT.

In the year leading up to the 2016 election, a campaign that would transform both major parties and the American political system, Biden knew he could win—and that his longtime senate and White House colleague Hillary Clinton could not.

But President Barack Obama, the man he had served faithfully for two terms as vice president, saw things differently. He made sure Biden got that message.

"My sense was there was every effort to have the political people around Barack Obama communicate directly to Joe Biden that this was not a smart political thing to do," a former Biden adviser said.

According to the adviser, Obama's people told Biden, "This isn't going to end well for you."

The reasons for Obama's doubts were obvious. Despite their two-term partnership, the pair were essentially political opposites. Biden had run for president twice—in 1988 and 2008—and lost. Obama, who had never run before, defeated Biden that second time after electrifying the nation with his promise of hope and change. While Obama was known for soaring rhetoric, Biden, who overcame a youthful stutter, was infamously prone to gaffes. Obama, who was in his forties when he became the first Black president, represented a new generation of leadership. Biden, already a senior citizen when the pair took office, was an old white man.

Obama saw Hillary Clinton, his former secretary of state, as a better bet than Biden. Clinton was only five years younger than Biden, and her husband was a former president. But she would have been something new for the party—the first woman in the White House—something many voters in the Democrats' base desperately wanted.

At that time, Biden's life had been rocked by a fresh tragedy. In May 2015, as the race was taking shape, Biden's oldest son, Beau, died at the age of forty-six after a battle with an aggressive form of brain cancer. Biden—who had already lost his first wife and a daughter—was known for his resilience, but this was the unimaginable. His pain was apparent in the brief public statement he issued on Beau's death. Biden called his son, "quite simply, the finest man any of us have ever known."

Biden was struggling and Obama had his own political debts to pay. While Biden had washed out of that 2008 race early, Clinton had not. Obama's charismatic, pragmatic progressivism brought together a coalition fortified by unprecedented turnout from youth and people of color. It ran headlong into the whiter, older, more institutional, and more conservative base of Clinton's support—a once-dominant wing of the Democratic Party that she and her husband had long cultivated.

Clinton battled Obama hard all the way into the summer, long after her practical pathways to the nomination had disappeared. She threatened to use delegate maneuvers and sheer will to take their battle all the way to the convention. The fight widened the gulf between the younger progressives in the party and its old guard. But as their feud started to turn truly toxic, Clinton backed down and gave Obama her support. Her endorsement that summer had been essential to unifying the party and delivering his victory. After winning the election, Obama chose to cool their rivalry by making Clinton secretary of state. The overture brought stability to his first term, but deeper tensions inside the party remained.

After two terms in office, Obama sought to return the favor by delivering a unified Democratic party to Clinton. As it turned out, party unity wasn't something he could control.

For his part, Biden had a gut feeling he could win. He also worried that Clinton—whom he liked well enough personally—could not forge a sufficiently strong bond with voters.

To most observers, Clinton seemed solid. She came into the race in April 2015 with near-universal name recognition from her time as a candidate, secretary of state, and, before that, senator from New York and First Lady. Clinton also had a pile of endorsements from the Democratic establishment and polls that firmly established her as the frontrunner by a huge margin. Months were ticking by. The first debate had already taken place. Biden's potential late entry into the race threatened to make things messy. Obama's team demanded Biden make an immediate decision.

The announcement came abruptly on October 21. Even some of Biden's top staffers only got a fifteen-minute warning. With his wife, Jill, and Obama by his side, Biden stepped out into the Rose Garden and declared he wouldn't run.

"Unfortunately, I believe we're out of time, the time necessary to mount a winning campaign for the nomination," Biden said.

Clinton became Obama's chosen successor. The sting of that moment produced lingering resentment for some on Biden's team.

"It is fair to say, and I believe it, that Joe Biden has been more politically loyal to Barack Obama than Barack Obama has been politically loyal to Joe Biden," one Biden adviser said.

When he reluctantly stepped to the sidelines, Biden became a passenger on an awful ride. He and Obama remained officially neutral during the extended primary campaign, but they watched with unease as Clinton's campaign once again faltered in the face of a surprisingly strong and divisive primary challenge from a progressive insurgent who appealed to young voters. Rather than the smooth and graceful Obama, however, Clinton found herself struggling to head off Bernie Sanders, a disheveled socialist senator from Vermont who espoused political "revolution" within the Democratic Party and promised to take down its elites.

With her political pedigree, vast personal fortune, and high-powered allies—including corporate donors and the network of consultants, advocacy groups, and officials that had long benefitted from their largesse—Clinton was the embodiment of the Big Dem establishment. It made her the perfect foil for Sanders. Voters who grew up with the frustrations of the financial crises, the growing wealth gap, and seemingly endless foreign wars that bloomed during the Bush and Obama years were drawn to Sanders's transformative politics.

Biden feared Sanders's promises to voters were unrealistic. But, more importantly, he was terrified by what was happening on the other side of the aisle. Donald Trump ran away with the Republican primary by building a cult of personality, beating up his rivals, and bashing minority groups. A demagogic real estate tycoon and TV personality, Trump rode a wave of racist reaction against Obama's presidency to prominence and then dominance in the Republican world. Once he secured the GOP nomination, Trump mounted a campaign of unrestrained savageness against Clinton.

Watching this fearsome right-wing momentum, Biden worried

that both Sanders and Clinton were ill-suited to woo the independent-minded voters needed to ward off Trump.

It took until the summer of 2016 for Clinton to secure the nomination. Along the way, a hack linked to Russian intelligence spilled the Democratic Party's internal communications into public view, revealing—in the eyes of Sanders supporters—a scandalous level of favoritism. The primary culminated with accusations of corruption and chaos at the party's convention. Faced with the threat of Trump, the Democrats were at war with one another.

When Biden returned to the trail to help with the general election campaign, he found it wasn't just the kids and die-hard Sanders supporters who had issues with Clinton. Her campaign dispatched Biden to locations she seemed to view as an afterthought. Biden could sense they were losing people.

"Biden got sent to all the Scrantons, and the Wisconsins, and the Ohios," his senior adviser Greg Schultz, recalled. "We saw all the Democrats who were upset about Hillary."

While the party relied on people of color and young people as its core base, white working-class voters were its vanguard in the swing states—the front line and the easiest group for the opposition to reach. Biden instinctually knew that the dissatisfaction fracturing the Obama coalition represented an existential threat to his party.

Clinton, famously, neglected to visit Wisconsin herself in the 2016 campaign, and wound up losing it to Donald Trump by the narrowest of margins. In the days before the election, Clinton's team had called Schultz to ask Biden to go and plant the flag there.

Biden flew out to Madison on November 4, 2016, just four days before the election. He held a rally for young voters at a theater near the University of Wisconsin campus with Senator Russ Feingold. Then he took the senator out for ice cream—a quintessential Biden touch. Back on Air Force Two, the vice president's official jet, he delivered an ominous verdict for Schultz.

"It just didn't feel right," Biden said.

No one had listened to him, and he had been underestimated by Obama, his longtime partner. Now, Biden was watching a slow-moving train wreck.

"If you're Biden, you've been in one thousand events for your own presidency, or potential presidency, or someone else's, so you can actually judge a room," Schultz said. "His gut is better than probably most polls because he's just lived it."

When the votes were counted, Biden's fears were confirmed. Disaffected Democrats who didn't show up to vote seem to have put Trump over the top. A poll of 100,000 registered voters conducted right after the election found that more who leaned Democratic stayed home than Republicans by a margin that likely would have changed the outcome.

Biden spent election night in 2016 with a small circle of advisers at the Naval Observatory, the vice president's official residence in Washington, DC. As the bitter reality of Trump's victory over Clinton became increasingly apparent, the mood turned mournful. Around 1:30 in the morning, Biden picked up the phone, called the switchboard at the White House, and asked to speak with Obama.

A source familiar with the call described their brief exchange. Biden had listened to the warnings from Obama's camp and stayed out of the race. But, apparently, Obama had not listened to the warnings from Biden.

"Boss, I told you," Biden said to Obama. "People just don't like her."

Four years later, Biden would get the chance to do it his way. Once again, he was underestimated and, once again, his political instincts proved strong. After nearly being counted out, Biden managed to surge past both Sanders and Trump to win the White House. Perhaps even more stunningly, as he took power, Biden managed to forge a truce with Sanders and the party's ascendant left flank—he achieved the party unity Obama could not bestow upon Clinton.

Yet the story of Biden's uneasy peace with progressives—a pause in the unfinished civil war of 2016—reveals the shakiness of the new Democratic alliance. While Biden managed to fend off Trump in 2020 and largely hold the line in 2022's midterms, he and his party are once again surrounded by doubts. The story of how the Democrats' warring factions came together behind Biden also reveals the existential questions the party faces going forward.

Biden, the man who finally brought the party together, is in his eighties. Neither he nor Sanders, who remains the most prominent leader of the left, have identified a clear heir. While bridges have been built between left and center, sharp divisions remain in the Democratic ranks. The party continues to feud over whether to present a transformative progressive message tuned to their base or a moderate one designed to cater to independents and have a broader appeal.

The question now is whether the current truce can hold. The Democratic Party is still struggling to find itself—and the future of the country is hanging in the balance.

Chapter 1

KALORAMA

BARACK OBAMA WAS LOOKING AT HIS LEGACY. IT WAS MARCH 25, 2019. The former president surveyed the newly elected Democratic members of Congress, face to face with the fractured, shaky future of the party he once led.

The congressional freshmen crowded in front of him were deeply divided, feuding, and facing a dangerous enemy in the White House. The group was looking to Obama for answers.

It was spring in Washington and the bright cherry blossoms that dotted the nation's capital were in peak bloom. Obama met with the new class at a home of the Democratic Party's old guard. The reception was held at the mansion of Esther Coopersmith, a doyenne of DC society for over seven decades.

Coopersmith's stately redbrick mansion was located on S Street, nestled between the Irish ambassador's residence and the Laotian embassy. Billionaire Jeff Bezos maintained a residence just up the block. This was Kalorama, the elegant neighborhood at the heart of Washington's diplomatic community, a key node in its influence ecosystem.

Unlike the many consulates, permanent missions, and organizations that dotted the leafy streets, Coopersmith's home never held an official role. Nevertheless, she had turned it into a regular gathering place for the city's most powerful and a museum of her own significance.

Coopersmith had met every modern US president since Harry S. Truman—all, that is, except the one who then held office, Trump. Signed photographs hung alongside the sumptuous oil paintings, antique vases sat atop marble mantels and mahogany tabletops. Her home had all the traditional trappings of power.

Though Coopersmith was a stalwart of the Democratic establishment, she had a bipartisan and international sense of hospitality. Over the years, her soirees have been attended by presidents, White House officials, a slew of foreign dignitaries, members of Congress, and even the infamous South Carolina segregationist Strom Thurmond. Coopersmith met everyone who was anyone in Washington, had probably invited them to her home more than once for an elegant luncheon or a relaxed dinner, and she had pictures to prove it hanging on the wall—alongside tickets for every presidential inauguration since 1961.

Coopersmith, then in her eighties, had reportedly broken into politics as a young woman in 1952 when she managed the ill-fated presidential campaign of liberal senator Estes Kefauver in Wisconsin. Two years later, Coopersmith came to Capitol Hill for a staff job. She married a wealthy lawyer and built a reputation as a Democratic fundraiser. Coopersmith went on to spend several years as a diplomat and ambassador under Presidents Carter, Reagan, and Clinton. She also earned a reputation as a hostess nonpareil. A *New York Times* profile from 1987 described Coopersmith as "one of the best at playing the Washington 'networking' game" and noted she "concedes that the real impetus for her party-giving is that she enjoys having power at her dinner table."

She was a major donor who paid for the privilege of mixing with politicians. The late senator William Proxmire, a Wisconsin Democrat, described her to the paper as "the Democratic political den mother of all fundraising."

"She really is, truly, a human catalyst," former Democratic House Speaker Nancy Pelosi once said at a birthday celebration for Coopersmith. "She just brings people together."

On this night, it was easy to see what Pelosi meant. The House freshmen stepped out of their cars in the mansion's trim forecourt, ascended the two white marble steps, strode between the tall cast-iron lampposts into Coopersmith's twenty-eight-room home, and crammed themselves into the living room with its lemon-colored walls, gold-framed mirrors, and candelabras. The centerpiece of the event wasn't Coopersmith or her lavish knickknacks, or even Pelosi, who had helped plan the evening. They were there to hear from Obama, the party's last great champion.

Near the beginning of his remarks, which we obtained in detail, Obama assured the new House members he knew what they were up against. He also acknowledged that Democrats were split on how to confront the urgent threats posed by President Donald Trump and his increasingly militant MAGA movement.

"I know that there are debates right now taking place among the presidential candidates and among the congressional candidates and all of us who care about this country about how do we confront some pretty bad stuff," Obama said. "How do we confront a resurgence of racist or misogynist attitudes? How do we confront things that we thought were no longer acceptable but have been made acceptable again?"

It was only natural the party would turn to Obama for guidance. He was one of its most politically skilled and popular leaders. Obama's rise to the presidency captivated the country and, after winning two terms, he left the White House with the approval of nearly nine out of ten Democrats.

As he addressed the intimate gathering in 2019, Obama admitted it had become a "different moment."

"The Republican Party is different," Obama said. "I don't want people to feel as if we have to harken back to what we did then in order to succeed now."

Obama's conversation with the freshmen came on a particularly rough day for the party faithful.

Shortly before Obama left office, the US intelligence community released a report showing Moscow had pushed propaganda designed to help Trump defeat Hillary Clinton. The Kremlin campaign included the email hack that inflamed the division between Democrats. In the two years since Obama's exit, distraught liberals had put their faith in Special Counsel Robert Mueller's investigation into Russian intervention in the 2016 election, holding out hope he would bring Trump down.

Mueller had delivered his final report to the Justice Department at the end of the previous week, and on the day before the dinner at Coopersmith's house, Attorney General William Barr released a brief letter summarizing it. Mueller's probe had already produced sweeping indictments of Russian officials and multiple convictions of key Trump allies. It had uncovered contacts between Trump's team and individuals linked to Russia. And it had documented myriad ways that Trump had tried to squash the investigation. However, Mueller had not found evidence that the Trump campaign conspired with the Russian government. Barr's letter—which was later revealed to be somewhat misleading—made clear that the Justice Department would not pursue charges against Trump.

Like many Democrats, Obama and his team viewed Trump as a uniquely insidious foe, not merely a political adversary but someone who might bring the whole American experiment to ruin. As Trump heedlessly broke norms in the White House, they considered what traditions they would be willing to set aside to rein him in. But even in this fevered climate, Obama made clear he hadn't lost his appetite for diplomacy.

"What I do believe is that the principle of reaching out beyond the people who completely agree with you is a good principle to follow," Obama said. "You know, as I tell sometimes when I talk to young people, if you don't talk to folks who aren't woke, they'll never wake up. You've got to be able to have some conversation with folks who don't align with you on every issue."

At this point, in March 2019, Obama had only recently come out of the political hibernation he had imposed on himself upon leaving office two years earlier. While Obama had largely left the public eye, he had stayed in Washington so that his daughters could finish school. Obama had once looked forward to a president's traditional retirement, working on the task of writing his memoirs, and letting the next president do his—or, preferably, her—job. But then Donald Trump had beaten Clinton and it complicated his plans.

Obama initially resisted the entreaties to help his fellow Democrats fight Trump. He had made all his arguments during the 2016 campaign, doing his best to summon the better angels of Americans' nature against Trump's demagoguery.

"He's betting that if he scares enough people, he might score just enough votes to win this election. And that's another bet that Donald Trump will lose," Obama had thundered during the Democrats' convention in Philadelphia. "And the reason he'll lose it is because he's selling the American people short. We're not a fragile people. We're not a frightful people."

But it was Obama who had bet wrong.

Obama's first public speech after leaving office, in April 2017, didn't once mention Trump's name. He largely avoided the midterm primaries. However, by the final months of the 2018 race, the former president had made appearances in multiple states and earned a reputation as a "closer" who could help secure victories for the Democrats.

Standing at a lectern in late October, Obama didn't need to stake out a place on the spectrum between Clinton's moderate establishment politics and Sanders's transformative reimagining of the American system. Obama could simply root for the Democrat on the general election ballot, and tout voting as the remedy for an ailing democracy.

Coupled with deep anxiety and dissatisfaction with Trump's daily parade of scandals, the late campaign appearances from Obama and his wife, Michelle (who may have been even more popular than he was at that point), helped the Democrats summon what was widely dubbed a "blue wave" that swept them into the majority in the House of Representatives.

At the Coopersmith residence in Kalorama, Obama met the new Democrats he had helped bring to power and faced their questions. His answers provided a unique glimpse into his closely guarded thinking on many of the party's core issues.

"I think that this was the most candid I had ever seen Obama, because it was a safe space," California's Katie Hill, who had handily won a race in a competitive district in Los Angeles's northern suburbs, said in an interview for this book.

Obama relished playing the party elder and cheerleader-in-chief. In front of the room alongside Pelosi, who had helped arrange the gathering and served as the master of ceremonies, he began the formal discussion of the evening by gushing to the new members, "I'm so proud of all of you."

"I think you are going to be outstanding. Not just for the remainder of this Congress, but for a long time to come," Obama said.

"And you have a really good example in the Speaker of the House," he continued. "Most of you know I love Nancy Pelosi. I mean [her husband] Paul knows it. Michelle knows it. I mean, I just love Nancy—I don't lie about it."

"I love you too," Pelosi shot back immediately.

The warm banter between the two of them sent a wave of laughter rolling through the crowd.

"Many of us had met President Obama before at various campaign events and other fundraisers or whatever, but this was definitely the most intimate setting, in somebody's living room," said Hill.

The night was Pelosi's as much as Obama's. At that time, the senior and most powerful elected Democrat in the nation, she had been in Congress since 1987—longer than some of the new members at the event had been alive. Pelosi had been Speaker once before during a stretch spanning the end of George W. Bush's presidency and Obama's first two years in office. It was a moment when the party had ridden the coattails of Obama's unique brand of celebrity to huge majorities in both houses of Congress. With that supermajority, Pelosi had wrestled the Affordable Care Act, Obama's signature health care bill, across the line.

"There is not a piece of legislation that I passed or an initiative that I was able to accomplish during the course of my presidency that [didn't] happen, in part, because of the extraordinary leadership that Nancy already showed," Obama said.

After losing the Speaker's gavel in the Tea Party–driven midterms rout Democrats suffered in 2010, Pelosi hung on as party leader for eight years in the minority. She gained the gavel back again thanks to this new group of Democrats, and she kicked the conversation off

by celebrating the fact they had made it the most diverse Congress
in history.

"Before we were fifty percent women, people of color, LGBTQ,"
Pelosi said. "With the arrival of this class we are now sixty percent
women, people of color, LGBTQ."

Pelosi had been there long before Obama, and she was still in power
years after he left office. To some Democrats, she was the lioness who
had saved Obamacare. For others, she had failed to do enough with that
rare supermajority. The left viewed her as a prime example of how the
party's aging leadership was blocking a younger generation from setting
ambitious new priorities.

Obama's choice to speak to the freshmen rather than the broader
Democratic caucus meant he wouldn't encounter any of the presidential
candidates who were already hatching campaigns in the halls of Congress that spring. A little over a month before the gathering at Coopersmith's home, Bernie Sanders had officially announced another White
House bid to "complete" the "political revolution" he had started in
2016. He would ultimately be joined in the field by five other sitting
senators as well as four House members who hoped to lead the party
against Trump.

By 2019, the question of an endorsement already hung over Obama.
Besides the many Democrats in Congress with dreams of the White
House, Obama had to consider his loyal vice president over two terms,
Joseph Robinette Biden Jr. About a week before Obama's reception
with the new members, Biden had telegraphed his own desire to run
with a slip of the tongue where he dubbed himself one of the candidates
who was "running" before correcting and reframing it as a hypothetical.

As the discussion began, Obama noted he and Coopersmith were
neighbors. Kalorama was supposed to be the site of his quiet retirement.
Obama and his wife had purchased an $8.1 million mansion of their

own shortly after signing a publishing deal that was reportedly worth over eight times that amount.

"This is a little more intimate group and my goal is not for us to have . . . speeches and sound bites but to actually have a conversation. And since this is really close to my house, we can hang out for a while," Obama quipped.

After the jokes and pleasantries, the questions began. Pelosi selected new members to stand and address the former president. They had only been sworn in about two months before, but the freshmen had already begun sorting themselves into the factions that made up the Democratic delegation.

There was the Congressional Progressive Caucus, or CPC, a large and heterogeneous collection of about one hundred left-leaning members. Others joined the New Democratic Coalition or New Dems, a similarly sized group of avowed centrists. Beyond those major ideological groups, there were racial and multiethnic organizations like the Congressional Black Caucus and the Congressional Hispanic Caucus, as well as smaller organizations like the Blue Dogs, a handful of the most conservative Democrats, and the Problem Solvers Caucus, a bipartisan group ostensibly focused on compromise.

It was the Capitol Hill equivalent of a high school lunchroom. As they joined the various groups, members needed to account for the poll numbers and preferences of the voters as much as their own personal preferences. Some were part of multiple coalitions, but there were also bitter rivalries. A member might, for example, join both the Blue Dogs and the New Dems. However, it would be hard to imagine a Blue Dog being part of the CPC.

Four of the freshmen had formed their own small group, which they called "the Squad." They were supported by an organization called Justice Democrats, which was founded by Sanders campaign alumni and dedicated to his mission of pulling the party leftward. Two of them—Alexandria Ocasio-Cortez and Ayanna Pressley—had won their seats after defeating powerful establishment incumbents. In the months since their primaries, the quartet had sparred noisily with party leaders while generating a maelstrom of media attention. Pelosi had a particularly fraught relationship with the group. While they were not necessarily following her lead, perhaps they might listen to Obama.

The first questions for the former president came from the center. Michigan's Haley Stevens and Texas's Colin Allred, a pair of New Dems who were presidents of the freshman class and had both served in Obama's administration, stepped up and asked how the party could maintain a "positive" message while taking on Trump. It was a fraught, fundamental question that indicated just how much Democrats were struggling to find their footing.

Obama admitted that it was a "different era" from his time in office and encouraged the pair to reach out to people with different views.

But, Obama said: "You don't have to sing 'Kumbaya' and pretend to paper over differences. You don't have to chase a phony bipartisanship that somehow—if we just split the difference between sane and crazy—that somehow, we're better off."

Nor did Obama think Democrats should adopt Trump's smashmouth rules.

"This idea that somehow, we can give as good as we get, I think, is a losing proposition. Because when we get that nasty and dishonest and make up stuff . . . unmoored from facts, that's playing in their field," Obama said.

Obama had direct experience with the sitting president's malice. Trump's transition from Page Six to presidential politics owed a great deal to his promotion of the racist and thoroughly debunked "birther" conspiracy theory, which held that Obama was actually born in Africa and, as a result, disqualified from the White House. The Republican Party's media ecosystem had stoked its audience's rage with racial and cultural resentment during Obama's time in office. Trump was the distilled expression of that anger.

Obama implied that race was at least part of why he, as a Black man, would not be able to practice Trump's angry and factually challenged brand of governance.

"Like I couldn't do what the guy in office currently does. . . . It's not just an issue that I couldn't get away with it, it's that—that's not who I am," explained Obama. "Don't fall into the trap of thinking that being tough involves being mean. Don't fall into the trap of thinking that being effective means that you have to set aside some core values that help get you here."

Then, Hill spoke. Fresh off an approximately nine-point victory against a Republican incumbent, she, like many of those in the room who needed independent and moderate voters to win, was worried about young people who demanded Democrats take a more aggressive, progressive approach.

"We've seen a gap of young people voting for Democrats by thirty-five points and we've seen historic turnout among young people in this past election," Hill began, adding: "But also, there are many of us who flipped districts in these more conservative seats, so when you're talking about progressive policies . . . that mobilize and inspire young people, they don't always align with those that might be the ones . . . you're most inclined to support if you're in a red to blue seat. So, I am just wondering if you had any thoughts on kind of balancing that."

Hill, who had been seen as a rising star by the party's establishment, would later become a vivid example of how some members of the party were seeking to hold their behavior to the higher standard Obama was advocating.

The issue wasn't limited to Trump's coarse language and many ethical lapses. At the time, society was in the midst of a broader reckoning. The MeToo movement that began with high-profile sexual assault and harassment cases in Hollywood was spreading to misconduct in government as well. During the Trump era, Democrats sought to cast themselves as the party that respects and believes women and lives by a higher standard of behavior. However, they also found taking the high road came with a political toll. In late 2017, Minnesota senator Al Franken, a popular figure among the Democratic base, stepped down after he faced accusations from multiple women. Franken's case played out abruptly and he would later say he wished that he had stuck around to see through an investigation of the claims against him, some of which were called into question by subsequent reporting. That feeling was shared by some Democratic politicians and wistful supporters.

Seven months after the night in Kalorama, Katie Hill herself would resign amid allegations she had inappropriate relationships with multiple staffers. Her choice to leave amid controversy rather than holding on to her seat and fighting off the scandal was driven in part by a desire to maintain the image of a Democratic Party that had more stringent ethical standards than their opponents.

"I didn't wanna give any other fodder to the motherfuckers on the other side," Hill said of her decision to resign.

Hill's story showed the price Democrats could pay for pursuing Obama's high-minded politics. Following her exit, the district flipped back to the Republicans.

In Ms. Coopersmith's ballroom, Obama responded to Hill's question by urging the freshmen to focus on hands-on leadership, and providing direct services. He related that the number-one suggestion of his first Senate chief of staff, the veteran Capitol Hill hand Pete Rouse, was to answer the mail from constituents.

"Somebody sent you here to do a job and you have to respond to them," Obama said. "You work for them. You don't work for CNN. You don't work for Twitter. You work for them. And that, I think, is a useful thing to remember."

Obama heard in Hill's question a genuine anxiety about how freshmen in purple districts might hold their seats. He warned them against being overly preoccupied with their poll numbers.

"Don't operate out of fear. One of [the] things that I was surprised about when I got here is, I'd met people who fought really hard to get into the Senate and they were afraid of their own shadow," he said, recalling senators he'd seen who were constantly hedging in light of their reelection prospects. "There has to be a time at which you're actually going to do something that you care about. And if it's significant then it means that . . . there are going to be some people who don't like it."

Growing philosophical, Obama advised that, for a politician, "the vanity of holding office should burn away fairly quickly; it's not lasting, it's insubstantial" compared to holding onto one's convictions and delivering for one's constituents.

In other words, they weren't in Washington simply to enjoy the perks of political notoriety.

"Remember why you got here and don't start thinking that the reason you want to stay here is because you got a pin on, and you got an office, you're on TV once in a while. First of all, nobody watches cable TV . . . ordinary people aren't reading Politico. If you want to be famous, go to Hollywood. Do something, you know, be a celebrity for the sake of being a celebrity. But it's not worth all the sacrifice your family makes; it's not worth calling donors—" Obama said, allowing a burst of laughter and applause from the young politicians to drown the end of that sentence.

Obama was reminding the members they were elected to perform a public service.

"All that stuff is only worth it if there's something that, at the end of the day, you feel like, 'Man, I'm proud of that, I know that helped somebody, I know that made the country better,'" he said.

As for the young voters that Hill had fretted about, Obama pointed out they "have a pretty good nose for who's in it for the right reasons and who's sincere." However, even as he urged the freshmen to be heartfelt, Obama admitted they can't entirely ignore political realities.

"I want to make sure that I'm not having all of you . . . go in front of the Capitol and set yourself on fire," Obama said. "You guys are also politicians and . . . you are obligated to think through how you can be effective. And for me, at least, the way I always used to think about it was that I would never compromise on my core positions, but I think strategically and tactically about 'How do I advance them?' and 'How do I talk about them?'"

As an example, Obama pointed to a maneuver from early on in his White House tenure. During his historic "HOPE" campaign in 2008, he had vowed to end the military's "Don't Ask, Don't Tell" policy, a compromise with the right made by President Bill Clinton that banned gay people from serving openly in the armed forces. Obama told the story of how he strategically took a slower path to that promise.

Ending "Don't Ask, Don't Tell" was "important" to him, he said, but he also worried it could be controversial. Obama described bringing together members of his cabinet to come up with a plan.

"So, I brought Bob Gates, the then defense secretary, and I told him, I said 'Look, we're going to end 'Don't Ask, Don't Tell,' but I recognize this is a transition that folks have to wrap their heads around, so how are we going to do this?'" Obama recalled. "Then I got the Joint Chiefs, and essentially Jeh Johnson who was an extraordinary lawyer

and African American who was general counsel over at the Pentagon . . . came up with the idea of, look, let's do like a year-long survey of
all the troops and find out how are they thinking."

The survey bought time. It also undermined a core argument from
opponents who had argued soldiers would be uncomfortable serving with
gay colleagues. The survey results helped give Obama the political capital
to end "Don't Ask, Don't Tell" two years into his first term. Speaking to
the new members, Obama framed the story as an example of how Democrats needed to find a "balance" between progressivism and pragmatism.

"I just want to make sure that you heard the point. The key point
is, you have to be principled. That doesn't mean you have to be absolut-
ist. That doesn't mean you have to be impatient. That doesn't mean you
have to be sanctimonious with your fellow Democrats," Obama said.

Lauren Underwood, a progressive who had taken out an established incumbent in the midterms, was up next. Her question returned
to one of the more pressing puzzles facing the party: young voters.

Voters under thirty overwhelmingly back Democrats, which
should theoretically cement a major advantage for the party. However,
older voters are far more likely to show up to the polls. Turnout rates
for the younger demographic are typically at least 10 percent lower than
they are for those above the mark. There are similar trends among voters
of color. Overall, the dynamic has made voter engagement something
of a holy grail for Democrats.

Those younger voters who did come out had been showing far more
enthusiasm for Sanders and the new wave of progressives. They also
had a sharp hunger for social justice and for increased equity for people of different races, religions, national backgrounds, sexualities, and
gender identities. Even some proponents of the progressive economic
agenda were wary of the identity issues and cultural concerns some
younger activists saw as urgent priorities. Embracing the needs of the

new generation risked potentially turning off more moderate voters or falling prey to Republicans eager to paint new political correctness and gender equality as a dangerous ideology.

When Underwood asked Obama for his "thoughts about engaging young people," the former president responded that there is "power in people just being seen and recognized."

"When we lose them, it's because they don't feel seen and they don't feel heard," he added.

Obama then harkened back to his roots as a community organizer.

"When I used to organize, one of the basic principles was, before you ask people to do something, no matter what it is, try listening to them first. Try. It's a magical thing. You take the time to listen to other people. Find out what is on their minds, find out what their issues are but, more importantly, find out what their stories are, right?" Obama said. "Because we have a story inside us that's sacred about how we see the world and meaning and our deepest values."

Obama also shared an anecdote from his first presidential race.

"One of the reasons my campaign back in '08 did well with young people: It wasn't just that I was young; we just put them in charge. We were all like, okay you figure this out. Go," Obama said. "So, they come to the office, yeah there [was] grunt work but there was also 'Oh, we're just going to drop you off in the middle of a cornfield, and you figure out how all those people are going to end up caucusing for Obama.' "

Rather than giving young staffers a "script," Obama said his campaign encouraged them to "just go talk to people and listen to them and find out what they care about." He made the case that being "predisposed to the power of those young people" and listening to them was how Democrats should operate on the Hill in between elections, as well as on the trail.

"That's true in campaigns, I think that's true as a party. That should be true in your office, by the way," said Obama.

Obama broke down the math that made young voters such a vital target for Democrats. Most Americans support the party's platform of reproductive rights, increased access to health care, gun control, and gay rights. It's just a question of who's actually motivated to vote.

"You're not going to get one hundred percent involved. It's never going to happen. But as all of you, I think, are aware, if you get a ten percent boost in the youth vote in the next election or in your district, then it is basically a different match," Obama explained. "This is not a fifty-fifty country. This is a sixty-forty country except older folks vote more. And our folks are distracted, discouraged, disempowered, and so we have to work to make them feel included and empowered. But if we do, they'll respond."

Obama was one of the few Democrats among his contemporaries who managed to captivate both young voters and older ones. As he talked to the freshmen at the Coopersmith mansion, he showed why he had been so good at bridging the party's many gaps. Obama could be both the progressive candidate who ran on hope and the enthusiasm of young Americans and the sober, sensible pragmatist who steered a safe course. In the years since his departure, the party had struggled to find a similarly unifying figure.

The next question came from Conor Lamb, who had been elected to Congress in a special election in March 2018. In an interview for this book, Lamb said he was caught "off guard" since Pelosi "cold-called" on him rather than letting him know he would be part of the event. And, like many of the new members in the room, he was somewhat awed by Obama.

"He was someone I really admired, obviously," Lamb said of Obama, adding, "This is a personal thing, . . . you know, when I was a

Marine officer, he was the commander in chief. . . . I just always looked
up to him."

Lamb's rise was held up as proof that a more moderate version of
the Democratic Party could deliver swing districts. He won an upset in
Western Pennsylvania, a hotly contested swath of a key battleground
state filled with shuttered steel mills and white working-class voters
who had ditched Democrats to back Trump. Those voters fascinated the
political press, as did Lamb. He was cast by pundits as living proof the
arguments espoused by Sanders and Ocasio-Cortez, and her progressive Squad, were losers on the national level. Lamb had won his seat by
presenting himself as a pro-gun and not-necessarily-pro-abortion independent who was against increasing the minimum wage and opposed
Sanders's vision for a single-payer health care system.

Over the next two years, Lamb would increasingly get drawn
into arguments with progressives. A little over a year later, Ocasio-
Cortez called him out by name in an interview where she criticized
his campaign strategies. Lamb fired back by suggesting her strident
progressivism was "damaging" in swing states. By 2021, Lamb was
running for Senate against a more progressive opponent, John Fetterman, and telling reporters he would not accept any endorsement
from Sanders. Fetterman ultimately won their race.

Yet, as he questioned Obama, Lamb said he was eager to focus
on common ground between the warring wings of the party. He
asked if Obama could offer advice on how to "focus" on policies like
social security.

"You know people in Western Pennsylvania, at least, overwhelmingly
asked about the same things over and over again: social security, Medicare, prescription drug prices. It is kind of amazing to come down here
and see how many other issues get put on the table day to day," Lamb said.

Expanding social security was an area where Lamb and the left were in agreement. He and Sanders were co-chairs of a caucus dedicated to the issue. At the moment he brought it up to Obama, Lamb said he was eager to see the policy—and economic concerns more broadly—become a central part of Democrats' public engagement.

"I felt like our day-to-day legislative focus was not very concrete and economic as far as the things that we were offering," Lamb recounted later on. "It may have been just because the Trump vortex made it impossible for us to set the agenda. But I think at the time I was hungry to see Democrats set an agenda that was not about Trump and that was more about the people we were representing in their basic economic concern."

Obama responded by acknowledging the larger debate Lamb had waded into.

"I will say—just a little bit editorializing—because I know there has been this discussion about—in the Democratic party, there's like super, super progressives versus the moderately progressive. And then there's the somewhat conservative progressives. Everybody wants progress," Obama began.

Obama continued by saying social security was an area where Democrats should be willing to make the kind of fundamental changes to the economic system that progressives clamored for.

"I think people feel deeply insecure about the economy right now in all sorts of ways despite the fact that we've got a great economy, relatively speaking. . . . I mean I left a really good economy but . . . we didn't fix some of the core structure stuff that is part of making people feel insecure. The wages still don't go up as fast as profits do. Inequality continues to rise," said Obama. "And so, I think it's important for us to protect things like social security that people care about, and they feel is like a lifeline for them. But I think it's entirely appropriate for us to try and reimagine what some of our social arrangement institutions are and update them for this new economy."

Even as Obama embraced the left's concerns about economic inequality, he trotted out the standard centrist rebuttal to the progressive agenda, that they had no way to fund their ambitious ideas. Obama said the voters in places like Lamb's district don't "believe in free lunch" and, if you're proposing to have the government give them something, they "kind of want to know 'well, how are you going to pay for it?'"

Progressives like Sanders and Ocasio-Cortez reject the suggestion they can't fund their proposals. Raise taxes on the wealthy and cut the defense budget, they argue, and the government will find it has abundant revenue to fund expanded social programs.

But Obama was zeroing in on a core component of those Pennsylvanians' stories. Those voters, he said, "have a responsibility gene"—one, Obama added, "that apparently doesn't apply to the folks who create trillion-dollar deficits."

It was likely a lightly veiled shot at Trump and Republicans in Congress, whose ambitious tax cuts—which were not offset by any reduction in outlays—had swollen the federal deficit by nearly 17 percent in the previous fiscal year, and would top a trillion dollars a year before the next presidential election. Of course, those Republicans would probably point out that Obama ran up some trillion-dollar deficits himself in the early years of his presidency.

Still, Obama deployed the Republican excesses as a cautionary tale for progressives.

"We have to think practically about how we imagine these big ideas, we have to think about how to pay for them," Obama said, adding, "None of us as Democrats should be afraid of big, bold ideas. But we should also hold ourselves accountable to think of the nitty-gritty of how those big bold ideas are going to work."

Obama also warned that even staunchly progressive voters might not "automatically sign on" if they were told a given policy would raise their taxes substantially.

The nuanced discourse at Esther Coopersmith's ballroom was typical of the forty-fourth president, who had joked early on in the reception about his "bad habit of giving too long of answers." As the one-time candidate of "hope," his remarks were, at the very least, sympathetic to the concerns of the left and their youthful base.

But a source who worked with the Squad said the group of progressive freshmen viewed the session with Obama as a "chastising." According to the source, the Squad members who were able to attend were "excited" to see Obama, who won the White House in 2008 as a progressive taking on the establishment. They left the room feeling let down by Obama's remarks, much as they did with his time in office.

"They felt like parts of it were targeted at the Squad and trying to get them to settle down," the source said. "It was disappointing. . . . Candidate Obama was who they were looking for, but second-term Obama showed up."

Despite his best efforts to stay above the fray, even Obama, the master tactician, was finding himself caught in the party's divisive new dynamics. DC's newest Democrats had come to Esther Coopersmith's mansion that night consumed by questions. Could they beat Trump? What was the path towards winning over young voters without losing purple states? How should they strike a balance between aspirational, transformational politics and cold, hard realities?

On that night in Kalorama, Obama attempted to give them a road map. He had a deep-seated desire to unify the party to unseat his successor, Trump. However, his answers hadn't sold everyone in the room. Which led to the biggest question of all: If Obama, the party's most magnetic leader, was not able to articulate a way forward, then who could?

Obama departed into the soft air of the spring evening, returning to his writing desk and his memoirs. The House freshmen filed out to an uncertain future. For now, this was Trump's Washington, the damage Democrats inflicted on themselves in 2016 remained unhealed, and the leader of hope and change had left the next generation to sort out the party's future on its own.

Chapter 2

JUSTICE DEMOCRATS

BERNIE SANDERS WANTED A "REVOLUTION." HE ENDED UP SPARK-ing a civil war inside the Democratic Party.

When the Vermont senator launched his first presidential bid in April 2015, he said it was designed to take on two major targets; the "immoral" and "unsustainable" economic system where "the top one percent owns almost as much wealth as the bottom ninety percent" and a "political situation where billionaires are literally able to buy elections and candidates."

Sanders knew his mission was dicey. At his very first announcement, he openly wondered whether it would even be possible for a candidate who railed against the rich and corporations to succeed in a time when presidential campaigns typically cost over a billion dollars and relied on wealthy backers. Sanders also alluded to the fact that, as an avowed socialist and the longest serving independent in Congress, he was operating outside of the two-party system that had dominated American elections for over a century.

"You are looking at a guy—indisputably—who has the most

unusual political history of anybody in the United States Congress," Sanders said to the small throng of reporters and curious onlookers who came to see his first announcement on a lawn outside the US Capitol.

However, the idea that a grumpy socialist in rumpled suits who relied on small-dollar donors could catch fire and shock the country's corporate establishment turned out not to be the most audacious aspect of Sanders's campaign. Sanders, who had caucused with the Democrats since he entered the Senate in 2007 but was not technically a party member, was trying to wrest the Democratic nomination from the party's leadership without throwing a punch.

At his announcement, the reporters pressed Sanders to criticize Hillary Clinton, who was widely seen as President Obama's chosen successor and the choice of the party elite. Sanders declined. He stressed that he detested "ugly thirty-second ads and vigorous personal attacks."

"I believe that, in a democracy, what elections are about are serious debates over serious issues, not political gossip, not making campaigns into soap operas," Sanders said.

Despite starting with those lofty aspirations, less than eight months later, before the voting even had begun, the Sanders campaign was feuding with Clinton's camp and the Democratic National Committee over debate scheduling and access to voter data. One late 2015 dispute saw the party committee lock Sanders's team out of some of its own files. The move led Sanders's campaign manager, Jeff Weaver, to hold a fiery press conference where he declared the "Democratic establishment" was engaged in "a heavy-handed attempt to undermine this campaign" in order to have a "coronation" for Clinton.

Amid the conflicts, Sanders put aside his initial reluctance to engage in arguments outside of the policy realm. Once the primary voting began in the first months of 2016, Clinton pulled ahead and Sanders himself described the race as unfair. He suggested that the DNC chair, Florida congresswoman Debbie Wasserman Schultz, needed to be removed and that the party needed to change its direction.

"Frankly, what the Democratic Party is about is running around to rich people's homes and raising obscene sums of money from wealthy people," Sanders said in a late May 2016 interview with CBS. "What we need to do is to say to working-class people—we are on your side."

Sanders had also begun to attack Clinton more directly. He criticized her on issues of criminal justice, on economics, on her past remarks that he said were "racist"—a strategic shift his advisers credited with achieving his late victories, particularly in Michigan, and prolonging the primary. Clinton fired right back.

The fight cracked a deep rift down the middle of the Democratic Party that led to ugly scenes at the national convention in July 2016. An email hack linked to Russian intelligence spilled the DNC's private communications into public view just ahead of that gathering, where Sanders was set to formally cede the nomination to Clinton. The trove of messages revealed Wasserman Schultz and her aides mocking Sanders's team, rejecting an offer to schedule an extra debate, and considering sending reporters negative narratives about Sanders's campaign operation. Sanders supporters reacted by staging loud protests outside the venue and on the convention floor.

Sanders ultimately lost the nomination to Clinton. However, his political revolution didn't entirely end in defeat. Under pressure from the scandal, Wasserman Schultz resigned as the convention began. The party's new leadership acceded to several reforms proposed by Sanders and his allies.

In the general election, Donald Trump, a businessman and reality TV star who ran on racially charged attacks on immigrants and minorities, took advantage of the Democrats' infighting to eke out a narrow victory over Clinton.

Exit polls from multiple news organizations indicated roughly nine out of ten Republicans voted for Trump and roughly nine out of ten Democrats voted for Clinton. In a starkly polarized nation, there was very little crossover. This landscape meant the infighting on the left was likely decisive. The division persisted after Trump took office.

Unlike the Republicans, who emerged from the cataclysmic campaign as, unquestionably, the party of Trump, Democrats came out of 2016 defeated and adrift. Trump's win had effectively prevented the race from being a definitive referendum on whether Clinton's politics or Sanders's should guide the party in the post-Obama era.

With the future of the party in question and the progressive movement galvanized by Sanders's run, a wave of socialist candidates staged their own battles against Democratic incumbents in the midterm elections two years later. Their most dramatic victory came in New York when Alexandria Ocasio-Cortez, who had been a volunteer on Sanders's 2016 campaign, took down a Democratic Party boss.

Ocasio-Cortez was not entirely a political neophyte. Before working on Sanders's race, she interned for the late Massachusetts senator Ted Kennedy, the old liberal lion of New England. However, her insurgency didn't start with Kennedy or even with Sanders.

It began with her little brother.

———

GABRIEL OCASIO-CORTEZ ENJOYED LISTENING TO PROGRESSIVE COMmentators on YouTube. As the left reeled from Sanders's 2016 primary loss and Donald Trump's subsequent victory in the general election, Gabriel watched two prominent digital rabble-rousers, Cenk Uygur and Kyle Kulinski, co-found a new political action committee: Justice Democrats. The group was explicitly designed to carry on Sanders's mission by recruiting progressive candidates who would reject corporate donations, primary incumbent Democrats, and shift Congress to the left. Gabriel latched onto the idea and nominated his sister for the project.

At the time, Alexandria Ocasio-Cortez was in the midst of a quarter-life transition. She'd graduated from Boston University and returned to New York City stuck in neutral, living in her mom's old apartment in the Bronx while serving cocktails at a bar in Manhattan. But she was, as anyone who met her could see, a superstar—brilliant, beautiful, engaging, and relatable. All she needed was a spark.

Corbin Trent, who was one of Justice Democrats' leaders and would go on to join Ocasio-Cortez's staff, remembered Gabriel's nomination.

"It got noticed," Trent said, in an interview for this book.

Justice Democrats fell short in several respects. They fielded far fewer candidates than they had initially hoped and lost almost all their races. Nevertheless, their impact was massive. Ocasio-Cortez won her race. Along with her, the organization also helped elect three other House members—Ilhan Omar, Rashida Tlaib, and Ayanna Pressley. The quartet joined together to form the progressive "Squad." With just those four victories, Justice Democrats had unquestionably transformed Congress.

Like the candidates they hoped to elect, the leaders of Justice Democrats came from unusual backgrounds. Along with Uygur and Kulinski, the group's founders included Zack Exley and Saikat Chakrabarti, who met while working for Sanders in 2016. The two campaign aides had started another group, Brand New Congress, as it was becoming clear that Sanders would lose to Clinton. By March 2017, they brought that organization into Justice Democrats.

The group's operations were led by Chakrabarti, Exley, and Trent. The three had met on Sanders's "distributed organizing" team, which used digital tools to encourage volunteers to knock doors and make phone calls.

Trent was a self-described "semi-right-winger from East Tennessee." He initially captured the attention of Sanders's team with cash.

"We had donation data for Bernie. And for the longest time, Corbin was one of four or five people that maxed out," recalled Chakrabarti, who was already working for the campaign. "So, we just assumed he was this super-rich heir of some southern billionaire or something."

That assumption turned out to be a mistake. Trent had grown up just outside the Smoky Mountains and worked in a factory that made furniture parts. That job vanished in the wake of the recession, along with so much of the region's manufacturing industry. Trent tried to reinvent himself as a trained chef. He went to New York for culinary school and ended up working in some of the most exclusive restaurants in the city and its suburbs.

Trent only had a casual interest in politics, but serving outrageously expensive cuisine to indifferent diners instilled in him a seething class rage. His tipping point came when he poured a thousand-dollar bottle of pinot noir only to watch it go to waste.

"It's one of my favorite grapes, one of my favorite wines, one of my favorite regions," Trent said, his drawl speeding into a staccato. "I'm kind of excited about it. I'm telling them about it all.... Then, when I'm clearing the table after a few hours, I notice they didn't even fucking take a sip of this wine."

He soon quit his job and returned home to open a food truck. When Trent came back to Tennessee, he found a community that had "collapsed." Many of his friends and family were using opiates to fill the holes left by the economic downturn. The pill demon would eventually climb onto his back too. Yet as Sanders caught on around the country, Trent saw reasons for hope and threw himself into the campaign.

"When Bernie showed up, he was living in a trailer," Chakrabarti said of Trent. "He sold his food truck ... and basically just used the savings to start driving around Tennessee, just organizing Tennessee, whatever he could do."

Chakrabarti had assumed Trent's money flowed from a family fortune, but it was just earned selling street food.

Unlike Trent, Zack Exley actually had political experience prior to working for Sanders. A tall, slender man with windblown white hair, Exley had a résumé that included work on John Kerry's 2004 White House run and at the progressive organization MoveOn.org. But even as he moved within the more traditional apparatus, Exley longed to subvert it. According to Trent, Exley was "like this mad scientist dreamer" who had pitched the idea of a congressional insurrection within the Democratic Party for years.

Exley had just needed a backer. Now, he had found one. Chakrabarti was a multimillionaire, a coder who left Silicon Valley to hack the political system.

The son of Bengali immigrants, Chakrabarti grew up in Texas. His grandfather was a professor whose work as an engineer at a nuclear power plant paved the family's path to America. Chakrabarti went to Harvard, where he studied computer science.

After school, Chakrabarti made his way to a hedge fund and, ultimately, to the West Coast where he started his own company before becoming the founding engineer at Stripe, a payments-processing firm. That made him one of the first few employees to earn equity at a business that's valued at over $50 billion as of this writing.

For Chakrabarti, the startup world was "amazing" because he could create something and see a real impact.

"I'm never going to downplay how much I enjoyed working at Stripe or doing my own company because it's so much fun to build stuff," Chakrabarti explained. "You feel like you're doing something that's helpful."

But while he liked starting businesses, Chakrabarti didn't necessarily enjoy running them. As he put it in an interview, "I wasn't really the guy to figure out like, you know, corporate culture and how to do management correctly and all that stuff."

However, after Chakrabarti founded Justice Democrats in the wake of Sanders's defeat, he and his colleagues would soon be managing a dozen political campaigns all at once.

IN EARLY 2017, AS DONALD TRUMP WAS REMAKING THE RIGHT IN HIS own image, Justice Democrats set out to build a new left. From its headquarters in Corbin Trent's home state, Tennessee, the group began trying to build a progressive alternative to the consulting firms, advocacy groups, and alphabet soup of committees at the heart of the Democratic Party apparatus.

With Brand New Congress, Trent, Exley, and Chakrabarti initially sought to back an army of about four hundred candidates who would run for almost every seat in the House.

"We were trying to run in every primary," Chakrabarti said. "We were going to run people as Republicans, as Democrats, Independents."

The trio wanted to leverage multiple races to solve what they called the "spotlight problem"—the challenge of getting voters to pay attention outside of a presidential election year. Compared to the high-wattage, eleven-figure frenzy of the presidential election, local and congressional elections are often dimly lit affairs, plagued by low interest and low turnout. Chakrabarti and his team were hoping that operating a slate of hundreds of candidates could turn congressional elections into a similarly big, captivating campaign. Attention was vital because they hoped to counter incumbents backed by the establishment donor network and expensive ads with digital organizing tools like the ones Sanders pioneered and a full-court media press.

"I think those are the only two things that matter," Trent said.

As Chakrabarti told Rachel Maddow in a 2016 interview, Brand New Congress would be "a single, unified, presidential-style campaign that's going to look a lot like the Bernie Sanders campaign." Like Sanders, they were hoping to galvanize an army of small-dollar donors.

It was a grandiose dream that would have to be scaled back multiple times. Their first wake-up call came when the group discovered that, amid the hyperpolarization of the Trump era, they could make no inroads into conservative areas. As the trio of strategists brought Brand New Congress under the umbrella of Justice Democrats, they abandoned the plan to take on the couple hundred staunchly red seats in Congress.

Instead, they narrowed the focus to blue districts, but Justice Democrats still thought they might be able to recruit hundreds of primary challengers. Armed with funding and resources from the organization, these progressive champions would primary "corporate Democrats," hoping to knock them out, win the general election, and establish a beachhead for the left on Capitol Hill.

The group was collecting nominations, meeting with candidates, and bringing the most promising recruits together at weekly retreats. These gatherings were held in Frankfort, Kentucky, where a Sanders campaign alum who volunteered for Justice Democrats, Mary Nishimuta, ran a coffee shop.

"She had space," Chakrabarti explained.

Chakrabarti described the multistep vetting process as "grueling as hell." In the end, though Justice Democrats would endorse over seventy House hopefuls in the 2018 midterms, they decided to cut back their ambitions again and focus on working with a dozen of the most promising prospects. It was the number they had ready to go when money—and time—started to run out.

"We couldn't keep funding doing those retreats," Chakrabarti said. "So we had what we had, and started basically announcing campaigns in the summer of 2017 because we didn't want to get to a point where we're at the end of 2017 and we haven't even launched a campaign yet."

Ocasio-Cortez would later say attending a Justice Democrats retreat in Frankfort convinced her to run for Congress. But not every candidate that the group wanted to back was committed. Justice Democrats didn't wait for them to pull the trigger.

According to one source, the activists at Justice Democrats filed declarations of candidacy with the Federal Election Commission without authorization from the candidates in question—forms that they falsely represented as signed by those candidates.

This certainly seems to have happened at least in the case of Ocasio-Cortez, since public records show that she filed in one district and then filed in a different district five days later.

"We filed Ocasio's paperwork to run against Serrano initially in New York," Trent said, referring to Jose Serrano, the member of Congress then representing the state's Fifteenth District.

Serrano was hardly an ideal opponent for her. Like Ocasio-Cortez, he was Puerto Rican and an icon of that community. The pair were also both to the left of the Democratic establishment. Serrano was one of the most reliably progressive House members, and, for that reason, never a figure in Democratic leadership.

An FEC filing made for Ocasio-Cortez to campaign against Serrano on May 10, 2017, confirms Trent's account. Ocasio-Cortez was ready to run, but she had her own idea about where to fight. Her paperwork was refiled in the Fourteenth District five days later, on May 15, 2017. She had set her sights on a far more natural enemy—Joe Crowley.

Chapter 3

THE PEOPLE'S REPUBLIC OF QUEENS

WITH HIS BARREL CHEST, RUDDY-FACED GRIN, AND THIN REM-nants of blond hair, Joe Crowley was the prototypical glad-handing political jock. But, other than appearances at parades and in back rooms, he had little presence on the ground in the parts of Queens and the Bronx that he represented. Nevertheless, he was a local party boss and a formidable figure in Washington.

As chairman of the House Democratic Caucus, Crowley was fifth in line in the party's leadership structure and a contender to succeed Nancy Pelosi as Speaker of the House one day. Crowley was also entrenched in New York City's power structure as chair of the Queens County Democratic organization, the local party apparatus that held sway over political offices and appointments in the borough.

The county party was one of the final vestiges of the old boss and machine system that powered the city's infamous Tammany Hall years. Crowley had an uncle, aunt, and cousin who also had positions in the local government.

The circumstances of his first election to Congress show the machine in action. By 1998, Crowley had spent a decade in the New York State Assembly when the sitting congressman, Thomas Manton, who had already filed paperwork to run for reelection, abruptly announced his retirement.

At the time, Manton was chair of the Queens County Democratic Party, which means he ran the committee that would select his replacement. Crowley was his handpicked successor. By dropping out at the last minute, literally one day before the deadline, Manton had blocked anyone else from running for the open seat. Crowley's name replaced Manton's on the ballot. The maneuver led to criticisms from the local press and politicians on both sides of the aisle, but Crowley won without much contest and was effectively installed in Congress. Soon after, Crowley assumed the Queens County chairmanship.

Crowley was emblematic of the aging leadership and anti-democratic party structures progressives often blamed for blocking popular reforms. He was also out of step with the changing face of the district. Manton and Crowley both had the Irish roots that were predominant in Queens and the Bronx for much of the last century. Yet, in more recent times, the area had seen an influx of immigrants from Africa, South Asia, and Latin America. The streets of the district teemed with halal butchers, South American food carts, and Caribbean restaurants. These new residents needed access to better health care, jobs, and an immigration system that worked—and they wanted leadership that looked more like them.

While Crowley and his traditionally moderate politics were becoming a bad fit for the district, he was still a fearsome rival. He had a million-dollar war chest and alliances with officials and unions who could put boots on the ground for him in a primary race.

Justice Democrats provided Ocasio-Cortez with impetus and

infrastructure, but their capabilities were limited—particularly with a dozen candidates around the country. The group's Tennessee headquarters was nearly a twelve-hour drive from Ocasio-Cortez's district. She initially pounded the pavement herself, weaving in and out of brown brick apartment buildings and elevated train tracks without professional staff by her side.

"I was bartending. I was going out in my community. The very first canvass that I did was out of a Trader Joe's bag," Ocasio-Cortez said to an audience of college students a year later.

For all her modesty, Ocasio-Cortez proved a solid strategist. She had identified Crowley's central weakness—he did not live in the district and owned a home in the DC suburbs with his wife and daughters. At local events and forums, Ocasio-Cortez blasted Crowley as disconnected and in thrall to corporate donors.

Back in Tennessee, some of the Justice Democrats' leaders were beginning to see unusual promise for her race. Few people outside of the organization believed Crowley could be seriously challenged. A relatively sleepy race usually favors the incumbent. But Ocasio-Cortez's backers saw low turnout as a potential asset.

"We don't gotta move that many people," Trent said of the race. "The win number was so low."

Eventually, Justice Democrats dispatched a veteran of the Sanders campaign, Waleed Shaheed, to join Ocasio-Cortez in September 2017.

Their first meeting was at a café in Union Square that had a long line to get in.

"And so I pointed to a restaurant across the street that looked empty and I was like, why don't we just go there?" Shaheed said in an interview for this book.

Ocasio-Cortez declined.

"Oh, I, uh, work there," she replied sheepishly.

It was the site of her now-famous job as a bartender. She was meeting her first staffer between shifts.

Even while working a day job, Ocasio-Cortez threw herself into the race. She initially struck Shaheed as highly motivated but new to the mechanics of campaigning.

"She was just learning a lot," he said.

A quick study, Ocasio-Cortez displayed a clear knack for messaging. The budding candidate was "doing her own oppo" and eager to share her own research about her chosen opponent.

"She was like, 'Oh, and I just found out this thing about Joe Crowley's record, or . . . this donation he got from this bank,'" Shaheed recalled. "She was just so excited."

But even with a uniquely talented candidate and the compelling narrative of a twentysomething taking on a party boss, Ocasio-Cortez's campaign struggled to gain traction. To make matters worse, by the end of 2017, the Justice Democrats organization was facing a crisis.

According to Trent, the group's leadership realized "we can't back twelve people. We're out of money and we're only bringing in . . . $50,000 a month or whatever."

The group would have to scale back its grand ambitions one more time. They needed to go from a dozen candidates to one who really had a chance.

"We had to pick the right one," Trent said. "We end up deciding in December . . . to go all in with Ocasio."

Within about a month, in early 2018, Chakrabarti headed to New York, taking on a full-time role as Ocasio-Cortez's campaign manager. That meant Justice Democrats would be largely abandoning the other candidates they had promised to support. This decision led to resentment behind the scenes. And Chakrabarti found a new crisis when he stepped off the plane. Just as they were pinning all their hopes on Ocasio-Cortez, she was thinking of quitting.

"It hadn't turned around yet," Trent explained.

After nearly a year of hard work, she had gained little visible traction. With Chakrabarti throwing himself into the race, Ocasio-Cortez decided to soldier on. Yet even her allies believed a victory was impossible.

Sean McElwee, a progressive pollster, was host of a weekly happy hour that functioned as a social hub of sorts for New York City's leftists. He bragged about having Ocasio-Cortez come by in the early days "when she had 8,000 Twitter followers."

"Even on the day of the election, I don't think anyone really thought she was serious or was going to win," McElwee said.

Ocasio-Cortez's campaign staff was looking at grim numbers put together by the respected Democratic pollster Celinda Lake. According to Trent, Lake's data never showed her within thirty-five points of Crowley.

Crowley seemed to share that dim view of Ocasio-Cortez's chances. He didn't rouse himself to catch the Acela back to the city for an initial debate with Ocasio-Cortez, and instead sent a surrogate to appear in his place. Ocasio-Cortez turned the occasion into a rout, politely dismissing the stand-in and pouring criticism on Crowley that he wasn't present to answer. Ocasio-Cortez's campaign had a fresh face and well-produced videos. People started to notice. The next time they were set to debate, Crowley actually showed up.

OCASIO-CORTEZ ALMOST CERTAINLY COULD NOT HAVE MADE IT TO Congress without the Democratic Socialists of America.

While nowhere near the size of the major parties, the DSA boasted of being the largest socialist organization in the country. With roots in early twentieth-century union movements and sixties radicalism, the organization blended the old left and the new. In May 2017 when Ocasio-Cortez launched her campaign, the DSA was enjoying a period of explosive growth fueled by Bernie Sanders's run the prior year and backlash to the subsequent election of President Trump. Many of the group's new members were younger, more modern progressives who were focused on identity and social issues.

In 2015, the DSA only had about six thousand members. Two years later, its ranks had swelled to roughly twenty-five thousand. That surge was being felt on the ground in Queens.

Prior to Trump's election, the Democratic Socialists of America had no outpost in the borough. In January 2017, as the Queens-bred Trump took office, the organization formed a local branch and held its first meeting organized by veterans of the Sanders campaign.

Aaron Taube, who would go on to briefly work for Ocasio-Cortez, was present for the first DSA meeting in Queens. His story is emblematic of how Sanders, and then Trump, drove the group's rise in New York City.

For Taube, a skinny, self-described "Jewish kid" who grew up in a Long Island suburb and wasn't politically active, Sanders's White House bid caused something to click.

"Oh wow, there's this thing beyond being a Democrat or even a progressive. There's this thing that's democratic socialism," Taube said of Sanders. "He spoke to a lot of these issues that I cared about and he showed me that there's this thing beyond liberalism."

While Taube supported Sanders and donated money, his admiration for the candidate didn't translate into in-person activism. That all changed after Trump's victory in the presidential race.

"I have to do something," Taube thought. "Everything is burning and bad."

Along with "abject fear," Trump's ascent added to Taube's dissatisfaction with the Democratic Party establishment.

"The Democrats had failed their one purpose, which is to protect us from the Republicans," Taube said. "Seeing this fall apart you're like, 'Oh yeah, actually everyone who is running the Democratic Party is a huge idiot.'"

Taube joined the DSA on November 9, 2016, the day after Trump was elected. He felt the Democrats were "not fit to stand up to this crisis."

"We need something stronger and better that really speaks to people," said Taube.

The DSA's national leadership similarly saw Trump's ascent as an indictment of the Democratic establishment. In 2018, when asked about the organization's post-Trump membership surge, DSA National Director Maria Svart described it as being motivated by opposition to both the Republicans and the mainstream left.

"People are excited by a bold vision and they're willing to fight for it. Neoliberal Democrats are afraid of what might happen if we build the powerful multiracial working-class movement that it will take to stand up to Trump because they know that this movement will also stand up to them, too," Svart said at the time.

Vigie Ramos Rios, a Puerto Rican woman who grew up as an "Army brat" and found her way to Sanders's organization after a layoff, was one of the initial organizers. Ramos Rios, who went from having not voted for over a decade to serving as one of Sanders's delegates at the 2016 Democratic National Convention, was eager to stay involved after Trump's victory. Nevertheless, she had moderate ambitions for that first Queens DSA meeting.

"There ended up being like ten of us who were planning it and we were like, 'If we get another ten people, this would be great,'" Ramos Rios remembered in an interview for this book.

The event exponentially exceeded her expectations. Ramos Rios said over 130 people showed up. Taube, who was one of the attendees, said the place was "packed."

At the meeting, people listed their priorities and concerns on over-size pads of paper. For Ramos Rios, the main takeaway was that they needed to establish an organization capable of exerting "political pressure" to help people achieve these goals. They also recognized the need for diplomacy since, as Ramos Rios put it, despite socialism's popularity with young people, "for Boomers and Gen Xers—the word socialist had been demonized."

"We needed to be able to establish an organization that could get people in our local communities involved," she said, adding, "When you talk about the aims and the goals of socialism, the vast majority of people in Queens agree but when you talk about it using that language, you alienate a good portion of the population. . . . So from what I recall, the group that was organizing things was really about how do we get people to come back?"

Ramos Rios ended up becoming Queens's representative to the citywide DSA steering committee. However, the initial momentum didn't last.

"There was a big drop off after that," Taube said of that first meeting. "It felt like there was a lot of people there and excitement, and then, it sort of fizzled."

Taube was one of the ones who stuck around, even though he was a newcomer to activism.

"I had sort of a limited understanding of political possibilities," explained Taube. "I was kind of like, well, you can have a revolution or an election and I don't know how to shoot a gun and probably would be really bad at that. . . . I'm going to go do this electoral thing."

Taube became a chair of the Queens DSA's electoral working

group. The position made him a key figure in Ocasio-Cortez's rise. It also thrust him into one of the organization's main internal schisms.

When Taube and the other new chairs took over the electoral operation, they figured endorsing candidates would be a natural first step.

"We were like, 'Oh, I guess we're leading this working group, I guess we should do a campaign,'" Taube said.

But the question of electoral participation was fraught within the DSA. Some members of the group prefer to prioritize other forms of activism like union and tenant organizing rather than campaigns for office. And, if the DSA was going to back a candidate, there were extensive questions about what kind of platform they should have and how closely tied to the organization that candidate should be.

Alexandria Ocasio-Cortez had joined the DSA, but she didn't have a long history with the group. Nor was she in lockstep with the policy positions the DSA included in its endorsement questionnaire. Namely, while she defended the movement to boycott and sanction Israel over the Palestinian occupation on free-speech grounds, Ocasio-Cortez did not explicitly support it. Lastly, she was running on the Democratic Party line.

All of these issues were controversial within the DSA. Still, when Taube and his colleagues first met Ocasio-Cortez in early 2018, they were completely sold.

"We were just blown away by what everyone sort of knows about her now, which is that she's this incredible public speaker who comes across as very sincere, and passionate, and smart," said Taube.

Along with being drawn to the candidate personally, the electoral working group liked the idea of an underdog taking on a Democratic Party machine. They also appreciated how Ocasio-Cortez stacked up against her initial opponent, Joe Crowley.

"You know, you have this dynamic young woman of color running against this really just totally frumpy old white guy with no swag," Taube said, adding that they thought, "She's got this, she's going to be the youngest woman elected to Congress."

While Taube and his cohort saw Ocasio-Cortez as an ideal future "ambassador for DSA," others in the organization had what he diplomatically described as "concerns." Mainly, some worried that the candidate was "a Democrat." Others wondered whether Ocasio-Cortez was "a real socialist" since she hadn't publicly identified as such before pursuing the group's endorsement.

Many DSA skeptics of Ocasio-Cortez balked at backing any candidate who was also on the major party line. They complained that the Democrats are "a party of capital," and, as a result, it didn't make sense for an anti-capitalist group like the DSA to back them in any way. According to Taube, the debate over endorsing was a microcosm of the larger questions among leftists over whether to work with more mainstream allies or make a more radical, and ideologically pure, stand. However, the radicals' reservations did not prevail this time. Ultimately, Taube said he and the Queens working group "led the process of convincing the New York City DSA to endorse her, which we did a little over two months before her election."

"It was a harder sell than it should have been," Taube added with a wry laugh.

The process took time due to the DSA's internal debates and the fact Ocasio-Cortez's district spans parts of both the Bronx and Queens. The DSA prides itself on democracy. For the city organization to support her, she would need to win at least 60 percent of the vote in either the Queens DSA branch, or the so-called "BUM Branch," which represents the Bronx and Upper Manhattan. Ocasio-Cortez fell short in the BUM Branch. However, she crossed the 60 percent threshold in Queens.

"We got what we needed," Taube said.

Ramos Rios was frustrated by the DSA's hand-wringing over whether to back Ocasio-Cortez and other potential candidates.

"I'm trying not to be disparaging, but I often think of it as navel-gazing because I'm like, we are so far from truly pulling in the vast majority of voters," Ramos Rios said. "It's part of the frustration of why I'm not as active a member anymore."

Rather than looking for perfect allies, she suggested the growing organization should "talk to people who are not members to continue to invite people in and welcome them once they're there."

"I hate the litmus test. I hate the arguments of who's a true socialist and who isn't," she explained. "Like how about we hold up what are our basic values on helping the community on universal health care, these sorts of things. And we can get back to the argument when we actually have political power."

Once the group decided to endorse, the DSA provided Ocasio-Cortez with over one hundred volunteers, which Taube said was about one-fifth of her ground game. The organization also helped connect her to Ramos Rios, who became her campaign manager.

Ramos Rios said she got the job after a call from Chakrabarti, who she knew "from the Bernie days." He reached out in early February 2018, just four months prior to the primary. Ramos Rios thought he was asking for her help organizing volunteers since it was late enough in the game that "they must have a campaign manager already."

"I realized three questions in, he was interviewing me to be her campaign manager," Ramos Rios said.

Once she was brought on to the team, Ramos Rios had questions about the campaign operation since deadlines were fast approaching. Was there a lawyer? Did they have a team to collect the signatures from voters that were needed to get on the ballot? The answer was no to all of the above.

"I'm like, okay, we have a lot of work to do in two weeks," Ramos Rios recalled.

Along with Ramos Rios and the team from Justice Democrats, Ocasio-Cortez's fledgling campaign had another key adviser: Alexandria's romantic partner, Riley Roberts.

The pair, who became engaged in 2022, initially began dating in college. During Ocasio-Cortez's 2018 campaign, they lived together in her Bronx apartment. Since-deleted webpages show Roberts dabbled in a variety of projects prior to Ocasio-Cortez's race. Roberts's personal home page described him as an "entrepreneur, sociologist, and contrarian." The site said Roberts had helped set up something called the "Cop Out Collective," which he called "a social project with the mission of shifting the public opinion about the role of cops in society."

"The influence of certain bureaucratic pressures creates some cops that abuse their power and dehumanize the members of society who [they're] supposed to be protecting," Roberts wrote, adding, "High end hemp t-shirts with our logo will be available for sale on our website."

Roberts also once built a website for a venture selling a brand of high-priced coffee culled from the droppings of the civet, a cat-like Indonesian mammal. His page for the exotic excrement brew featured a testimonial from Ocasio-Cortez alongside her smiling photo.

"I was skeptical at first, but this Civet coffee has a unique, smooth and full-bodied flavor that I really enjoyed trying," Ocasio-Cortez declared, according to the page.

A source close to the couple described the site as a mock-up that Roberts, who was freelancing at the time, made to build his web design portfolio.

Roberts's digital experience came in handy as Ocasio-Cortez ran for Congress. According to Ramos Rios, the campaign manager,

Roberts was Ocasio-Cortez's "major adviser and supporter." She also said he was "the linchpin" of their digital fundraising operation. Ramos Rios described his contributions as "vital" and "integral."

While Roberts's presence was felt on the campaign, the staff rarely interacted with him in person.

"He was a force and he was active, but . . . I think Riley's an extreme introvert," Ramos Rios said. "He's really quiet. In fact, he worked out of their apartment. . . . Riley was like, Boo Radley, half the time you didn't see Riley. You didn't hear Riley."

Ramos Rios and multiple other veterans of that campaign said Ocasio-Cortez also had a shy streak.

"She's a writer, she's an introvert," Ramos Rios said of Ocasio-Cortez. "Introverts lose their energy talking to people. So if she's done a big rally or talking to a bunch of people, she needs time alone to recoup that energy."

This personality trait meant Ocasio-Cortez was absolutely overwhelmed by what happened next.

***

OCASIO-CORTEZ AND HER CAMPAIGN WERE SET TO SPEND ELECTION night at a pool hall in the Bronx. Pink neon lights blared down from the ceiling as volunteers and supporters weaved between the bar and scuffed billiards tables. As the polls closed, a local news station, NY1, had a camera trained on Ocasio-Cortez when the first results filled the television screens. She was *crushing* Crowley.

Her reaction was instantly iconic. Her jaw dropped, she shook, screamed, and covered her open mouth with her hands. Her eyes remained locked on the screen, blazing out utter shock and delight.

"She's looking at herself on television right now," the NY1 reporter, Ruschell Boone, explained to the audience at home.

Ocasio-Cortez was literally reeling. A smiling woman put a hand on her back to help her keep steady.

"How are you feeling?" Boone asked. "Can you put it into words?"

"Nope," she answered instantly, shaking her head with her jaw still half dropped. "I cannot put this into words."

Ocasio-Cortez's eyes stayed wide, riveted by the numbers that were coming in. Her breath was ragged as though her astonishment had knocked the wind from her small frame.

"This was a grassroots campaign. Can you believe these numbers that you're seeing right now?" Boone asked.

"I cannot believe these numbers right now," Ocasio-Cortez replied. But even in her apparent shock, she pulled herself on message. "But I do know that every single person here has worked their butt off to change the future of the Bronx and Queens. That's what I know."

Boone pointed out that she had gone up "against the Queens machine."

"Well you know what?" Ocasio-Cortez answered, "We meet a machine with a movement."

The eyes of the world were on her now. That dramatic first interview kicked off an avalanche. Reporters who had not planned to cover the long-shot challenger rushed up to the pool hall. Camera flashes broke through the lights with a disorienting rhythm as the mix of press and supporters surged towards the woman of the hour.

Trent, Ocasio-Cortez's communications director, remembers seeing Ocasio-Cortez try to huddle with Roberts in a roped-off area by the pool tables.

"The thing that happened instantly was . . . now she had become a magnet," Trent recounted in a series of interviews for this book. He described the people in the crowd as a "sea of iron shavings" that were flying at Ocasio-Cortez.

"They're just drawn to her," Trent said. "And they all want a little bit."

People crushed around her asking for selfies, autographs, interviews, and hugs.

"She had to, like, take a break," Trent said. "It's such a physically draining, and mentally and emotionally draining experience for her to do this with people."

And it wasn't going to stop any time soon.

As the waves of admirers came down on Ocasio-Cortez, Trent had a major problem of his own. Throughout the campaign, he had been struggling with an opiate addiction. Trent put it more bluntly.

"I was hooked on fucking pain pills," he said.

He had not told Ocasio-Cortez any of this. And as election night approached, Trent ran out of the medication he had come to rely on.

"I was on Suboxone, which is the shit you take to get off of Oxycontin and opiates, until election night—until, literally until, the night that Ocasio won her primary," said Trent.

If she lost, Trent's time in New York would have been over, but the shocking upset victory meant he couldn't return home to Tennessee the next day to refill his prescription. He was wracked with withdrawal symptoms as he and Ocasio-Cortez dealt with an onslaught of media requests and press coverage. But the whir of international attention afforded to America's rising socialist star was its own kind of buzz.

"I got off Suboxone with fucking adrenaline," Trent said.

Chapter 4

PULLING TEETH

NORMALLY, A PRIMARY WIN IS JUST THE FIRST HALF OF A CAM-paign. But, in a deep blue metropolis like New York, where roughly 80 percent of the electorate votes on the Democratic line, Ocasio-Cortez's victory over Crowley made her a presumed congress-woman. The long-shot win combined with her youth and the sharply opinionated, made-for-social-media quality of her campaign ignited a political supernova.

Throughout the rest of her election and her first year in office, liberal and conservative media elevated her into a main character in the ongoing political soap opera. She did the late-night talk show circuit and made the cover of *Time* magazine. Clips of her grilling witnesses in congressional hearings racked up millions of views online.

By the fall of 2019, Ocasio-Cortez's star had not stopped rising. Meanwhile, Bernie Sanders, the man who helped inspire her campaign, was at a low point.

After his electrifying 2016 primary campaign and Clinton's humiliating general election defeat, the left had high hopes Sanders would run again. "Bernie," as his armies of online supporters insisted, "would've won." It became a recurring taunt to the Democrats who had denied him the nomination.

Sanders and his supporters believed it would be different this time. All the fundamentals had changed. His prior run had made Sanders one of the most famous people in the country. He had legions of fans who knew the core parts of his platform; "Medicare for All," elimination of student debt, and an aggressive desire to take on the "millionaires and billionaires." Sanders's ideas were no longer radical and he was not just some eccentric outsider. He was a familiar and popular figure with new allies all over the country. Most importantly, his 2016 campaign proved that his vision of funding a White House bid with millions of small-dollar donors could work.

By late 2018, Sanders was pulling together his staff and getting ready to fire up that record-breaking fundraising machine once again. His team was confident. They had momentum and had learned from the mistakes of 2016. Sanders officially announced his second run in February 2019 and came into the race with high expectations.

But Sanders spent that September polling behind Joe Biden and another progressive, Massachusetts senator Elizabeth Warren, in Iowa. And Pete Buttigieg, the young, moderate, Midwestern mayor, was gaining on him. What could Sanders do to make a difference—to win some headlines—besides continuing to shake hands, give speeches, and raise cash? His campaign needed an injection of energy. He needed an endorsement from the most visible star on the left.

The Sanders campaign pressed Ocasio-Cortez's office on the subject. And some on her staff—which now included multiple veterans of both Justice Democrats and Sanders's operation—were eager to have her give him public support. But important fall weeks clicked by with no action.

The benefit to Sanders was obvious. The youngest and most famous woman in Congress could offer a vital boost. This election wasn't like 2016, when it was essentially just a one-on-one race between Bernie and Hillary, democratic socialism versus the centrist party establishment. In 2020, Sanders was mired in third place while competing against an ideologically diverse field of candidates, many of whom had adopted at least some of his ideas.

For Ocasio-Cortez, the value proposition wasn't quite so apparent. With her surging national profile and seat in a staunchly blue district, Ocasio-Cortez didn't appear to need Sanders. Nevertheless, some on her team reasoned that his support was crucial. If Ocasio-Cortez did ultimately want to run for higher office, she might need to win state-wide in New York, which included tens of thousands of square miles of relatively conservative suburban and rural areas. In these purple and red counties, and across the country, Sanders had much more pull than the new congresswoman.

"Bernie brought a lot to the table for her. Period," a former Ocasio-Cortez staffer said. "She brought lots for Bernie. It was a very mutually beneficial connection."

Surprisingly, Sanders also had stronger support than Ocasio-Cortez among Latinos. Despite her Puerto Rican roots, Latinos—particularly older men—were an unexpected and persistent soft spot for the congresswoman in her own district.

A member of her team drafted a strategy memo arguing that, not only should she endorse Sanders, but it should be a central theme of her own 2020 reelection campaign. Ocasio-Cortez remained unconvinced.

Part of the issue was Ocasio-Cortez's desire to stand out. Before her arrival, Sanders had been the standard-bearer of the Democratic Party's progressive wing. He also was a core part of her story. In most of her retellings, Ocasio-Cortez's political life began as a volunteer on

Sanders's campaign in 2016. Between her own work and Justice Democrats' ties to his campaign, Ocasio-Cortez's links to Sanders's movement were foundational and undeniable. Now, she was eager to cement
her own separate legacy.

Warren's presence in the race also complicated any potential
endorsement. Sanders's decline had come just as Warren was surging,
briefly sprinting into first place in Iowa.

Both Sanders and Warren wanted single-payer health care, both
wanted to attack income inequality, both sought an aggressive, comprehensive approach to climate change, and both, in their own ways,
proposed seismic overhauls of the American system. For Sanders, it was
a "revolution." For Warren, it was "big structural change."

Along with her progressive platform, Warren had a strong relationship with one of "the Squad" members, Ayanna Pressley, who
was also from Massachusetts. Pressley, one of Ocasio-Cortez's closest allies, would soon endorse the senator from Massachusetts and
become a co-chair of her campaign. And, of course, Warren had something Sanders never did. She was running to be the first woman in the
White House. All of that made it fraught for Ocasio-Cortez to stand
in Warren's way.

Wasn't it time to shatter the glass ceiling? There were so many bad
feelings when Sanders contested Hillary Clinton's attempt to break
that barrier in 2016. Hadn't Bernie already had his chance?

Ocasio-Cortez knew some of her supporters—particularly
women—hoped to see her back Warren. And, at times, sources close
to her said she was genuinely leaning in that direction. Yet, a former
staffer on Warren's campaign said they didn't actively court Ocasio-
Cortez. For Warren and her team, it would have been enough if she
simply stayed neutral.

In the end, a brush with death tipped her to Sanders.

SANDERS WAS ON THE ROAD EXTENSIVELY IN SEPTEMBER 2019 WITH over thirty appearances in nine states. He finished the month doing four rallies in one day in New Hampshire. On October 1, he flew to Las Vegas. There were two events scheduled that day. The final one was a fundraiser at a Middle Eastern and South Asian restaurant in a shopping center a few blocks off the Strip.

The event was set to be a question and answer session. Sanders was speaking at a lectern on a small stage in the dining room. Bulbous modernist lamps hung down from exposed pipes on the ceiling. Mismatched metallic statues lined the walls.

According to the restaurant's owner, Raja Majid, Sanders kept noting that it had been a "long day."

"He looked tired. His voice was breaking," Majid told a newscaster for FOX5 Las Vegas after the event.

Sanders got about four questions in before stopping. Arm outstretched, Sanders called for his aide, Ari Rabin-Havt.

"Ari, could you do me a favor? Where's Ari?" Sanders' voice cracked. "Get me a chair over here for a moment."

Sanders plopped down and took a deep breath. He then returned to the question he had been answering. But Rabin-Havt could tell something was wrong. He cut the fundraiser short and got the senator back in the car.

On the road back to their hotel, Sanders began complaining of tightness in his chest. His team scrambled to find an urgent care clinic. Once there, doctors confirmed Sanders was having a heart attack. Within hours he was having a blocked artery cleared at the hospital.

The health scare subsided quickly. Sanders was back on his feet within a couple of days. Nevertheless, it shook a campaign that was already struggling to gain traction.

"People don't remember that we were circling the drain in September," Tyson Brody, Sanders's director of research, recalled in an interview for this book.

Sanders's poll numbers were plummeting and he was in danger of losing his third-place spot. The race was entering the home stretch, and Sanders was fading.

"We had a long summer where we were never the exciting thing. And then Bernie literally has a heart attack," Brody said. "We weren't certain what was going to happen those few days."

While Sanders was in the hospital, his team held its breath. Events were canceled, Facebook ads were paused, and a slate of television commercials was delayed. Sanders's wife, Jane Sanders, and his campaign manager, Faiz Shakir, rushed to Nevada to be by his side. Shakir would get flashbacks of these moments for months. They feared the harsh realities of biology would abruptly end the dream.

But Sanders was undeterred. By the time Shakir landed in Vegas, Sanders was sitting up in his bed eager to get back to work. He wanted one more shot in front of the voters. He needed to convince them of his vision.

The heart attack gave Ocasio-Cortez a vision of her own. She had nearly lost the man who was so foundational to her career. Ocasio-Cortez realized there might not be another chance to stand with him. She called Sanders and told him he had her support.

"Bernie's in the hospital. She talks to Bernie," a former Ocasio-Cortez staffer told us, and the new message was: "Okay, we're going to do it."

"She had the epiphany when he had the heart attack," the staffer added.

But soon after the endorsement, her doubts allegedly began to creep back in.

Sanders's team wanted to have a huge event for Ocasio-Cortez to make her formal, public endorsement later that month in her district. There was an outdoor park in Queens with a stunning view of the Fifty-Ninth Street Bridge and Manhattan skyline. Thousands of people would show up. But soon, Ocasio-Cortez's inner circle started to worry the congresswoman was getting cold feet.

"We had planned to have this Bernie rally in Queens in October," the former Ocasio-Cortez staffer said, adding, "There starts to be this sort of feeling they're going to delay the event right? 'Let's not do October; let's wait.' . . . I'd been through this before and what 'let's wait' means is it probably isn't going to happen."

The delay led to drama behind the scenes. Corbin Trent, who had become the communications director in her House office, even threatened to quit. He remembered a "big argument" with the congresswoman about delaying the event in Queens. "I was a prick, I'm sure," said Trent.

A member of Ocasio-Cortez's congressional team said the idea she had any reluctance to support Sanders was "heavily overstated."

"To the staffer in question, her endorsement may have felt 'late' but she endorsed in the fall of 2019—months before the first primary states," said the Ocasio-Cortez aide, who requested anonymity and added, "This was also her very first year in Congress, so she had other very legitimate things to focus on like setting up her office and figuring out the ropes of legislating."

While some of those close to Ocasio-Cortez believed her reticence about campaigning for Sanders stemmed from concerns about optics, there was something else too. Ocasio-Cortez was still dealing with her discomfort with crowds. And for months Trent and Chakrabarti, who was now her chief of staff, had been pushing her in front of every audience they could. That dynamic was a constant source of tension.

Trent and the team were consistently booking major events and media appearances. For an introvert like Ocasio-Cortez, the spotlight was taxing.

"She would be so pissed off," Trent said of Ocasio-Cortez. "The person who put her in that position in her mind was me, so she's pissed at me."

Ocasio-Cortez ultimately agreed to attend the massive "Bernie's Back" rally in Queens in October 2019. Yet even after that initial endorsement, Trent said she repeatedly balked at adding more Sanders campaign events to her schedule.

Just a year after her own election, Ocasio-Cortez was uncomfortable wielding her newfound fame. She was also intensely protective of her nascent brand. With one wrong move, Ocasio-Cortez feared she could lose megastardom as quickly as she gained it. She felt at once incredibly powerful and fragile. Trent recalled her openly worrying about being outshined even as she agreed to campaign for Sanders.

Nevertheless, she hit the trail for him in November 2019. Ocasio-Cortez joined Sanders for two on-stage events in Iowa. Their first stop was a community college gym in Council Bluffs, a small city on the banks of the Missouri River.

"Who here is ready for the revolution?" Ocasio-Cortez asked as she bounded onto the stage. "I know I sure am."

The crowd roared. They always did that for her now. Only a year after being elected, Ocasio-Cortez was arguably the most famous woman in politics. Her upset victory had vaulted her to the kind of celebrity status that comes along once a decade, at most. Her face graced countless magazine covers, TV screens, and T-shirts. And here she was, live, on the western edge of Iowa, standing under banners for fifth- and eighth-place sports teams in a junior college arena.

According to the Sanders campaign, the pair drew a crowd of 2,400 that was "the largest rally in Iowa" at that point in the primary. The gym's bleachers had been folded away for the event, leaving the audience standing shoulder to shoulder on the basketball court. The crowd, a mixture of old hippies and bright-eyed kids that reflected the nearly fifty-year age gap between Sanders and the young congresswoman, beamed up at her on stage.

An unusually large pack of photographers crouched down in front of the lectern with their long lenses upturned. Shutters hissed each time she moved. Editors in New York and DC knew it was worth the price of a flight to capture scenes from Ocasio-Cortez's first trip to Iowa. This was a generational political talent stepping onto the traditional proving ground for presidents.

With her trepidation about crowds, rallies weren't Ocasio-Cortez's strong suit. In more intimate rooms, her small frame radiated power. Ocasio-Cortez translated that energy into social media broadcasts, making online audiences of hundreds of thousands feel as though they're sitting beside her.

It's hard to capture that same electricity alone in front of a large audience. Nevertheless, her speech had a smooth delivery, tight message, and magnetism that most politicians can't hit on their best night.

Ocasio-Cortez paced the stage wearing a tan motorcycle jacket over all black. Her hair was in a tight ponytail and she sported her signature bright red lipstick, a nod to her Puerto Rican roots. As Ocasio-Cortez talked, her eyes and smile grew wide. She transitioned seamlessly from her life story as "the daughter of a housekeeper" who waited tables to put herself through college into a stream of memorable calls to action. Slogan-worthy sound bites spilled from every few sentences of her speech.

"We don't watch the polls. We change the polls," she said, punctuating each point with her hands. "This is not a movie. This is a movement."

The room fell into reverent silence as she spoke. When she'd land on an idea, the crowd cheered approval and waved their blue and white "Bernie" signs. The applause bounced off the hardwood and echoed around the arena. It was exactly the response any campaign would want from a stump speech. But Ocasio-Cortez didn't seem to have rehearsed. All of a sudden the remarks took on the confessional familiarity of her livestreams. At one point, after declaring, "Here's the deal," she began to sputter.

"I'm—you know—and what is also—and so the deal is. Sorry," she said, bent over and slapping her thigh as the words failed to come.

She stood up and composed herself, deftly turning the moment into an opportunity to forge a closer bond with the thousands in the packed gym.

"I've got so much going on in my mind, because I'm just *talking* to you all this evening," she said.

"I was trying to prepare some remarks on the plane," Ocasio-Cortez continued. Then she dismissed the idea of a scripted speech with a wave of her hand. "I was like, I'm just going to *talk* to them. OK?"

The crowd was hooked. Then she picked up where she left off.

"The deal is that we have to stitch ourselves together. We have to connect ourselves to one another. . . . Our destinies are tied," Ocasio-Cortez said, reaching a crescendo.

"All of us need health care! . . . All of us need college! . . . All of us need to save this planet!" she shouted.

Her soliloquy about shared struggle and solidarity culminated with an introduction of the man of the hour.

Ocasio-Cortez called Sanders her "tío," Spanish for uncle. It was a phrase she had used as she endorsed him on video the month before. The Sanders campaign had it printed on shirts that they debuted during the Iowa trip. This was a moment that merited dedicated souvenirs.

"I want to introduce to you all my tío, our tío, but also the senator who has paved the path for us to talk about this today who has helped create the space," Ocasio-Cortez said.

Sanders strode out with a tight smile. His standard entrance music blared, "Power to the people, right on!" Sanders had none of Ocasio-Cortez's finesse. He dropped the file folder containing his typed-up stump speech as they shared a quick hug. Ocasio-Cortez quickly ducked down to recover it for him. When she popped back up, he grabbed her wrist, held it aloft like she'd won a boxing match, and waved both their hands to the crowd.

The press and the public gave their endearing odd-couple performance rave reviews. The *New York Times* called it an "Iowa Buddy Movie." Twitter and Instagram overflowed with hearts and gleeful emoji.

Ocasio-Cortez and Sanders were basking in each other's reflected glow. Many of the people in attendance, Iowans who understand the significance of a trial mission to a key early primary state, were envisioning the day she might mount a White House bid of her own.

"I think it's just a matter of time," Kacey Davis, a nurse, declared after Ocasio-Cortez's second appearance with Sanders in Des Moines. "I think definitely she'll run for president."

Ocasio-Cortez was still just twenty-nine years old, too young to make a White House run. The Constitution requires a commander in chief to be at least thirty-five when they're sworn in. But 2024 was another story. Some of the people watching her in Iowa pointed out that Ocasio-Cortez's thirty-fifth birthday would be exactly one hundred days before the inauguration. They were in awe. Another bit of destiny was on her side.

Even members of Ocasio-Cortez's team were overwhelmed by the weight of the moment. Aaron Taube, the DSA activist, who was now a staffer on her campaign, fainted backstage at one of her events with Sanders. He attributed the swooning to "being in the presence of the two giants of the resurgent US left."

Ocasio-Cortez's early November Iowa trip lasted two days and included three events, immediately boosting Sanders's poll numbers. By the start of 2020, Sanders had surged to the head of the primary pack.

But it wasn't all smiles, laughs, and excitement. Behind the scenes, Ocasio-Cortez remained deeply conflicted about pulling too close to Sanders. In fact, she almost didn't make the trip to Iowa at all.

In January 2020, Ocasio-Cortez returned to Iowa during the weeks before the caucus. Sanders had been pulled off the campaign trail by the first Trump impeachment trial, and she was his most powerful surrogate. Yet at an event in Iowa City, Ocasio-Cortez gave an entire speech without mentioning Sanders by name.

Her omission was glaring enough to provoke a handful of news stories. The member of Ocasio-Cortez's congressional team, who requested anonymity to discuss the issue, insists that she "didn't intentionally leave out Bernie's name."

All of the attention on the missed mention might have seemed frivolous. After all, Sanders had only called into the event. Yet Corbin Trent, who accompanied her to Iowa that second time, said Ocasio-Cortez had taken some deliberate distance from Sanders.

"That's not an accident," Trent said.

Chapter 5

FOR THE PEOPLE

THE SAME MONTH ALEXANDRIA OCASIO-CORTEZ HIT THE ROAD FOR
Bernie Sanders in 2019, Kamala Harris was shutting down her campaign. Harris's early departure from the trail stunned many observers.

As one of her senior campaign staffers said, "If you ask Democratic voters to describe their ideal presidential candidate, they'd basically describe Kamala." Her campaign was confident that Democrats were eager, as this staffer put it, for "a young, Black woman who is tough and can take the fight to Donald Trump and is going to be the face of America."

Harris promised to synthesize the most appealing attributes of Barack Obama and Hillary Clinton. She bridged the Democratic Party's yearning for representation of women and people of color in the Oval Office, with its need for a leader who had substantial experience in government. She was also a fighter. Harris had thrown some memorable elbows in court as a prosecutor and in Senate hearing rooms. She was someone who could both fire people's hearts and land a haymaker on the opposition.

Harris can lay claim to a remarkable number of firsts. The daughter of a Tamil Indian mother and a Jamaican father, she is the first Black person, the first South Asian person, and the first woman to be vice president of the United States. Even before ascending to that post, she was the first Black and first Asian-American senator from California. Harris was also the first woman or person of color to serve as California's attorney general or as San Francisco's district attorney. She is a pioneer many times over.

Harris and those close to her say that experience blazing a trail through the ranks of American life informed her work and left her with a dedication to ensure others would have an easier time following in her footsteps. A White House official described Harris to us as being focused on "opportunity, and justice, and access."

"That's the foundation of who she is," the official said. "She's the daughter of folks who were in the civil rights movement, she comes from a perspective and a vantage point of fighting for those who can't fight for themselves."

In light of that legacy, it's staggering how little trust her record of electoral accomplishment has earned her as a potential standard-bearer for Democrats. Biden's selection of Harris as his running mate seemed to set her up as his natural successor. However, soon after Biden took office, a consensus began to emerge that—despite his age—he would have to run for a second term. The fear was Kamala Harris could not win a race against Donald Trump, or perhaps against any Republican at all, and there was no other obvious heir. Democrat after Democrat who we interviewed in the run-up to 2024—including members of Biden and Harris's own teams—ascribed to this conventional wisdom.

"Kamala is not ready for prime time," one senior White House staffer said, adding, "She ain't made for this."

But why, despite all her accomplishments, did Harris's party have so little confidence in her? And where will that leave the Democratic Party when Joe Biden inevitably exits the White House?

Many of the doubts were rooted in her stunning campaign collapse.

———

BEFORE SHE WAS A CANDIDATE IN CRISIS, HARRIS WAS A CHILD OF the movement.

She grew up in West Berkeley in the flatlands between the Cal campus and the Bay, ensconced in one of the most enduringly progressive districts of the country. Her mother Shyamala was a pioneering biologist at the Lawrence Berkeley National Laboratory, and her father Donald was a professor of economics at Stanford. The couple met in graduate school as civil rights activists. In her memoir, *The Truths We Hold*, Harris described spending most Thursday nights with her mother and sister at The Rainbow Sign, a center of Black activism where Nina Simone sang and James Baldwin read. Famously, as part of Berkeley's effort to integrate its school system, Harris regularly rode a bus across the color line to an elementary school in a leafier, whiter part of town.

A politician emerging from that milieu might easily become an anti-establishment leftist. Indeed, her local congressman, elected when Harris was seven years old, had done just that.

Ron Dellums represented Harris's East Bay district in Congress throughout her adolescence and teenage years and into her adulthood. Dellums had grown up in Oakland. Some of the early organizing for his campaigns took place at The Rainbow Sign in Berkeley. In 1970, Dellums became the first socialist elected to Congress in at least twenty years after he was recruited to run by anti-war activists. He would serve in the House until 1998, followed later by a stint as the mayor of Oakland. Towards the end of his life, in 2012, Dellums sat for a multipart oral history interview that was published by the House of

Representatives' historian. In that conversation, Dellums described his radical politics as a natural reflection of his upbringing.

"I happened to come from a place where every movement of the sixties emerged in close proximity and in great simultaneity," Dellums said. "Some places, it was primarily the civil rights movement. But in Oakland, Berkeley, Bay Area—every movement. The civil rights movement, the nationalist movement, the [Black] Panther movement, the feminist movement, the gay liberation movement, the environmental movement, the peace movement, all of it."

He wrote in his memoir that he arrived in Washington in 1971 trailed by a perception popularized by Spiro Agnew, Nixon's first vice president, that he was an "Afro-topped, bell-bottomed radical" from the "commie-pinko left-wing community of 'Berzerkeley.'" Dellums, the first Black man to represent a majority white district in the House, didn't run away from that characterization. He wholeheartedly embraced radical politics.

As the first democratic socialist in Congress since Vito Marcantonio, a New York representative and labor activist who was pushed out in 1951 amid the rising anti-communist sentiment of the "Red Scare," Dellums was a forerunner to Alexandria Ocasio-Cortez and "the Squad." His experience in the House also showed how the new left might gain power. During his time on Capitol Hill, Dellums managed to confront the waning segregationist wing of the Democratic party in the House, win the confidence of his fellow members, and rise to the chairmanship of the Armed Services Committee.

Dellums also racked up meaningful progressive wins. As a freshman member in the Congressional Black Caucus, Dellums attended a meeting of Polaroid workers protesting the use of their products in South Africa's apartheid passes. Taken with their cause, Dellums wrote the first bill targeting the South African regime with sanctions. He introduced the bill in the early '70s, drawing only one co-sponsor. But he kept reintroducing versions of it, shifting its focus to banning US investment in South Africa, and gradually building support.

In 1986, both houses of Congress passed the Comprehensive Anti-Apartheid Act—a compromise sanctions measure—which became law over President Reagan's veto. The South African leader Nelson Mandela would later thank Dellums for the constancy of his efforts to put political pressure on the apartheid regime. Mandela, who was held as a political prisoner for decades, saw Dellums as a crucial ally. In his oral history, Dellums described Mandela grasping him by both arms and declaring: "You gave us hope. You kept us alive."

"The reason why I introduced the disinvestment bill," Dellums said in the oral history interview, "was because I'm a very firm believer that there are only two factors over which any of us have control . . . your fidelity, your faithfulness to what you believe in, and your willingness to show up every day for the fight. With those as the guiding principles, I kept introducing the disinvestment bill even though people said, 'There's no way this is going to happen. This is outside the realm of reality. It's way too radical.'"

Dellums, here, is discussing what's now known as the "Overton Window." That political model suggests there is a range of policies that are considered socially acceptable in a given moment and that politicians are bound by that range. Dellums felt that engagement at the margins drives change. Fighting for policies to the left of the mainstream would help open the window and broaden what might be considered acceptable. Building political momentum towards a preferred outcome, in other words, is not a matter of adopting broadly popular positions, or being personally popular, but of sticking with what you believe in and pushing the whole debate in the right direction.

"People often think that the center of American politics is a real place, that it's a static place, that some way you could discover the center of American politics," Dellums said, in comments that seem aimed at politicians like Harris. "My view is that there's no such place—that the center is contingent upon who shows up for the fight."

If Harris's longtime congressman, perhaps the most influential progressive ever to hold federal office, had any impact on her, there's little evidence of it. As far as we could discover, she has only spoken about Ron Dellums publicly once, sending a tweet of condolence on the day of his death in 2018.

Though they emerged from the same milieu and both claimed the mantle of "progressivism," Dellums's approach could not be more different than Harris's. The gulf between them is a stark illustration of how Generation X strayed from the revolutionary politics of their parents' generation and how, under the Democrats of the 2000s, the definition of "progressive" became muddied as moderates and centrists wrapped themselves in the term; it provided an inviting refuge from the perhaps more accurate description "liberal," which had been under withering assault from both the right and left for decades.

While Dellums abhorred moderation, Harris kept reaching for the illusory center. She seemed to dismiss every substantive choice as a false one that a politician need only transcend. And even though she hailed from one of the most distinctively progressive regions of the country, by simultaneously trying to stake out the middle ground and a progressive brand, she risked becoming a woman from nowhere, or worse still, letting her adversaries define her in clearer, more straightforward terms.

―――――

ON THE WAY INTO THE CALIFORNIA ATTORNEY GENERAL'S OFFICE IN Sacramento, there's a lengthy corridor lined with framed portraits of all the previous occupants of the position, one after another.

"It's just a giant long wall of really old white guys," said Nick Pacilio, who spent four years as a staff member for Kamala Harris when she held the post. "With no exception, every single attorney general had been an old white man, until her. Reporters couldn't even fit in their ledes how different she was from her predecessors."

Harris has a tendency to dial in on statistics and intricate details that aides attribute to her unique background. After breaking down so many barriers herself, a White House official interviewed for this book said Harris often describes herself as "walking in the room for others" who can't be there.

"She is standing in the gap for so many," the official said of Harris. "So, yeah, she is going to get down in the weeds. She wants to make sure she has all the data so she can stand up for the people who aren't in the room."

That wonky approach means Harris doesn't embrace the labels like "progressive" and "moderate" that often wrap around political debates. The White House official said that adopting a simple brand is not Harris's "style" and, instead, she prefers to be judged on her policies and priorities.

"She knows exactly who she is and the work that she focuses on tells that story," the official said of Harris. "She doesn't need to overqualify herself in that way because of her record."

Harris's effort to transcend traditional political terms has been apparent since the early days of her career. In 2008, the website for her San Francisco district attorney campaign, which has since been deleted, explicitly noted Harris was trying to strike a middle way between the dominant modes for discussing criminal justice. It painted Harris as both a reformer and an aggressive guardian of law and order who boasted of her record locking up criminals.

"Her pledge is to move beyond the false choice of being 'tough' or 'weak' on crime," the site said. "Kamala Harris is smart on crime . . . and it's working."

A technocratic sleight of hand, the phrase "smart on crime" suggested that the growing divide between criminal justice reformers and Democrats scarred by race-baiting attacks that painted them as weak on crime could be overcome by a savvy politician.

Yet, on criminal justice and other issues, that effort to be "smart" also meant avoiding the fundamental questions about crime and how to order society.

"Most of the conversations throughout the years with her have never really focused on 'progressive' or 'moderate,'" one longtime adviser told us when asked how Harris viewed her brand. In Harris's world, according to this adviser, those terms would only be used to describe different advocacy groups. Harris opted for an approach that was more "pragmatic" and viewed the landscape in terms of issues and goals rather than ideology.

"She'll often say in a briefing with her team, 'What is the value statement we are all in agreement about?'" the adviser continued, paraphrasing Harris. "And it's an exercise for all of us to be like, 'Okay, we believe there should be . . . economic security for families.' Then working backwards from that, you can build in different policies."

Focusing on individual values and issues rather than choosing to align herself more broadly as a progressive or a centrist also meant that Harris was rejecting the vocabulary the Democratic voter base had been using to define their loyalties and choices for years.

In the decades before Harris's campaign, a number of Democratic politicians had made a specialty of so-called "triangulation." The technique involved situating themselves roughly equidistant from the left and right wings—i.e., approximately in the middle of the Overton Window—on a given subject, garnering partial credit for adopting a version of each side's ideas and insulating the politician from either side's attacks. The most famous practitioner of this art was Bill Clinton.

Harris's effort to adopt an approach that was separate from the two poles of the party seemed to be a form of triangulation, and it worked during her rise in California politics. She also had the good sense to align herself with a core institution in Golden State politics: Bearstar Strategies.

Bearstar is a fixture in the lives of West Coast Democrats. It was founded under the name SCN Public Relations in 1997 by three executives named Ace Smith, Sean Clegg, and Dan Newman. Newman was a veteran spokesman and message minder for Democratic candidates. Smith and Clegg met while running Barbara Boxer's campaign for Senate in 1992, the so-called "Year of the Woman."

In 2019, the firm changed its name to SCRB Strategies. The company settled on its current moniker Bearstar, an allusion to the California state flag that features a grizzly bear walking under a lone red star, in March 2021.

Bearstar's client list has featured some of the most powerful figures in the Golden State including Governor Gavin Newsom, former governor Jerry Brown, former Los Angeles mayors Antonio Villaraigosa and Eric Garcetti, Boxer, former San Francisco mayor Ed Lee, and Alex Padilla, the man who replaced Harris as California's junior senator when she became vice president.

"If you weren't working with them, you were not gonna win," Pacilio said of Bearstar's influence in the state. "It was everyone—it was everyone in politics they picked, and that's how Democratic politics worked," he added. Other consultants we spoke to who work in California pushed back on this notion and raised the question of whether Bearstar was simply adept at attaching itself to winning campaigns.

Pacilio described Bearstar as part of a largely white "good old boys club mentality" that dominated California politics, and, he said, Harris "had to be in the center of [that mindset] for her entire career."

Though Harris had found a way to work within this boys club while she held city and statewide positions, she worked hard to ensure the next generation that came after her would experience a different landscape. In the run-up to her presidential campaign, multiple sources said Harris pushed her consultants, most likely including her team at Bearstar, to diversify their leadership.

"Kamala is, and I say this with reverence, she pushes for diversity in every conversation," said one consultant who worked with her. "She cared less about how much money I was raising for her and more about what I was doing to create a good inclusive workspace."

In 2017, shortly after Harris's victory in her Senate race and while her planning for a presidential campaign was already underway, Bearstar brought in Juan Rodriguez as the first new partner since the firm's formation. Rodriguez had worked as Harris's senior adviser in the California Attorney General's Office. The next year, Bearstar added labor leader Laphonza Butler to the partnership as well. With Harris on the rise, California's old boys club culture was breaking, or at least bending.

As her White House bid came together, Bearstar was not Harris's sole adviser. A candidate's family must always figure in any politician's career—either as advocates or props. However, Kamala's sister Maya Harris, Maya's husband Tony West, and Maya's daughter Meena Harris have all taken far more involved roles in her campaigns, formally and informally, than a typical candidate's relatives. Maya, as chairman, occupied the top post on Harris's campaign from the official launch in January 2019. (Maya Harris did not respond to extensive requests for comment on this book.) The family faction would ultimately clash with Bearstar in spectacular ways.

Some staffers felt the tug-of-war between the Harris family and Bearstar pulled the team apart.

"Pretty quickly, the campaign got splintered off into factions. It was two warring camps and then everyone was trying their best to find a spot in the middle," one campaign aide said.

Others felt the tensions between Bearstar and the family were overstated. A source familiar with the matter pointed out that the relationship between Bearstar and Harris's family members stretched back "a really long time," and they had worked together on a number of Harris's winning campaigns.

"They [Bearstar] were involved in Senate races and AG races, and family comes in and out of everything," this person said. "It was not like this was the first time they had worked together."

However, the source also acknowledged some staff felt there were tensions and chose to air their concerns to reporters. The resulting coverage had a corrosive effect on the team as they read the negative headlines and speculated about who was responsible for the leaks.

Competition between Bearstar and Maya was ongoing, but it always had a clear winner. The top Harris aide who described the dynamic as "two warring camps" said Rodriguez, a junior partner in the firm serving as the campaign manager, "got bowled over a ton by Maya Harris."

Rodriguez worked to assert himself. According to a senior staffer, the divisions eventually manifested themselves geographically. Maya Harris and Rodriguez had offices on opposite sides of campaign headquarters. As Harris's poll numbers sagged, Maya and Rodriguez separately called staffers in for audit interviews to assess the state of the campaign.

"It was the most awkward day of my life," the senior staffer said. "People were literally having a thirty-minute audit meeting with Juan about how the campaign was going," they added, "and then they were walking across the hall into the same meeting with Maya.... I remember Juan popping into my office to find out how the meeting with Maya went."

Most campaigns, of course, have disagreements among their leadership, and they eventually get sorted out—or someone gets fired. Neither of these things happened on Harris's team.

The tensions between Maya Harris and Rodriguez seemed uniquely unresolvable. Kamala, the thinking went, could hardly dismiss her own cherished sister, and removing Rodriguez probably would have led to the equally unthinkable resignations of the whole Bearstar team, essential allies for a California politician. With the candidate remaining neutral, the rest of the staff was forced to choose a side.

Others pointed out that the main tension wasn't the family versus Bearstar, but between the campaign's aspirations and the financial realities of the race. Campaigns—like all businesses—run on cash. Managing the balance between fundraising, spending, and momentum is a delicate calculus that is essential in a presidential race. On Harris's team, the source said, senior staff had not kept careful track of their resource allocations.

Another Harris backer made a similar point, suggesting her campaign was "too big too early" with an unnecessarily sprawling national footprint and insufficient focus on South Carolina.

"The focus early on in the campaign was obviously Iowa.... Her campaign also invested in a bunch of places really early on. I mean, she had the office in California, she had a Washington office."

Still, according to the source, it was money management that was the key issue. Rifts between top advisers were only part of a larger toxic climate. In a resignation letter that, of course, leaked publicly in late 2019, the campaign's state operations manager Kelly Mehlenbacher wrote: "Campaigns have highs and lows, mistakes and miscalculations, lessons learned and adjustments made. But, because we have refused to confront our mistakes, foster an environment of critical thinking and honest feedback, or trust the expertise of talented staff, we find ourselves making the same unforced errors over and over."

This portrayal of Harris's leadership struggles is drawn from extensive conversations with staff who worked with her in San Francisco, the Senate, during her campaign, and in the Biden administration. It's natural to ask whether the critical elements of the account are simply a manifestation of the racism and sexism that she has spent her career overcoming. However, the stories of mismanagement shared by our sources on Harris's various teams were substantive, nuanced, and consistent. And they came from sources who signed up to work for her and, at least at one point, wanted her to succeed. It's impossible to dismiss all of their critiques as entirely the result of prejudice.

Other veterans of Harris's White House bid didn't criticize how it was run. They just kept quiet. In a brief phone call, Bearstar partner Ace Smith said simply, "I don't talk about that campaign."

———

DESPITE THE TURBULENCE BEHIND THE SCENES, AT HER CAMPAIGN launch event, Harris drew a crowd of 20,000 Californians outside Oakland City Hall. The location embodied some of the tensions swirling around the campaign. It was literally the site of battles between the institutional Democratic Party and the activist left.

The beautiful Beaux Arts building that serves as the seat of government in Oakland overlooks a plaza that was ground zero for the Occupy Wall Street protests which rocked that city in 2011. Those demonstrations were some of the biggest in the country and—under a Democratic mayor—provoked one of the most violent responses from law enforcement.

Harris, who had been California's top prosecutor at the time, had her office picketed by Occupiers who deemed her a "sell-out" for not doing more to punish banks for the foreclosure crisis. Now, she was surrounded by American flags, standing where those demonstrations were beaten, making a progressive pitch and declaring that "our economy today is not working for working people" and vowing to be a champion for the "battle ahead."

"We are here knowing that we are at an inflection point in the history of our world. We are at an inflection point in the history of our nation," Harris said. "We are here because the American Dream and our American democracy are under attack and on the line like never before. We are here at this moment in time because we must answer a fundamental question. Who are we? Who are we as Americans?"

These were questions Harris never seemed quite able to answer about herself.

In 2003, the website for her successful run at the San Francisco District Attorney's Office attributed Harris's politics to her upbringing in the progressive movement.

"I grew up during the often-contentious civil rights movement of the sixties—my parents carted me to protest marches in Berkeley and Oakland and instilled in me a strong sense of justice," she wrote. "I chose to become a prosecutor because I wanted to ensure that justice is done on both sides of the law—which requires that crime victims and defendants are both accorded the rights they deserve."

Yet, as she touted progressive bona fides, Harris steadfastly continued her career-long refusal to engage with policy debates on the terms that were increasingly defining politics within the Democratic Party.

In her memoir, Harris declared herself a "progressive prosecutor." But her definition of the phrase—"someone who used the power of the office with a sense of fairness, perspective, and experience, someone who was clear about the need to hold serious criminals accountable and who understood that the best way to create safe communities was to prevent crime in the first place"—sounded conventional, and not discernibly progressive.

After Harris launched her presidential campaign, critics from her left mounted a withering assault on her actual record in office in op-ed pages and through news articles. They noted that she had pushed for harsher sentences for drug offenses, fought to uphold patently wrongful convictions, championed legislation to punish the parents of habitually truant children, appealed a ruling that the death penalty was unconstitutional, and resisted systemic reforms.

Harris had not chosen a broad brand for herself, and her opponents on the left were more than happy to give her one. They called her, quite simply, "a cop."

At the Oakland City Hall launch event, Harris laid out her vision "to be president of the people, by the people, and for all people." Contrasting herself with President Trump, she highlighted her commitments to unity and fighting for ordinary people, and she pledged to support popular progressive initiatives like government-provided single-payer health insurance.

"America's story has always been written by people who can see what can be unburdened by what has been. That is our story," Harris told the excited crowd.

The audience punctuated each applause line by waving bright yellow banners decorated with the slogan: "Kamala Harris for the People."

"So, let's do this!" Harris exclaimed, and laughed in delight. The crowd roared its approval. "And let's do it together! And let's start now! And I thank you, and God bless you, and God bless the United States of America!" Harris concluded.

Harris began to make her way off the stage, shaking hands, as The

Roots's mixtape version of the song "My Shot" from the Broadway musical *Hamilton* played over the loudspeakers. "I'm not throwing away my shot," the hook insisted, over and over.

But despite the rousing start, the Kamala 2020 campaign soon floundered. The campaign slogan itself was evidence of the deeper problem. As a phrase, "for the people" sounded like a clarion call to classic progressives, the radicals of Berkeley's People's Park and Oakland's Occupy movements. However, Harris's "for the people" was rooted in her work as a prosecutor, a vocation that earned her skepticism and anger from the left.

In her memoir, Harris wrote that she used the phrase to introduce herself in Alameda County Superior Court when she worked as a line prosecutor. Those appearances began with her declaring, "Kamala Harris, for the people." To her, it was a reminder that, in court, the prosecution acted for society at large, not just the victim of the alleged crime. She relished the universality of the idea and wrote that it was her "compass."

She recounted one speech where she told a group of newly recruited young prosecutors, "Let's be clear. You represent the people. So I expect you to get to know exactly who the people are."

" 'For the people' means for *them*," Harris said. "All of them."

As she rose through California and the US Senate, Harris had a particular focus on standing up for women, children, and the poor. A White House official told us the slogan was a clear reflection of Harris's core values.

"At the end of the day she's a fighter and she's been fighting for people in her entire career," the official said. "There was no mistake in making her campaign slogan 'for the people,' because that's who she's always represented."

But in hoping to represent *all* people rather than aligning herself with one of the major brands that defined Democratic politics, Harris had forgotten the lessons Dellums had articulated. By focusing too much on what a broad swath of the public wanted, she now failed to articulate her own positions on key issues. Her core values may have been clear to Harris and her team, but as she ran for president, her policy positions and rationale were far less precise.

On health care, over a year before she launched her presidential campaign, Harris added her name to Bernie Sanders's "Medicare for All" bill. For a mainstream Democratic candidate, it was a daring move and an attention-getter. Harris was staking out a position substantially to the left of where Barack Obama and Hillary Clinton situated their own health care policies. Sanders's Medicare for All plan—a cornerstone of his presidential campaigns—would enroll the whole country automatically in the single-payer insurance scheme and forbid private insurance policies that offered similar coverage, almost entirely displacing the system of private, largely employer-provided insurance that America has had since World War II. This one move meant Harris was running to the left of the institutional Democratic Party.

Within days of Harris's opening speech, reporters sought to put the spotlight on her bold policy. Pressed in a town hall appearance in Des Moines about whether people who like their private insurance plans would get to keep them—the same question that vexed Obama as he pursued more modest public health care expansions—Harris initially dug in her heels.

"The idea is everyone gets access to medical care," she said, "and you don't have to go through the process of going through an insurance company, having them give you approval, going through the paperwork, all of the delay that may require. . . . Let's eliminate all of that. Let's move on."

Republicans pounced, hoping to capitalize on voters' uneasiness about changes to an already precarious health care regime. Harris soon recalibrated her position. Rather than talking about how Medicare for All would eliminate the injustice and ruinous costs of the private insurance system, she pulled her punches, emphasizing the fact that Medicare for All actually *preserved* a role for private insurers. They would, she promised, be allowed to offer supplemental coverage for certain treatments and procedures. For the rest of her campaign, it was difficult to discern a clear position on health care at all.

Harris's ending position on health care—a version of Medicare for All that paradoxically retained a sizable role for private insurers— might well have been the outcome of strategic triangulation. But her manner of arriving there lacked the grace that Bill Clinton or Barack Obama brought to the maneuver. It more nearly resembled a far less exalted political trick: the flip-flop.

"Walking back from it, that hurt us," a staffer on the digital team said of Medicare for All. "That hurt our fundraising numbers. That hurt us with Democratic activists, and that's a problem. The last thing you ever want to be seen as is wishy-washy or flip-floppy."

———

HARRIS CAME TO THE FIRST DEBATE OF THE 2020 DEMOCRATIC PRESI- dential primary in late June 2019 loaded for bear but unsure about the hunt.

Biden had blundered several days before by bragging about his working relationships with segregationists in the early years of his long Senate career. Harris publicly needled Biden on the remark for days, and at the debate, she launched the withering attack. While the other candidates were engaged in a back-and-forth on police reform, Harris cut in.

"As the only Black person on this stage, I would like to speak on the issue of race," Harris declared, as the crowd applauded.

Then Harris directed her attention towards Biden. She paired his comment about the segregationists in the old Senate with his past record of opposing court-ordered busing for school integration in the 1970s. While Harris granted Biden that she believed he was not "a racist," she called his behavior "hurtful" and stressed that the pain was personal.

"There was a little girl in California who was part of the second class to integrate her public schools and she was bused to school every day, and that little girl was me," Harris said.

The line was a showstopper, and it worked to stupendous effect. The confrontation instantly became the defining moment of the debate and dominated coverage afterward. At campaign headquarters, the digital team immediately saw the fundraising numbers spike.

"It was an explosion," said a staffer on the digital team. "Everything we did for like a week turned to gold. It was just like we couldn't do any wrong for fundraising. Our ads took off; our email program took off. And it was after a dry spell. . . . sixty-three thousand people donated within twenty-four hours, fifty-eight percent were first-time donors, [and the] average contribution was thirty dollars."

Harris, in other words, garnered $1.9 million from small-dollar donors in a single day after the debate, and over $1 million of that haul was from people giving her money for the first time. The momentum was real.

"What I recall was, either the day after or two days after, everybody's fucking excited; the campaign's got life again," a senior staffer said. "We were raising a shit-ton of money."

Her masterstroke on the debate stage rejuvenated Harris's operation, brought her legions of new fans, and appeared to offer her a chance to make inroads with Black voters—a crucial voting bloc for

Biden. Federally mandated busing had not been a live political issue for decades, but it roared back to relevance and instantly focused the primary's simmering tensions about race around a genuine question of policy. But the boost did not last. Once again, Harris failed to maintain her compelling, bold stance.

A scrambling Biden staff had made a raft of phone calls to reporters on the Harris campaign beat to ensure she was asked her precise position on busing. When the question came, the senior staffer said, Harris didn't "have an answer for it."

"I would say it's a pretty important piece. If you attack someone for their position—" Biden's campaign manager Greg Schultz began to say when asked about this post-debate counterattack in a 2023 interview, before stopping himself short. "I don't want to relitigate. She's vice president. She's great. She's loyal to [Biden]. But, if you attack somebody for a policy position, it's fair for you to ask, 'What's your policy position?'"

The questions to Harris about busing dogged her for several days. On debate night, she had signaled support for federal mandates, saying to Biden that there had been a "failure of states to integrate public schools in America" in the 1970s. By the following week, she had retreated, saying at a picnic in Des Moines that local school districts should consider busing to achieve more diverse schools, but that she wouldn't necessarily support federal mandates if local authorities decided they preferred de facto segregation in their schools after all. A day later, Harris tacked again, telling reporters in Indianola that, while she would have supported federally mandated busing in circumstances like those that existed in the '70s, she wouldn't support it in contemporary America.

"Thankfully, that's not where we are today," Harris said. As she had at the debate, she called on Biden to apologize for having been wrong decades ago, but at the same time, she unmistakably aligned herself with his current position.

As with the Medicare for All debacle, Harris seemed to be trying to straddle the left flank and middle ground, but she ended up nowhere. But this moment would be remembered by her campaign as the beginning of the end.

"That's the focal point of where it all falls apart," a senior staffer said about her shifting stances on the busing issue.

The debate moment had propelled Harris to the head of the pack.

"She rose to the top of the polls, I remember some poll that had her in first place with like 30 percent," the senior staffer said. "People were ready to fucking go. It was the only real movement of the whole race. Otherwise, the race never moved."

The heat Harris generated at the late June debate evaporated as she waffled on the very issue that had ignited her campaign. That stalled momentum also applied to the all-important fundraising numbers.

"We had an explosive couple of days and then it just disappeared," the staffer said. "To the point that in August we couldn't scrape together two nickels."

In a few short months, Harris went from a front-runner to a complete bust.

The ineffectiveness of Harris's campaign, which she suspended in December 2019, and the alienation felt by some of her staff didn't stop her national ascent. Instead of finding a significant constituency on the ground, she ultimately found one among the leaders of the Democratic party. The following August, Joe Biden—who had promised to pick a woman as his running mate—anointed her.

While Harris's campaign was unquestionably successful in the sense that it elevated her to the second-highest office in the land, those closest to it were left with deep-seated doubts about her ability to lead.

As Democrats fretted over whether Harris could serve as a successful successor to Biden, some of the staffers who had worked most closely with her were among the most afraid.

"It was rotten from the start," one top aide on the 2020 campaign said. "A lot of us, at least folks that I was friends with on the campaign, all realized that: 'Yeah, this person should not be president of the United States.'"

As she ran for office, Harris had trouble managing money and competing personalities. But perhaps more importantly, she suffered from a lack of overall purpose.

Harris struggled to decide what she was offering voters beyond her compelling persona.

"That's a lot of the reason people support her," a senior staffer said of Harris's backstory. "But you've got to back that up with: 'What are you going to do?'"

Ultimately, at a moment when the Democratic Party was wracked by a genuine debate over its policy course, Harris had not picked a direction.

Chapter 6

WAR ROOM

TWO MONTHS AFTER KAMALA HARRIS'S CAMPAIGN COLLAPSED, the night of the Iowa caucus arrived. Bernie Sanders had every reason to expect good news. He was set to win.

The Vermont senator was deep in his election-night ritual, with his lanky, crooked frame stalking around a hotel suite filled with his family and Faiz Shakir, his campaign manager. Sanders constantly checked the television, refreshed news sites, and worked the phones to get the latest numbers, ideally ones that would confirm his victory. He peppered his people for scraps of information about the turnout.

"How are we doing?" Sanders asked, insistently and incessantly. "How are we winning?"

But the answers never came. Instead, everything went sideways.

Iowa was the beginning of the end for Bernie Sanders. A night where he imagined triumph ended in something even worse than defeat.

We captured the experience of Sanders and his top campaign staff through a series of interviews. Sanders came to the state expecting it to vault him towards the presidency. But a perfect storm of incompetence, technical glitches, and sheer bad luck opened old wounds and dealt a shattering blow to his quest to steer the Democratic Party on a revolutionary course.

He spent the evening at two hotels in Iowa's capital city. The night started at the Hilton DoubleTree, which was Sanders's standard destination in Des Moines. For the caucus, his campaign planned its main event at an airport Holiday Inn. At some point, Sanders switched between the two venues but it was hard for Shakir to remember exactly when.

The campaign trail is a grueling, lonely slog, particularly brutal in the key early primaries when life is lived almost exclusively in a dizzying succession of bland, dated hotel rooms. The off-white walls, fake woods, scratchy curtains, and bad abstract art begin to blend together in a dim haze.

Daytime offers small tastes of place glimpsed through rental car windows. Iowa's flat, gray, wintry plains. New Hampshire's high forests blazing bright with snow and ice. Nevada, baking in the dry heat of the desert under impossibly blue, wide-open skies, an overexposed photograph brought to life.

But nights are all the same: liminal hotel purgatory. Then there are the rallies.

People in pain made pilgrimages to Sanders's speeches. His crowds at high school gyms, small colleges, and well-worn community centers were filled with men and women experiencing a melancholy American story: lost jobs, low wages, illnesses, and lost opportunity. They rushed towards him every time he stepped down from the podium, desperate to share their concerns. Their hands reached out from the crush eager to briefly touch a man who offered them hope.

But Sanders's tent wasn't just filled with the work-weary people his idol Eugene Debs, the turn-of-the-century socialist presidential candidate, had dubbed "Fountain Proletaire." Along with tie-dyed Boomers and working-class heroes, Sanders's rallies drew young people with boundless optimism about the fairer, more economically just society they could build if their man ran the government. In the final eight days of the race, polls showed Sanders a few points ahead of a crowded field thanks largely to support from those young voters. Their presence in his base hardened Sanders's conviction that his path offered the best future for the country.

Sanders had the wind at his back. The centrist establishment that had tried to cut him down in 2016 was losing ground. Every Bernie event had become a swirl of adoring fans, cheers, bright lights, and cameras. When he looked out at the world, his own face stared back at him from T-shirts, front pages, and television screens. Journalists were—for the first time—calling him the front-runner. Sanders couldn't help but imagine his improbable dream might actually be coming true. Victory was in sight.

It's almost impossible to overstate how much the Hawkeye State meant to Bernie Sanders and his campaign at this moment. As Shakir put it months later, they had it "all plotted out" after a win in the traditional first caucus.

But that night, as Sanders paced in that Des Moines Holiday Inn, waves of bad news rolled in. Across town, in a squat, redbrick building that served as the nerve center for his campaign leadership, senior aides were panicking.

"There was chaos. Everyone was freaking out," Sanders's deputy campaign manager, Arianna Jones, recounted. "Bernie was pissed too."

Back at the hotel suite, Shakir said he found the candidate sitting with his hands at his temples and a thousand-yard stare glaring from behind his glasses.

"The only thing I remember is towards the end of the night . . . how upset—like really upset—he was," Shakir said of Sanders. The candidate grimaced with a mixture of what Shakir described as searing pain and "seething anger."

"We were just despondent about the situation," Shakir said. "He felt robbed."

━━━━━

POLITICAL CAMPAIGNS ARE DELICATE CREATURES.

An old adage compares them to a jumbo jet assembled on the runway during takeoff. To survive, a campaign requires a precise chemistry of talented people seizing fleeting opportunities. Presidential bids, some of which cost over a billion dollars, are the biggest—and most fickle—beasts of them all.

Sanders's White House run was particularly audacious. Before rising to national fame, Sanders was one of just two independents in the US Senate and the only one in history to identify as a socialist, one of the most consistently demonized ideologies in American politics. Yet he was vying to lead the Democratic Party, one of two major political institutions that have dominated American government since the Civil War.

Sanders's first presidential race, in 2016, was a bitter battle against Hillary Clinton, whose hundred-million-dollar fortune garnered from the global conference circuit and connections accrued over decades as First Lady, senator from New York, and secretary of state made her the living embodiment of the elite, centrist mainstream Sanders despised.

He almost won it, too.

Even though he was convinced the Democratic Party stacked the deck against him, Sanders's little rebellion still took off.

He drew massive crowds at raucous rallies where he barked out a blueprint for a progressive transformation of the American government.

In a gravelly accent that betrayed his Brooklyn roots, Sanders called for a political revolution that would transform America into a nation that taxed inequality out of existence, expanded the social safety net to include free college and health care, and fought the climate crisis instead of foreign wars.

But Sanders was no opportunist. He had pursued these goals for nearly half a century. The difference was that the country had finally begun to see the appeal (and the glaring logic) of his platform. A rising post–Cold War generation was more open-minded about socialism and disillusioned after decades of Wall Street excesses and foreign wars. Never giving an inch on his principles, Sanders went from an oddball underdog to a close second-place finisher against Clinton's imperial machine. His vision of a new politics captivated millions and built him a base within the Democratic Party.

Four years later, Sanders had gone from a relatively obscure independent to a powerful senator with supporters in Congress, in city and state capitals around the country, and, with Clinton swept aside by Donald Trump, even in the party leadership. The same institutions that once tried to stop Sanders had begun to make concessions and work with him. Sanders was starting the 2020 race in a far stronger position, and a win in Iowa would establish enormous momentum out of the gate.

Compared to the rest of the field, Sanders had the biggest team in Iowa and the most money in his war chest. Next up was New Hampshire, which Sanders had won in 2016, and then Nevada, where his robust operation had connected with the state's large Latino population. Based on the known poll numbers, a streak of three early state victories seemed almost inevitable. And, in a primary system where momentum is the coin of the realm, a trio of early wins could be enough to wrap up the Democratic nomination.

Sanders's strategy—and route to victory—made sense, but it all depended on Iowa. And on that night, the state delivered Sanders and his staff an almost unthinkable outcome.

"Devastating is an understatement," Shakir, the campaign manager, said when asked about what happened next. "I can't tell you how much we invested to win that state."

———

IOWA OCCUPIES A PECULIAR PLACE IN AMERICAN POLITICS. ITS CAUCUS had been guaranteed primacy in the nominating process by both major parties since 1972. That special status has afforded voters in the state, who are less than 1 percent of the US population, an immense degree of influence over the last twelve presidential races.

Detractors of this system argue it's wrong to give a relatively insignificant, overwhelmingly white, and rural group of voters such dramatic sway over our elections. Supporters of the caucus counter that Iowa's Midwestern charms and small size mean candidates can reach each of the ninety-nine counties and be welcomed into voters' homes without having to pay for luxuries like private jets and major market television commercials.

Caucus lore is filled with tales of long shots blanketing the state and winning over voters one by one on the way to Washington. Jimmy Carter famously biked his way through in 1976, shaking hands and propelling himself to the nomination. Iowa was also the place where Barack Obama caught fire in 2008.

Along with a special place on the primary calendar, Iowa has had an eccentric voting system. Caucuses are not simple votes. The Democrats' process has involved people gathering at an appointed hour in over 1,600 sites around the state including churches, community centers, at least one meatpacker's union hall, and a Shriners Temple.

Traditonally, when the action starts, there are speeches and the crowd separates into groups supporting each candidate. It's like a high-stakes version of musical chairs. Then, administrators take a head count. Any contingent that falls below a designated viability threshold is disbanded. Supporters of the other candidates then lobby the members of the losing factions to join their side. The process can take hours. Ties are sometimes decided with a coin flip. It's a messy, imprecise system—and it's a major part of how America picks its presidents.

In years past, the Iowa Democratic Party did not announce the raw vote totals. Instead, for public consumption on caucus night, it solely reported a metric called "state delegate equivalents," which was calculated based on the location of the site, turnout in recent elections, and lastly, the actual vote totals captured by the two head counts. Those figures were then filtered through a separate formula to determine how many of Iowa's delegates will back a given candidate at the Democratic National Convention.

Those elaborate calculations include multiple points where numbers must be rounded, which pulls the state delegate equivalent figure further away from the raw vote total. Campaigns had previously reported discrepancies between the official results and their data from caucus sites, raising questions about how the state party volunteers executed the math. Small mistakes could make a major difference. In 2012, for example, the Republican caucus came down to one-tenth of a state delegate equivalent.

In 2016, Sanders's loss to Clinton was tight as well—one-quarter of a percentage point in the state delegate equivalents. Sanders's campaign compiled their own data from the caucus sites that year. Based on their internal numbers, some Sanders aides were convinced he won the popular vote and possibly the delegate metric as well. However, since the state party didn't report the vote totals, there was no way to check.

With his strong showing and Clinton's ultimate loss to Trump in

2016, Sanders earned a degree of pull behind the scenes. He used it to chip away at some of the structures that preserved backroom influence and, he was convinced, had cost him the White House, including the black box that previously surrounded the raw count. In 2020, after a push from Sanders and his allies, the Iowa Democratic Party had agreed to announce the number of actual votes along with the state delegate equivalents.

Some observers warned that this could lead to a mess where one candidate was victorious in the popular vote and another won more delegate equivalents. Of course, such messes were equally possible in previous election years. There had just been no way to prove it.

There was one other wrinkle in 2020. Along with reporting a whole new set of numbers, Iowa's Democrats launched an app to transmit the results from the more than 1,600 caucus sites across the state. It was designed by Silicon Valley entrepreneurs with deep party ties, and it crashed spectacularly.

━━━

HOUR AFTER HOUR, AS THE CAUCUS SITES EMPTIED OUT, FOLDING tables were put away, and the world waited, the Iowa Democratic Party released no results. Television screens showed empty boxes where the candidates' running tallies should have been—zero percent reporting.

As it became apparent something had gone very wrong with the caucus, an explosive battle erupted among Sanders's staff as they scrambled to salvage the moment that was supposed to catapult him to victory. Sanders's former senior adviser Chuck Rocha was one of many who remembered the debacle vividly—and painfully.

"I was in Iowa that night when all hell broke loose," Rocha said.

A self-described "Mexican redneck," Rocha was a swaggering presence who woke up early each morning to lift weights. Tall and gregarious, with a clean-shaven head, he ran a consulting firm that specialized in Spanish-language advertising.

Rocha boasted of buying a beaver fur cowboy hat that cost about a thousand dollars after he signed his first big contract with Sanders in 2016. He was blunt about the team's failings and bombastic about its successes, which he usually attributed, at least in part, to his own work. In an East Texas drawl peppered with colorful euphemisms, he offered his assessment of the highs and lows of caucus night in Iowa: "There's good. That's about twenty percent," Rocha said. "Then there's eighty percent that is the most horrific thing I've ever lived through in my life."

Rocha's brash approach was emblematic of the entire Sanders team. On both sides of the aisle, political operatives are usually cut from a relatively similar cloth: well-scrubbed student-government-types. Straight-A kids who turn into cheerful stewards of the status quo. Sanders's team was different.

The candidate himself was famously unkempt, sporting cheap suits, a skewed tie, and shocks of white hair sticking out from his bald pate.

Many of his allies and operatives were similarly uncomfortable in dress clothes. Their anti-establishment bent was apparent the second you walked into one of the campaign trail hotels. Sanders's brain trust often crowded the lobby bars until late each night. A large contingent chain-smoked. Some opted for weed, which they all thought should be legal.

That night, Sanders's senior team was mostly in the war room in the redbrick building in downtown Des Moines. Other staff gathered at the ballroom at the Des Moines airport Holiday Inn for the party. Ostensibly the election-night reception is a place for supporters to celebrate a victory or commiserate after a loss. But, as with so many other things in politics, the real purpose was to put on a show for the national media camped out in the back of the room. Election-night fêtes are an opportunity for the candidate to grab some free broadcast real estate, called "earned media," with a speech either reveling in their triumph or spinning a loss.

These early primary contests are about "The Narrative" at least as much as the actual results. As results come in, particularly in a crowded race, campaigns begin jockeying with each other and the networks to secure precious on-air minutes to amplify their message about the contest. Ideally, a candidate is able to ice out their competitors and get on air early to claim some measure of victory. It would be Faiz Shakir's job to coordinate this process for Sanders and bring him from the hotel suite to the ballroom.

A Harvard graduate with closely cropped black hair and boyish looks that made him appear far younger than thirty-nine, Shakir was an outlier on the Sanders campaign. He had not been on the team in 2016. During that race, he worked as a top adviser to Democratic Senate Leader Harry Reid, the kind of politician who passed for progressive before Sanders's socialism caught fire. Shakir informally consulted with Sanders's campaign during that first race, which drew the ire of many of his colleagues on Capitol Hill, who were uniformly aligned behind Clinton.

While Shakir was a recent arrival to the inner circle, he was known as someone who could soothe Sanders, who often raged after missteps or defeats.

But even Shakir couldn't keep Sanders calm on caucus night. Sanders was glued to his screens, his phone, and the TV in his suite. Frantic, he called the war room and yelled out to Shakir for updates, but there were none. Something was off.

Counting normally begins at 7 p.m. at most sites around the states. Caucus results typically start pouring in an hour or so later. With no numbers posting and party officials ignoring requests for information, Shakir began to realize the evening was becoming, as he put it—bowdlerizing himself—"kind of a cluster."

"And then it just, clearly, it turns out to be like a much more massive cluster than we ever could have imagined," Shakir said.

The other top Sanders staffers were mostly camped out in the downtown war room taking in reports from the field, putting out fires, and fielding Sanders's constant requests for information. Often, the man on the other end of the line was Jeff Weaver. Sanders's calls took on a panicked urgency as the hours dragged on.

"Jeff, why aren't there numbers yet?" he implored.

Jeff Weaver never says a bad word about Bernie Sanders. A staunch loyalist since Sanders was mayor of Burlington, Vermont, Weaver had been in charge of Bernie's war rooms for decades. The laconic native of Vermont's Northern woods was a former Marine with a white beard and a dry sense of humor. When discussing his boss, Weaver resorts to clipped understatement—if you can get him to talk at all.

Weaver had run Sanders's campaign in 2016 and, this time around, was serving a more amorphous role as senior adviser. Multiple members of the team said that was, at least in part, because, amid mounting diversity pressure, it wouldn't do to have a white man running the show. Yet while Weaver had formally stepped aside, his place in Sanders's universe transcended title. Weaver was like family. He was both right-hand man and main attack dog.

Weaver's sparring with the Democratic establishment had earned him a national reputation as a combative political operative. But for colleagues, he was—at least outwardly—a far steadier presence. Weaver's ability to appear unruffled under fire would be sorely tested as the caucus night deteriorated.

Each time Sanders called, Weaver would offer a matter-of-fact reply, giving Sanders the information he had—which wasn't much. It wasn't enough.

Asked about his experience on that night, Weaver offered a typically spartan assessment, saying it was his job to "manage any problems" that came up.

"And, you know, the problems that occurred," said Weaver, "I don't think any of us could have anticipated."

Others who were in the war room remembered the evening in far starker terms.

"Things started to go to shit," Arianna Jones, the deputy campaign manager, recalled. "The vote wasn't coming in."

———

SANDERS'S ISSUES IN THE CAUCUS BEGAN WELL BEFORE THE IOWA Democratic Party's app crashed, and many stemmed from his longstanding frustration with the Democratic Party itself.

The candidate's 2020 launch speech framed his campaign as dedicated to fighting the "powerful special interests who control so much of our economic and political life." Such "special interests" included the supposedly liberal party, which he felt protected the advantages enjoyed by the elites through mechanisms designed to frustrate the will of the voters, like the arcane superdelegate system that allowed insiders to pick presidential nominees at the national convention. The Iowa caucus, with its complex counting system and weighted delegates, was another party apparatus that thwarted majority rule.

Sanders and Weaver had little patience for the complicated formula and how it could weight votes from rural caucus sites more heavily than the bigger cities and college towns. They were confident the popular vote numbers would make him a clear winner now that the totals would be public.

While Sanders's top staff shared his frustration, some feared that his disdain for the Iowa process could hurt his chances. Brendan Summers, who was Sanders's caucus director in 2016, remembered difficulties trying to school Weaver on the complexities of caucus-ology.

"You can say I was a very bad teacher," Summers said with a laugh. "Or Jeff may not have been the best caucus student."

The disdain for the arcane delegate math set the stage for a dangerously close night. While Sanders had fixated on the popular vote, some of his staff feared that this had created an opening for a rival. Sanders would no doubt run up big margins in Iowa's cities and college towns, but a competitor could outflank him in more sparsely populated corners of the state and earn a victory in the delegate count.

Indeed, in the weeks leading up to the caucus, one of his opponents, Pete Buttigieg, had gained in the polls with a barnstorming rural bus tour. With a crew cut, Rhodes Scholarship, and twinkling blue eyes, the former Naval intelligence officer was the fully evolved apex version of the typical, chipper Democratic staffer. Buttigieg's position as the chief executive of South Bend, Indiana, earned him the nickname "Mayor Pete." It was an impressive job for the thirty-eight-year-old Buttigieg, but not exactly preparation for being leader of the free world. At least that's what some of Buttigieg's critics felt—including Sanders and some of the other primary contenders—as they bristled at his rapid ascent.

But voters were charmed by Buttigieg. Many rallied behind the Midwestern mayor with the sparkling résumé and an inflection that seemed like a well-rehearsed imitation of Obama's smooth cadence. The first openly gay candidate to mount a serious primary bid, Buttigieg carved a clear lane for himself as a moderate alternative to Sanders. Mayor Pete leapt from relative obscurity to averaging just a few points behind Sanders—and at times leading the polls—in the weeks before the caucus.

Sanders also had his own strategies for exploiting the process in Iowa.

Matt Berg was an election lawyer whose official title was "director of delegates and ballot access" for Sanders's campaign in 2020. He was tasked with ensuring that Sanders qualified for the election in each state and territory. But Berg also used his mastery of voting laws to dabble in the political dark arts—identifying advantages for Sanders in locales that, like Iowa, employed a process that wasn't a straight vote count.

"In the presidential primary you win . . . by winning the most delegates to the national convention," Berg said. "If you are a competent campaign running in a presidential primary, you have to hire someone who is expert in understanding these rules."

A thin, soft-spoken man with sharp features and waves of blond hair, Berg doesn't come off as a political street fighter. However, his subdued nature belies his effectiveness. Berg's ability to game various electoral systems was so significant that he was one of the only Sanders staffers Clinton brought on to her general election operation after their bitter primary fight in 2016.

Ahead of the caucus, Berg had a pet project. As part of its changes to the 2020 process, the Iowa Democratic Party planned a tele-caucus to allow state residents who were not home on the day of voting to participate by phone. The system didn't survive a security check from the Democratic National Committee.

"The technology was so insecure," Berg said. "It took them like a minute to hack it."

In hindsight, that failure was an ominous indication of the Iowa Democratic Party's preparation and technical prowess.

Following the failure of the phone system, the state party created a remote caucus plan with sites around the country—and even abroad. Berg quickly realized there was "an edge to be gained" by focusing on those so-called satellite caucus sites. Worried the race was closer than the campaign realized, Berg went to Weaver.

"I realize the goal is to win Iowa by like five points, Jeff," Berg said. "But, if Iowa is a one- or two-point race, this is one or two percentage points."

Weaver let Berg hire an operative to find Sanders supporters from Iowa who lived out of state and could organize satellite caucuses in Sanders-friendly territory. Berg's operation was one example of how many resources Sanders had at his disposal compared to his opponents and to his 2016 operation.

"We were doing stuff like we would FOIA the student list from public universities and look for students with Iowa area codes and we would text them, and call them, and get them to show up to satellite caucuses," Berg said.

The first votes were cast in the former Soviet bloc at a satellite site in the living room of a freelance foreign policy journalist in Tbilisi, Georgia. It turned out that Iowa expats tended to like Bernie. All three voters there went for Sanders, netting him approximately one-one-hundredth of a percentage point of a state delegate equivalent. Berg's plan had given Sanders a strong start to caucus night.

As the voting rolled westward past Europe and over the Atlantic, it was all going his way.

The voting at these early events concluded before the majority of the caucuses in Iowa began. There were no apparent issues with the results. When the main event began, the party's app cratered and a backup phone system became jammed. At this point, the Iowa caucus broke down.

Meanwhile, the Sanders campaign was experiencing technical difficulties with its own app.

Claire Sandberg, Sanders's national organizing director, led a digital team that planned to use a project management program called Basecamp to have their caucus captains at each site report results. This would allow them to track the outcomes in real time rather than waiting for the state party's official numbers.

Using an app that the Sanders camp built on Basecamp would provide a slicker, more high-tech version of what Sanders's team did four years earlier—simply having caucus captains call in to campaign headquarters. Sandberg's team presented the Basecamp app to Weaver and Rocha weeks ahead of the caucus. Rocha was skeptical and wondered, "What's the backup?" According to him, the digital crew "hemmed and hawed" but he was insistent that "we've got to have a backup."

"They were supposed to have fixed all of that," Rocha recounted in his inimitable drawl. "Well, I'll kiss your ass, none of that shit worked on caucus night."

Berg was also wary of Basecamp and unsure whether the Sanders campaign implementation had ever been stress tested with hundreds of people trying to use it at once. And about forty-five minutes before the caucuses began, it went down.

"I could not log in to Basecamp," Berg said, with the air of someone describing a great crime to a jury. "Our app did not work."

For Berg, it was part of a long-gestating frustration with Sandberg and the digital shop. While he saw their work as "smoke and mirrors," others on the team viewed them as indispensable. It was another example of the many fissures that wracked Bernieworld. Berg curtly told Sandberg the app would be abandoned.

"Rather than screaming my head off at Claire," said Berg. "I just made a decision that we weren't using her thing any longer, even if she got it up and running again."

Part of Berg's frustration came from a belief they could have developed an effective reporting system with more old-fashioned means.

And that's exactly what he tried to do as the clock ticked down to the caucus.

Berg scrambled to get an alternative system working with Tim Tagaris and Robin Curran, a pair of strategists who led Sanders's fundraising operation and were there in the war room. Returning to a method the campaign had employed in 2016, they created eight different shared Google spreadsheets so the caucus captains at each site could log their results without so many signing in at once that it all went haywire. Then, they texted the sheets out to all of their people in the field, enabling them to begin inputting data.

Berg and his crew thought they had saved the day with the last-ditch maneuver. However, there was one more crucial technical error.

"At one point, we discovered that we forgot to turn one of them on," Berg said of the shared spreadsheets. "One of the forms wasn't set up to accept responses, but all of the other ones worked perfectly."

This minor oversight—familiar to many people who work with online document sharing—was fixed as soon as it was discovered. But this issue with the ad hoc spreadsheet system had major implications; it meant Sanders only had incomplete internal data to rely on. That was crucial when the party's data systems went dark.

CAUCUSES HAVE THEIR OWN RHYTHM. TYPICAL ELECTION DAYS MEAN frenetic activity from the morning when the polls open until the candidate's speech late at night. In Iowa, little transpires until the caucus sites open, which means campaign staff have a quiet day before the storm breaks in the evening.

As Sanders's team headed to work, they were feeling optimistic.

"We were like crushing the satellite caucuses," Berg said, adding, "I think we all felt good. I think we all felt like we were going to win Iowa."

Iowa's winters are brutal, and caucus night in early February was no exception. Gusts of icy wind blew through downtown Des Moines past the redbrick war room building.

Sanders's official headquarters was largely deserted. Local staff were out working at caucus sites and the main area of the office was strewn with signs and other election detritus.

Inside, tables were set up facing a television to watch the coverage. About a dozen senior aides filed in and out throughout the night. The caucus was well underway and it was obvious things were not going as planned.

Berg had been texting with Patrice Taylor, director of party affairs for the Democratic National Committee, and Dave Huynh, who is better known in political circles as "Delegate Dave." Huynh was Berg's counterpart working ballot access for Joe Biden's campaign. Berg and the other aides initially were "cracking jokes at each other" poking fun at the Sanders camp's persistent belief the party establishment was working against them.

"Is it just taking a long time because you're waiting until Bernie's not winning anymore to report the results?" he quipped.

But as one hour stretched into two, the text thread turned serious.

"The app crashed didn't it?" Berg asked the DNC official.

There was no answer. According to Berg, Taylor "went dead."

AS THE EVENING WORE ON, THE IOWA DEMOCRATIC PARTY LEADERSHIP finally announced it would be having a conference call with all of the campaigns.

"That's when we knew that it was, like, bad," Berg said.

On that call, the officials admitted the party's own app had failed. Nevertheless, the state party insisted the integrity of the results would not be impacted and that they would ultimately be able to declare a winner after recovering all the hand-counted results from the caucus sites. The campaign staffers were indignant and began to vent their frustrations. But the party leadership hung up. There would be no final results on caucus night.

That delay was critical. Tim Tagaris—Sanders's fundraiser—was waiting for the final numbers to send out a mass email requesting donations. Every hour that fundraising message didn't go out meant less cash would come in. It was agony.

"He knows that the later he sends out his fundraising email, the less money he raises," Berg said. "The life is slowly draining out of Tim Tagaris as the night wears on."

Tagaris and his partner, Robin Curran, had made a model showing they could have raised a decent sum even if Sanders came in second. "We would have raised a lot more money even if we had certainty of that result that night," Tagaris said.

The odd ambiguity of not having any outcome at all was a different story.

"Uncertainty really cast a pall over the fundraising for a few days," he explained.

Donations are the lifeblood of campaigns, which burn through vast sums each day. Tagaris's anguish was palpable.

"You have staffers who spent eight, nine, ten months every day, every day, working," Tagaris said. "You spend millions and millions of dollars, and it meant nothing."

And the money was just one of the problems generated by the lack of a definitive result. There was also the question of The Narrative—and that led to a full-scale blowup in Sanders's war room.

Ben Tulchin, the campaign's pollster and one of its key strategists, was adamant Sanders should simply declare victory. Based on the

partial numbers the campaign had received, they were certain Sanders was in a strong position—particularly when it came to the popular
vote—and Buttigieg was in second. Tulchin wanted Sanders to get on
stage, go on air, and claim a win before Buttigieg might do the same.

Tulchin was a veteran of progressive campaigns. He got his start
with Howard Dean's infamous insurgency in 2004. In an interview,
Tulchin said he saw himself and Weaver as "the main holdover strategists" from Sanders's 2016 run and as instrumental in "Bernie's success,
quite frankly."

"If you look at the Democratic Party and the impact Bernie has
had, Jeff Weaver and I are kind of major figures in that," he said.

Tulchin's desire to get on stage early was shaped by a memory of
Sanders's close Iowa finish with Clinton in 2016. While Tulchin had
advocated for an early declaration of victory then, too, Sanders wanted
to be "respectful of the process." Rather than prematurely declare victory in 2016, Sanders called it a "tie" as Clinton ultimately came out
ever so slightly ahead.

In 2020, with official results not only inconclusive but wholly
unavailable, Weaver was insistent that Sanders refrain from making what
might be an inaccurate victory speech. The failure of the campaign's own
Basecamp app (separately and in addition to the crash of the state party
app) was a factor. It left them with limited data and shaky confidence.

When he called into the war room, Sanders was also reluctant to
plant a triumphant flag on the night without official numbers. Resid-
ual trauma from 2016, when many establishment Democrats accused
Sanders of being a bad actor, weighed on him. Shakir, the campaign
manager, said Sanders was adamant his credibility would be ruined if
he declared victory and didn't win on every possible metric.

"He's hyper aware and sensitive that, if we say we won, it's going to be different than Pete saying he won," Shakir said of Sanders. "In his mind, the media will eat us alive."

Weaver was on the same page with Shakir and Sanders. He told an increasingly agitated Tulchin that, in the absence of official results, a victory speech was not happening.

Tulchin was already on thin ice—in two ways. For one, in Sanders's view, he was too well paid. Sanders has an innate distrust for high-priced operatives. The candidate had always touted his appeal to average working people. He was intensely proud that most of his donations were modest ones, made by people with small bank balances. He hated to see their money wasted or funneled into any one person's fortune. Sanders's award-winning ad-makers from 2016 had stepped aside amid strategic differences including disputes over their fees. Now, Weaver and Rocha were crafting his television commercials.

The second strike on Tulchin was something he couldn't do anything about: Bernie's confidence in his own instincts when it came to polling. He often wondered why he should pay for advice rather than rely on his gut.

It was an odd paradox. Sanders, the political animal who studied his poll numbers at every opportunity, had little use for the people who generated the data. Tulchin, who worked out of his Bay Area office, often fumed that his ideas were marginalized on the campaign.

But Tulchin, wiry, with curly hair, and the standard Silicon Valley business casual uniform of button-downs and fleece, likely contributed to his own ostracization, often cranking the volume to eleven when it wasn't called for. As the caucus fiasco unspooled, the pollster was apoplectic.

"It's a classic Ben Tulchin," Berg said. "We have to do this thing right now or the world is going to end."

Weaver eventually lost his patience. His standard war-room calm shattered.

"I've never in my life seen Jeff Weaver scream at someone the way he screamed at Ben Tulchin that night," Arianna Jones, the deputy campaign manager, said.

Bald head beet red, Weaver ordered Tulchin out of the room.

"At that point Ben took a step back like he was going to exit the room and sort of stood in the doorway but then continued to argue his points," Berg said. "There was a lot of cursing and name-calling going on."

Weaver got out of his chair. "Get out of the room now!" he bellowed.

"Ben's flight instinct kicked in," said Berg. "I think Ben thought Jeff was going to shove him through the door."

While Tulchin confirmed the substance of the disagreement, he didn't recall it quite the way Jones and Berg did.

"We had a difference of opinion," Tulchin said, "but I think everyone was on edge is the way I would describe it. I mean, the whole party was on edge, everyone in Iowa—everybody was on edge. . . . The whole world was on edge. And here we are once again, getting screwed over."

Weaver, ever the Sanders loyalist, offered a decidedly sparse assessment of the shouting match. "It was fine," Weaver said. "He's excitable."

Excitable or not, Tulchin had a point. Buttigieg ultimately seized on the exact stratagem Tulchin had envisioned.

"We knew that we needed to meet reporters' deadlines for the morning," said Lis Smith, Buttigieg's campaign manager, in an interview. "We also had to make a plane to New Hampshire because we had a full day of campaign events in New Hampshire the next day starting in the early morning, and so we had to get on that plane. So there were a lot of factors that were sort of pushing us to go out there, but we wanted to be a part of the story. And we did want that visual for the next

morning, and for newspapers, of Pete in front of a throng of supporters claiming—not claiming victory, but claiming . . . a strong showing."

There was one key difference between the two campaigns that
boosted their comfort with the aggressive move. Buttigieg's team,
according to Smith, had been receiving real-time reports throughout
the day. Their technology had not crashed, and they were confident in
their internal data showing Buttigieg's standing.

"We knew that we had built a really formidable operation in Iowa,"
Smith boasted. "I think our internal reporting ended up being within
one percent, or something like that, of the official reporting that came
back, so it was really accurate."

SHORTLY BEFORE ELEVEN, SANDERS TOOK THE STAGE AT THE CAM-
paign's election-night party. As he approached the microphone, he
quickly pumped his fist before taking a deep, frustrated breath and bit-
ing the inside of his lip. He stared down at the podium and gripped its
sides for a moment before looking up to survey the crowd. Seeing the
faithful gave Sanders a boost. He pulled Jane close and broke into a
genuine smile.

"I imagine, I have a strong feeling that, at some point, the results
will be announced," Sanders said, dragging out each word in exaspera-
tion. "And when those results are announced I have a good feeling we're
going to be doing very, very well here in Iowa."

Buttigieg was far less circumspect. After Sanders spoke, he took
to Twitter and declared, "By all indications, we are going on to New
Hampshire victorious." Soon after, on stage at his own event, Buttigieg
reiterated his claim.

Smith pointed out that Buttigieg had used artful language, saying he was going to "emerge victorious," which the campaign felt more

comfortable defending, even though they weren't sure whether Buttigieg would come out ahead of Sanders or not.

They were shaping The Narrative.

"We didn't claim outright victory . . . but, by any standard, the fact the . . . thirty-eight-year-old openly gay mayor of a town of 100,000 people was either in first or really close second place, that's victorious in anyone's book," Smith said.

Sanders didn't watch Buttigieg's speech.

As Buttigieg spoke, a staffer on Mayor Pete's team fired off texts to leading reporters citing internal figures to reinforce the claim of victory. About ten minutes later, as tweets and cable chyrons began to spread Buttigieg's confident assessment, the Sanders campaign sent an email with their own partial numbers, undercutting Buttigieg. Yet for all the posturing, neither side had the data to support a definitive declaration.

Sanders may have won the popular vote, but when the official results were finally announced three days later he was down by one-tenth of a state delegate equivalent. More importantly, he had also lost The Narrative and the momentum.

Tagaris, the fundraiser, said the uncertainty "denied" Sanders "any semblance of a bounce" in the polls or fundraising dollars.

"I think what every campaign hopes for out of Iowa is that earned media bounce, more than anything else," Tagaris said. "Nothing convinces voters that a candidate can win more than watching them win."

Instead, to the dismay of Sanders and his team, the boost seemed to go to Buttigieg.

"There was very little conversation about who had received more votes that night," Tagaris said.

Questions remained about every aspect of the actual result.

While some news outlets followed the state party's lead and declared Buttigieg the winner, the *New York Times*, the Associated

Press, and others declined to name a victor due to issues with the party's underlying data. The Democratic National Committee and the state party would proceed to battle in a blame game that went on for months.

On one of the many conference calls between officials and the campaigns that took place in the small hours of the morning after caucus night, Weaver unloaded on Iowa Democratic Party Chairman Troy Price. Weaver called the party's initial explanations for the catastrophe "bogus" and blasted the impenetrable nature of the caucus.

"The whole process has been a fraud for one hundred years," Weaver said on the call.

Even more than Buttigieg, the aspect of the fiasco that truly worried Sanders's team was the way coverage of the chaos distracted from the fact Biden, once a front-runner, finished a dismal fourth place. In hindsight, it was the first of many strokes of luck for Biden.

"The person it saved was Joe Biden," Tagaris said. "Just spared him from coverage of what should have been just an absolute, unmitigated disaster of a result."

Shakir, the campaign manager, agreed that losing focus on Biden's poor showing cost Sanders. "We get robbed of the opportunity to say that we won and we get robbed of the opportunity to stick daggers into the Biden campaign."

Sanders's Iowa implosion played a pivotal part in Biden's ultimate ascendancy to the presidency. But Sanders still ended up getting his victory in the Hawkeye State—technically.

Though the party's official results were questionable, they still dictated the makeup of Iowa's delegation to the Democratic National Convention, which took place six months after the caucus. The razor-thin lead the official results gave Buttigieg meant he would get two more delegates than Sanders on the floor of the party's nominating convention.

Sanders and his team disputed one of these delegates and argued he earned the same number as Buttigieg in Iowa.

As Biden secured the Democratic nomination, Sanders was his sole remaining challenger. The pair took pains to avoid a reprise of the last election's infighting, which included Sanders supporters staging protests on the floor of the quadrennial convention. This time, Sanders quickly and unambiguously endorsed. And Biden created a series of unity task forces designed to give Sanders and his allies input on policy. Their teams held talks ironing out every aspect of the convention.

Those calls found Berg back on the phone with "Delegate Dave." During negotiations over a separate issue, Berg decided to ask for the disputed Iowa delegate. If Berg could pull this off, Sanders would have the same number of Iowa delegates as Buttigieg to go with his popular vote victory.

In other words, Berg was trying to belatedly win (or at least tie) the caucus for Sanders with the exact kind of backroom maneuvering the candidate had always abhorred. It worked.

"I gave him something that he wanted that I didn't want to give up. And I said, 'I'll give this to you. If you give me my statewide delegates in Iowa,'" Berg said of his talks with Dave, adding, "I wasn't even fully serious about it. It was kind of a joke, but he gave it to me, so I took it."

The caucus came to an end on that call. There was finally a result.

Chapter 7

REGIME CHANGE

LONG AFTER THE 2020 PRIMARY WAS OVER—AND EVEN AFTER THEIR candidate emerged victorious—campaign aides to President Joe Biden still felt the sting of the lowest moments from the humbling early stages of the race. The emotions, as emotions tend to do, got wrapped up with food.

"If I see a District Taco, I cross the street," one staffer reminisced to a friend who had gone on to work in the White House.

The restaurant that haunted Biden's team was a modest Mexican fast-casual chain. One of the locations was near Biden's early campaign offices in Washington, DC. For staff, it became a bad-luck charm.

Debate season for the Democratic presidential hopefuls began in late June 2019. The initial skirmish was a bruising experience for Biden, who announced his race two months earlier and had been the front-runner in the polls ever since. The candidate stood dead center on that first debate stage and received incoming fire from all sides—most memorably, Kamala Harris launched her busing attack at that first encounter, arguably the pinnacle of her campaign. The other would-be presidents took turns painting him as old and out of touch as staffers in Washington headquarters picked at a lukewarm buffet of District Taco.

That downtown DC office, which was located just a block from District Taco, was always supposed to be temporary. In a nod to his working-class Scranton, Pennsylvania, roots, Biden planned to establish his home base in Philadelphia. The team moved there in July 2019 hoping the change in scene could bring new energy. Yet when they arrived in the City of Brotherly Love, a District Taco stood just on the other side of Penn Square.

Worse, the new headquarters were boring. One staffer described walking into the building and thinking that the stale, corporate space was exactly what the online left might have imagined for a stuffed suit like Biden.

"When I got there . . . someone told me that the Biden campaign has the office that Twitter thinks the Biden campaign has," the staffer said. "It was just drab. There's nothing on the walls . . . The water wasn't potable; it was brown water," and the campaign manager Greg Schultz "didn't pay for a water cooler."

In an interview for this book, Schultz dismissed the complaints about the water out of hand.

"I drank that water every single day, and it was fine," Schultz said. "I grew up in Cleveland, where a few years before I was born the river caught on fire, and I'm fine," he added, "That's so funny. . . . I don't know what people complain about."

A longtime loyalist who made his way from both of the Obama campaigns to Biden's vice-presidential team, Schultz was a fast talker with a head of short hair gone prematurely gray. He'd been involved in planning discussions for the race since 2018 and was close enough to Biden that he'd never had to interview for the campaign manager post. It began as a quiet assumption that Schultz probably would be tapped to run a potential campaign, and then one day "the verb tenses changed." And they were off.

As Biden's campaign manager, it was Schultz's job to strategize and manage resources. Being in charge of the budget meant Schultz had to nix various requests. The role helped make him a divisive figure for some of Biden's team even as, by his account, he came up with the strategy that ultimately brought them success.

"What I have to remind headquarters teams," Schultz said, "is that most of the campaign is nowhere near a big city, with no resources, in some field office with probably little heat and shoddy internet. Headquarters can't be splurging like we're a Silicon Valley startup, in particular until money comes in."

To all outside appearances, however, the campaign wasn't just scrimping and being patient; it was genuinely struggling. Polling showed Biden had failed to gain traction with Iowa voters after campaigning heavily in the state. It was shaping up to be a potentially disastrous setback.

Schultz said he was unfazed by Biden's poor standing. His plan for the race did not rely on the first two states on the primary calendar. Biden's prior presidential campaigns proved he was no favorite among the mostly white, largely non-union voters who made up the bulk of the electorate in Iowa and New Hampshire.

Schultz believed South Carolina, the third state to vote, was where it would come together for Biden. Focus groups showed Biden's standing was strong among Black voters, and Schultz believed that was his essential advantage. "The way to be the nominee of the party is to do okay among most groups and do really well among Black voters," Schultz said. South Carolina, where roughly 60 percent of Democratic primary voters are Black, was the key to the race.

There were hard numbers behind this strategy. New Jersey

senator Cory Booker said that he and Kamala Harris, the top Black candidates in the race, saw data as they prepped their campaigns that showed Black communities were particularly delegate-rich and that they tended to consolidate around one candidate after the first three states on the primary calendar. The theory behind the numbers presented to Booker and Harris was that, as Black candidates, they had a natural edge with this decisive base. However, Biden had his connection to Obama—and he had South Carolina, where his campaign was confident that history and a key ally would push him over the line.

In spite of his confidence in South Carolina, as Schultz planned the campaign, he confronted a number of hurdles. Biden had never been a particularly strong fundraiser. He lacked whatever magnetism attracted the rush of small-dollar donations to Bernie Sanders. Biden was also not a master of the big-money circuit. Democratic donors at every level, it seemed, underestimated Biden politically.

With limited resources, Biden needed to survive Iowa and New Hampshire with enough gas in the tank to compete in South Carolina. That meant pinching pennies. It meant there was no room for a plush headquarters or bottled water. It meant calling the donors he did have, soothing their anxieties, and asking for patience during early losses. And it meant beseeching the press to ignore Iowa and New Hampshire and not to write Biden off.

Schultz believed in the plan. He had faith, and he had data to back it up.

However, Schultz's staff didn't all share his confidence. Those lean early days had a grinding effect on the team's morale.

As the Iowa caucus approached, Biden was polling well behind Sanders, and his team was already seeing numbers indicating they would fare poorly in New Hampshire, which was set to vote just over a week later. Biden was staring down two straight losses. The Narrative was turning dark. And there was another dire omen: on caucus night, the campaign ordered Mexican. When they "saw District Taco in the office," one campaign operative said, "people thought it was going to go bad."

"It was literally one of the most depressing nights of my life," the operative continued. "We knew we were not going to win, but just the reality of the entire thing was . . . you're thinking 'Shit, we're in really big trouble.' . . . We knew we were going to lose New Hampshire. And we knew that just getting reports from the ground, our organization was in bad shape."

Even though the exact caucus results were lost to the app-crash chaos, there was enough data to know Biden did not have a strong showing. When the smoke cleared days later, he officially stood in fourth place, nearly five points behind Elizabeth Warren, the third-place finisher. Biden was more than ten points behind Sanders and Buttigieg.

In hindsight, the Iowa Democratic Party's meltdown that night might have saved Biden's campaign. Neither Buttigieg nor Sanders got a definitive boost, and the confusion blunted the impact of Biden's loss. Had his opponents been able to sink a knife in him after Iowa, or following the subsequent loss in New Hampshire, Biden might not have made it. In the moment, however, it looked like a disaster.

During his time leading Biden's team, Schultz enjoyed military metaphors.

"He'd be like, 'We are Spartans. This is Sparta. We are Spartans and we are fighting against everybody. It's everyone versus us. This is Sparta,'" a senior Biden campaign staffer recalled, before adding, "But dude, do you know what happened to the Spartans? They all die."

ULTIMATELY, THE CAMPAIGN DID SURVIVE. SOMEHOW, OVER THE THREE
weeks following New Hampshire, Biden managed to vault from a trail-
ing position in a six-way race to a dominant lead in a two-way contest.

In Schultz's view, Biden's rapid rebound was always the plan. That
may have been true, but, shortly after losing New Hampshire, Biden
shook up his staff and sidelined Schultz.

One staffer was relieved. They had compared "the Greg regime" to
the situation in Afghanistan: "There was a weak—a nominal—federal
government, but it was really ruled by a series of warring warlords."

This criticism was valid—but it also may have been more on Biden
than Schultz. This was generally how Biden's world worked. Biden sur-
rounds himself with key advisers, many of whom have been with him
for a very long time. The setup ensures multiple power centers.

Among those key advisers were Mike Donilon and Steve Ricchetti,
who had been inner-circle aides during Biden's vice presidency. In 2015,
during Biden's previous flirtation with running for president, Anita
Dunn and her husband Bob Bauer joined that inner circle. Both had
come into the White House working for Obama—Bauer was White
House Counsel—but, according to a *New York Times* profile of the
couple, they stood by Biden as the Obama team tried to usher him out
of the 2016 race, and with that show of loyalty, had earned his enduring
gratitude. Dunn, a forty-year veteran of Democratic presidential campaigns, was a force unto herself. She had staff from SKDK, the "strategic communications firm" where she is a partner, installed throughout
Biden's team. Bauer, in addition to being a close Biden confidant, was
the campaign's lawyer.

After the loss in New Hampshire, Biden opted for a regime change
and effectively replaced Schultz as campaign manager with Dunn. The

change had been brewing for some time. Even before voting started in the primaries, according to some aides, Dunn had been overruling Schultz on specific management and personnel decisions. Schultz would nominally hold the position of "campaign manager" through Super Tuesday. But after New Hampshire, Dunn was in charge.

Biden aides tend to reach for diplomatic platitudes when asked to compare Schultz and Dunn.

"He's a pretty good person," one staffer said of Schultz. "But I just think that Anita had been through so many experiences, she's a more battle-hardened type. And I think that ended up serving us extremely well."

After Anita Dunn took control, this person said, "Things just started to flow more quickly. I think part of it was that she just knew: This is do or die, and I'm going to make some fucking decisions."

Another member of Biden's team praised Dunn's almost unnerving calm.

"Anita was so chill about Iowa, and I thought that she was insane," they said.

For his part, Schultz maintains that, whoever was in charge, they were following his roadmap: "I would say the strategy, the campaign theme, the focus on the Democratic primary vote that was actually the path to victory, was established well before the campaign launch and continued on that established trajectory through securing the nomination."

But Dunn didn't just keep calm and carry on with the initial plan. After taking charge, she immediately shook up the Nevada organization. One staffer reported, "She made crucial choices about how they're going to redeploy folks to Nevada, because it was essential that we have a strong showing there."

Losing the first two states was one thing, but to make it to the friendly confines of South Carolina, Dunn knew Biden would have to survive Nevada—and Bernie was set to win big.

━━━━━

THE BIDEN CAMPAIGN, FOR ALL OF ITS SNAKEBITTEN LUCK IN THE EARLY days, knew that the party would line up behind him if he managed to get on track. That's one of the perks of running with a former VP and party elder as the candidate. Aides to Sanders, his anti-establishment rival, on the other hand, sometimes had nagging doubts.

Sanders had his own lingering trauma from 2016, when he had felt cheated by Clinton and party officials. Four years later, even when things were going well for Sanders, he and his team sometimes had trouble convincing themselves he could actually win the nomination. They always assumed that the Democratic establishment would some-how snatch it away from him. The night of the Nevada caucus, February 22, 2020, was one rare moment where they truly dared to dream.

Arianna Jones was quieter than her mostly male colleagues, and one of the more pragmatic figures in the organization. With a back-ground as an MSNBC producer, she had a more traditional political résumé than many of them as well. And she prided herself on seeing the big picture.

"I think I did a good job . . . never buying into the idea that we could ever win, because the whole point was we could never win. . . . It was an impossible task," she said. The night of Nevada, she added, "was probably the closest I've ever come working for him and being like, 'Wait a second, could it happen?'"

In Nevada, everything seemed to go right for Bernie Sanders. He was coming fresh off the victory he had earned less than two weeks ear-lier in New Hampshire, his northern New England home turf. Powered by a Spanish-speaking field operation that courted Latino voters door to door with a message of shared economic struggle, the campaign was going so well that the message often outran the boots on the ground. Volunteers would routinely visit homes only to find Sanders signs or residents who'd already voted for the man they called "Tío Bernie." Sanders managed to win Nevada by over twenty-six points and dispel the notion he struggled with voters of color.

After starting his morning in Las Vegas, Sanders had already flown on to Texas. He was holding an evening rally in Austin when Nevada was called. Sanders's voice was piped from Texas to the backyard of a bar his campaign had taken over in Las Vegas's arts district. He framed the win as vindication, "an historic victory because we won it in one of the most diverse states in the country."

Sanders couldn't hear the crowd at the bar, who drowned the next sentences with cheers. For many who were at the Sanders campaign's watch party that night, the memory would become uniquely crisp—images of stormy blue desert night sky, glowing bar lights, the joy of the packed crowd. In the weeks to come, the idea of standing with people packed shoulder to shoulder would become surreal.

An ocean away from the Sanders faithful, multiple cities in China had been on lockdown for weeks due to a little-understood "novel coronavirus" that was causing outbreaks and hopping continents. Italy had emerged as a hotspot in Europe, and the day of the Nevada caucuses, ten municipalities in Lombardy had joined several Chinese cities in shutting down.

Months later, as lockdowns spread across the United States and the death toll climbed, Sanders's team would remember that Nevada night as one of the last of the Before Times. It was also the first—and last—moment it seemed like Bernie Sanders could actually become president.

Sanders supporters and staffers in Vegas paid little attention to the virus. Some in the crowd talked about the recent headlines and wondered whether it would be a passing situation, another SARS or swine flu. Their anxiety was focused instead on the Democratic Party, and what it might do to stop Sanders's rise.

Asked about the campaign's feelings that Nevada night, Arianna Jones said, "We had just seen already what people were doing in terms of their reactions to him having success." The Democratic establishment was afraid of Sanders's revolution. Some doubted his electability. Others resented the threat he posed to the established order and their way of doing business, which relied heavily on corporate donors who were not eager to support Sanders's socialized tax schemes. There was a barrage of attacks as Sanders vaulted to front-runner status.

"We risk nominating a candidate who cannot beat Donald Trump in November," one fundraising text from the Buttigieg campaign had said, taking aim at Sanders, "and that's a risk we can't take."

For Sanders's team, their strong position after the big Nevada victory heightened the worries they would face an all-out assault from the mainline party.

"I think it was also a little bit of fear of like, people think we can win now, which is a scary place to be," Jones recalled.

Those worries were valid. As Jeff Weaver later said, "I certainly knew that there would be a last-ditch effort to sort of stop him, which there was."

SANDERS MAY HAVE WON NEVADA BY TWENTY-SIX POINTS, BUT THE Biden team was feeling quietly confident. They had "survived" after all. And their survival had come with an unexpected gift: strategic obscurity.

For weeks, the former front-runner had been counted out. One senior staffer recalled that the media wasn't even bothering to write negative stories about Biden—"incoming," in campaign operative parlance.

"After Iowa, we really stopped getting incoming because reporters were writing us off," a senior Biden staffer said.

Biden's team used this time to their advantage.

Michael Bloomberg, the billionaire former mayor of New York City, made a relatively late entry to the race in November 2019. He had an unconventional strategy to go with his unusual schedule. Bloomberg planned to skip the early races—Iowa, New Hampshire, Nevada, and South Carolina—to focus on Super Tuesday, March 3, 2020, when voters in fourteen states and the territory of American Samoa head to the polls. Bloomberg's massive fortune bought lavish advertising campaigns and sushi lunches for his staff. It also dominated the headlines.

"The whole conversation between Iowa and really South Carolina—a lot of it was focused on Bloomberg and not Biden. He was kind of like an afterthought during that period of time," recalled Sanders aide Tim Tagaris.

Bloomberg's cash—and the fact he was presenting himself as an experienced, moderate alternative to Sanders—were problems for Biden.

"Bloomberg was the biggest threat to us because he was gunning directly for our base," the senior Biden staffer said. "He was trying to essentially buy our base off."

With the focus off of Biden, his campaign team launched a hidden offensive against Bloomberg.

"So suddenly our bandwidth exploded, right? . . . And so the rapid response and research teams basically became an anti-Bloomberg super PAC for several weeks," the staffer explained. "The press interest in him was at its highest point. And there was so much on him."

Bloomberg's long history in government and business meant the Biden opposition research team had a lot to work with. They blasted unflattering stories about Bloomberg's record throughout the media landscape.

"He said a whole bunch of extremely offensive stuff," the Biden staffer said of Bloomberg. "He said that the financial crisis in 2008 was caused by the end of redlining, aka Black people being able to buy houses. We got that out there and it was a big hit."

During this time, Bloomberg made his own daring and secret overture to shake up the race. Shortly after New Hampshire voted, he sent a delegation to Cory Booker's house in Newark, New Jersey. According to high-level sources on the Booker campaign, Bloomberg wanted to convince Booker, who had ended his own presidential bid ahead of the Iowa caucuses, to be his running mate.

"They said they ran the numbers," one source who attended the meeting said, "they polled everybody—Kamala, Cory—and that Cory would give them the biggest boost and give them the chance to secure the nomination."

The announcement of a vice president to run on the ticket before sewing up the nomination is a rare, and some would say desperate, move for a presidential candidate. On the Republican side, Ted Cruz and Carly Fiorina tried to team up during the primaries in 2020 to head off Donald Trump. It didn't work.

According to the source, the pitch Bloomberg and his team made to Booker was all about thwarting Sanders.

"We're worrying now. Biden can't win. Bernie looks like the strongest candidate," Bloomberg's aide said, according to the source. "The only way to stop Bernie is for him to come out with a popular vice-presidential candidate. You've got the best numbers and you got some great history. Let's announce that you're a team."

Booker turned Bloomberg down out of hand.

While Bloomberg's drastic gambit failed, the Biden team's strategy of piling on the former mayor from behind the scenes was paying off spectacularly. The press that had obsessed over

Bloomberg's late entry to the race ate up the controversies Biden's researchers unearthed.

"I've never seen anything like it," the staffer recalled many months later, with still-evident glee. "It was NBC, AP, *Wall Street Journal*, boom, boom, boom, boom. Just shelling these motherfuckers. Torpedo to the hull!"

The Biden team took special pride when the 2008 remarks they had uncovered about redlining policy formed part of Elizabeth Warren's devastating assault on Bloomberg's record and character during one of the debates.

Warren had struck at the outset of the February 19 debate, with three days remaining before the Nevada caucus. She started in on Bloomberg's alleged history of sexist remarks, before digging into his other similarities to the sitting president.

"So I'd like to talk about who we're running against, a billionaire who calls women 'fat broads' and 'horse-faced lesbians.' And, no, I'm not talking about Donald Trump. I'm talking about Mayor Bloomberg," Warren said, with prosecutorial precision. "Democrats are not going to win if we have a nominee who has a history of hiding his tax returns, of harassing women, and of supporting racist policies like redlining and stop and frisk," she added, concluding, "Democrats take a huge risk if we just substitute one arrogant billionaire for another."

Warren's takedown over the course of that evening was widely credited with destroying Bloomberg's campaign. For political observers, the impression that she'd landed a debate death blow was immediate. But it wouldn't be ratified by data until Super Tuesday, when the billionaire lost everywhere, except American Samoa—a group of remote islands in the South Pacific spanning approximately seventy-seven square miles, population 55,000. He suspended his candidacy the next day.

In the meantime, significant things were happening at the front of the primary pack. On the day of the Nevada caucus, while Sanders's team was focused on its own win—and moving to the Western states that were poised to be his stronghold on Super Tuesday, Biden's team was entering the phase of the campaign where his strategic patience would begin to pay off.

Sanders was ascendant, but Biden was too. He had managed to climb up from fifth place in New Hampshire to second place in Nevada. It was a lifeline of precious momentum, enough for Biden to hang on until South Carolina, where his team was certain he had an advantage.

Two Bidenworld insiders described the Nevada caucus as the best night of the whole campaign, a moment filled with incredible promise, with Dunn and her lieutenant Jennifer O'Malley Dillon in command. It also happened to be the birthday of the campaign's top lawyer, Dunn's husband, Bob Bauer.

Bauer's birthday party turned into an ecstatic celebration in Philadelphia and inaugurated a new tradition for Biden's team.

"There was this birthday cake to celebrate Bob's birthday, and the entire campaign sang 'Happy Birthday' to him with a sheet cake," the campaign operative said. "And ever since then, everyone sings 'Happy Birthday' on a big Biden night to Bob Bauer."

In the weeks to come, Bauer's birth would be serenaded again and again.

Chapter 8

COUP DE GRÂCE

JIM CLYBURN HAS A VIVID MEMORY OF WHEN THE FIRST FREEDOM
Riders came to South Carolina. It was May 1961, and the activists
planned a bus tour through the South where they would enter "Whites
Only" facilities at bus stations. They intended to put pressure on federal
authorities to enforce a Supreme Court ruling that banned racial segregation in interstate commerce, and they knew their presence would
provoke a violent reaction from local segregationists.

The group departed from Washington on May 4 and passed through
Virginia and North Carolina without incident. Five days later, the thir-
teen activists reached Rock Hill, South Carolina. Two of the Riders—
including civil rights icon and future congressman John Lewis—tried
to enter the waiting room there. They were attacked by a group of
Klansmen. Lewis and his compatriot were left battered and bleeding.

Nearly sixty years later, Clyburn recalled the scene for *Good Trouble,* a documentary on Lewis's life. He described it as a vivid example of
the "different paths" the two Black leaders took to Washington.

"They were coming through South Carolina and I said to my wife that I thought I would meet the bus in Rock Hill," Clyburn recounted to the film crew in a slow, deep drawl. "She reminded me that I was no longer a college student at that time. We were expecting our first child. So, I did not meet the bus."

Clyburn had been arrested for organizing a sit-in one year earlier. He had, however, met his future wife in jail. Things were different now that he was getting older and becoming a family man. The cautious approach to the civil rights movement that he grew into was emblematic of the practical politics that would help him amass power without direct confrontation in his later career. This pragmatism helped deliver Clyburn's endorsement and his home state to Biden.

Clyburn, who was first elected to the House of Representatives in 1993, rose to become majority whip—the number-three-ranked Democratic leader in Congress—in 2006. He was one third of a triumvirate—along with Nancy Pelosi and Steny Hoyer—whose long tenure ensured that no one below retirement age had the top spots in the party's congressional delegation between 2007 and 2022. Along with his powerful position in Washington, during his more than fifty-year political career, Clyburn was also the face of the Democratic Party in the Palmetto State.

Clyburn's "World Famous Fish Fry" is an annual celebration of his status as South Carolina's Democratic kingmaker. He started the cookout in the early 1990s as a treat for his supporters and staffers who couldn't afford to attend the high-dollar fundraising dinners held in conjunction with the state party convention. As Clyburn's stature grew, so did his signature event. It became an elaborate ritual of respect for Clyburn, fueled by cold beer and thousands of pounds of hot whitetail. In presidential years, it was a required pilgrimage for White House hopefuls eager to woo South Carolinians. Clyburn makes an elaborate show of his own neutrality before the primary and thus invites every candidate to speak at the fish fry, so long as they keep their remarks brief.

In 2019, the fish fry was held on a warm night in late June. There were still more than two hundred days to go before the first votes would be cast and the field had yet to be thinned. Twenty-two presidential candidates showed up to speak to the crowd that packed in under the pines. All of them—from Joe Biden and Kamala Harris all the way down to lesser-knowns like Wayne Messam, the mayor of Miramar, Florida—put on the required uniform, a blue T-shirt with Clyburn's name emblazoned across the chest and a fish fry logo on the back.

One of the candidates, Senator Cory Booker, immediately remembered the sweltering heat, which made it "one of [his] least favorite events" of the campaign. "We just stood there for what seemed to be interminably long on a hot, thick, steamy night," Booker recalled.

Booker also remembered the imperative for the candidates to make a good showing for Clyburn.

"I began to love watching all these people under pressure," he added. "You can really tell a lot about a person under pressure."

All twenty-two hopefuls got up on the small outdoor stage and said their piece. Bernie Sanders was the only one who didn't have his Clyburn T-shirt on for his speech. By the time he got back up on stage for the group photo, that had been remedied.

When Biden's turn came to speak he, too, kissed the ring. Biden pointed out it was his "third fish fry" and praised Clyburn as "the highest-ranking African American in the history of the United States of America other than the guy I worked with for eight years."

After leaning on his Obama connection, Biden framed the election as a critical tipping point in the fight against Donald Trump, which required a unified party.

"You all know in your gut this election is more important than any . . . you've ever been involved in. Not because of any of us [who] are running, but because of the man who occupies that office. We can make up the four years of damage he's done, but eight years of damage will be almost impossible to get back," Biden said, squinting hard and raising his voice into a hoarse shout. "I hope to be your nominee. I'm going to work as hard as I can to get your support, but here's the deal, whomever the Democratic nominee is, we have to stay together and elect a Democrat."

As he walked off the stage, Biden and Clyburn shared a quick embrace.

"I did it in a minute," Biden boasted in a stage whisper as he handed back the microphone. Clyburn took the cue.

"We might have to put this as a day down in history," Clyburn said to the crowd. "That's the shortest speech Joe Biden ever made!"

The audience roared their approval.

"I really liked Biden," Booker said, still reminiscing about the fish fry. "He was kind to people. He would pay attention to the person delivering the water. . . . You see character a lot under stress and under pressure. And we got a good guy—we got a good guy in the White House."

JA MOORE IS A SOUTH CAROLINA STATE REPRESENTATIVE WHO WAS elected in 2018 at the age of thirty-three. As an influential young leader in a bellwether primary state, Moore was in demand during the primary as campaigns vied for the endorsements and support of local officials and operatives. In Iowa, New Hampshire, Nevada, and South Carolina, there's a grand tradition of lawmakers like Moore being wooed by the future leaders of the free world.

For Moore, calls from the candidates started coming in fall of 2018, two years before voters would head to the polls.

"I think the first person to, like, actively reach out was Cory Booker," Moore said, describing the experience of receiving calls from the New Jersey senator as "humbling." "I remember almost like it was yesterday. . . . Like I had his cell number and he would just hit me up. . . . He was trying to build a relationship with me as a . . . newly elected legislator from South Carolina."

Biden and his team were not that aggressive. According to Moore, they "actually started reaching out later on in the mix."

In the end, it wasn't a campaign pitch that sealed the deal. Moore decided to endorse Kamala Harris after learning he was having a daughter.

Moore received the news in March 2019. "That next day I just went to church that morning and just called Kamala right afterwards," Moore said, later adding, "I was going to be raising a little Black girl. . . . I wanted my daughter to grow up in a country where she could see someone who looks like her as president."

Both Booker and Julián Castro had worked hard to win over Moore. Calling them about the decision was tough.

"It was very, very, very difficult because I had built a really strong relationship with both Cory in particular and with Julián," Moore explained. "I had more direct contact with them than the other candidates quite frankly, more so than Kamala at the time."

Much of the political class—inside and outside of South Carolina—initially saw the race coming down to the two top Black candidates, Booker and Harris. Black voters make up the largest bloc in the state's Democratic primaries. They are typically unified and decisive. Harris had a natural appeal, but the implosion of her candidacy in December 2019 meant she never got to compete.

Booker dropped out a month after Harris, having never gained much traction in the polls. "Running for president is not a thing that you earn," he observed in an interview for this book where he reflected on his campaign. "It's really a moment. There's a larger zeitgeist that has to be flowing in your direction. And I respect that."

As the primary campaign entered its final week in February 2020, seven candidates remained in the race, with both Sanders and Warren running strong campaigns from the left.

And, despite the wooing of younger lawmakers like JA Moore, there is one endorsement that matters more than any other in South Carolina politics: Big Jim Clyburn. One local Democratic legislator offered a simple assessment of the state's political landscape. "South Carolina Democratic politics, for the most part, is Jim Clyburn," the lawmaker said.

"Almost to get anything done, like from a national perspective, you've got to go through Jim," said the lawmaker. Because of his influential position in Democrats' congressional leadership, "everything goes through him. If it's like political appointments at the federal level, if it's funds that can come directly, everything goes through Jim Clyburn."

All of that clout had—quite literally—paid off for Clyburn's family. He and his wife had three daughters. Two were appointed to federal commissions and the third had a post with the South Carolina Democratic Party. During the 2020 race, billionaire Tom Steyer—whose short campaign focused on the Palmetto State and rained down cash in the process—spent over $40,000 to rent an office from a company owned by one of Clyburn's daughters.

For decades, Clyburn had been coy and calculating about how to wield his singular power in South Carolina's primary. In 2004, he gave an early endorsement to Dick Gephardt, a close congressional colleague that Clyburn described as "number one in my heart." Gephardt, a former House leader, flamed out in Iowa. As Clyburn watched the caucus returns while sipping Jack Daniels and munching pork rinds, he was swamped with calls from other candidates who were eager to be his second choice. Clyburn chose John Kerry, who eventually won the nomination. The other leading candidate, John Edwards, a native South Carolinian, had rankled Clyburn by leaving the fish fry early.

Four years later, in 2008, Clyburn was in a bind. As part of negotiations that earned the Palmetto State its early place on the primary calendar that year, Clyburn had promised to stay neutral. But he also faced a particularly difficult choice. Hillary Clinton and her husband, Bill, were both old friends, but Barack Obama had put in time wooing Clyburn and seeking his counsel. And, of course, many of the Black voters who made up the Democratic base in South Carolina were eager to see a president who looked like them. Indeed, the state went heavily for Obama in 2008. Clyburn finally endorsed the Illinois senator in June 2008, over four months after South Carolina voted, on the day Obama secured enough delegates to pass Clinton.

In 2016, as Clinton faced off with Sanders, Clyburn broke his neutrality pledge. He endorsed Clinton about a week before the primary. Clyburn insisted it had been his "intention" to stay out of the race and when critics denounced the move he responded with a deflection: he was on his way out.

"I'm seventy-five years old, so I doubt very seriously. . . . If anybody would worry about me doing this again in the future, it would be somebody else," Clyburn said.

And yet, four years later, Big Jim was back at it, wheeling, dealing, and making his presence felt in the middle of a heated campaign. As Clyburn considered his options, he confessed that he was worried about a bitter fight splitting the party. Clyburn had been a delegate to the 1972 convention when divisive disputes over delegates, procedures, and young activists and minorities clamoring for representation led to infighting that was later seen as helping Republican Richard Nixon win the race. Now, Clyburn told reporters he feared a repeat of that rancor.

Almost everyone expected Clyburn's endorsement would go to Biden. The pair were close and—as Sanders surged to front-runner status in Nevada—Clyburn had made it plain that he was uncomfortable with the Vermont senator's brand of progressive politics. In an interview that aired on ABC, Clyburn suggested having Sanders lead the way might make it hard to win in "moderate and conservative districts."

"This is South Carolina, and South Carolinians are pretty leery about that title 'socialist,'" Clyburn said.

Unlike 2016, there was no pretense of neutrality. Clyburn only said he would hold back his choice until after the South Carolina primary debate, four days before the election. This decision gave him strategic leverage.

Clyburn had told Biden he wanted him to promise to nominate a Black woman to the Supreme Court during the debate. Nearly two hours in, Biden hadn't made the pledge. Clyburn reportedly ran backstage during a commercial break to make his case.

A few minutes later, Biden came through: "We talked about the Supreme Court. I'm looking forward to making sure there's a Black woman on the Supreme Court, to make sure we in fact get every representation." The next morning, Clyburn gave Biden his backing.

Clyburn's handling of the endorsement was indicative of the shrewdness that helped cement his dominance in South Carolina and his accumulation of power in Washington.

One South Carolina lawmaker explained: "In a lot of ways, what makes Jim Clyburn so successful is that, I mean especially when you think about a policy perspective . . . he's not really going to rock the boat or challenge the status quo, . . . What made Jim successful over his time and political life is he's always well-positioned."

It also highlighted something else that made Clyburn a force in the Palmetto State: most voters there share his moderate politics.

JA Moore, the state representative who had been in the thick of the endorsement scramble, describes the state's Democratic voters as "pragmatic progressives."

"We want working people to be able to . . . pay their mortgage, or their rent, and have enough money to take care of their prescription drugs and do child care," Moore said. "We want all of those things. We want clean water and air, but the pragmatism piece comes in because we live in a state that is dominated by Republicans."

South Carolina's governor and both of its US senators are Republicans. Clyburn is the sole Democrat in the state's House delegation. And the current conservative dominance isn't the only thing that has Democratic voters there feeling defensive.

The majority of South Carolina's Democrats are Black and staunchly middle-class. They have vivid memories of a dark, painful history of discrimination, segregation, and violence. Moore said voters there are cognizant of the "decades of work" it took to obtain some measure of equality.

"Progress to us looks a lot different than progress in other places," Moore explained. "We would rather take the inch knowing that the mile is impossible, but if you keep chipping away at that inch, eventually it becomes a mile."

For many South Carolinians, the past reverberates painfully in the present. Moore's own sister, Myra Thompson, was among the nine members of a Black bible study group who were killed by Dylann Roof, a white supremacist gunman, in 2015. His voice used to quake with apparent anger when he discussed her killing. Now, years later, he adopted a more rueful, wistful tone.

"Progress takes time," Moore said. "It takes generations."

In Moore's assessment, as the state's presidential primary approached in 2020, Biden seemed to most South Carolina Democrats like a far more realistic, less risky option than Pete Buttigieg, the then thirty-eight-year-old openly gay former mayor, and Bernie Sanders, the socialist.

"I think the Clyburn endorsement was just a manifestation of how the majority of South Carolina Democrats are in general. We're pragmatic like, you know, focused on who can actually win. I think that's what it comes down to," Moore said. "People did not in South Carolina see that Bernie could take it all the way or, you know, Pete could." Biden, he said, "was actually just a pragmatic choice."

South Carolinians were also making their pick in the shadow of Trump.

With a president in office who spouted divisive rhetoric, opposed spending on the safety net, and stoked culture wars, Moore argued voters there were looking for a rival who looked likely to win over moderate independents in a general election.

"It was less about inspiration at that point," Moore said. Backing Biden, according to Moore, was a calculated desire for "this country to continue to move forward and not be regressive."

SANDERS NEVER HAD MUCH HOPE FOR SOUTH CAROLINA. IN 2016, armed with Clyburn's endorsement, Hillary Clinton had beaten him there by nearly fifty points. That defeat led his senior campaign leadership to make minimal investments there in 2020.

"We were in the worst fucking situation in South Carolina because people were drunk off Nevada," said Tyson Brody, the campaign's head of research. "We raised expectations with a state we had not invested heavily in. [Campaign pollster Ben] Tulchin's whole fucking strategy was to win without South Carolina, which was always, always a long shot."

With Clyburn's endorsement and Sanders ceding the state, the primary voters of South Carolina delivered a thundering result for Joe Biden. On leap day, Saturday, February 29, 2020, every single county went for Biden. Sanders, who finished second, scored fewer than half as many votes as Biden did.

While it was a landslide, the exit polls still showed the rift in the party. Even in a centrist stronghold, Biden may have won, but Sanders beat him by nearly twenty points among voters under thirty. Clyburn had been wrong. All South Carolinians weren't afraid of socialism. Just the majority of those over forty-five.

Across three presidential campaigns, Joe Biden had never won a single contest until this one. Now, the path to the White House opened before him. With his victory in South Carolina, Biden had won thirty-nine delegates to the national convention—a tiny percentage of the 1,991 required to secure the nomination. But he had seized The Narrative by demonstrating the sturdiness of his connection with Black voters and more conservative Democrats. He also reinforced the idea that Sanders's relative weakness in those categories would translate to issues in a general election against Trump. That logic drove other moderate candidates into Biden's corner as they thought about leaving the race.

Pete Buttigieg, who had come in third in Nevada and South Carolina, knew he was finished after Biden's big win. According to his campaign manager, Lis Smith, Buttigieg had a conference call with his advisers on the night of the Palmetto State primary. She recalled his words in an interview:

"Guys, it's over," Buttigieg said. "Let's start planning my announcement to drop out."

"The next morning," Smith continued, "as we were planning that event, that's when we started to discuss who he was going to endorse. And there's just no question. There was no alternative. He was going to endorse Biden just because Biden was the strongest candidate left who was closest to him sort of both ideologically, tonally, et cetera."

For Biden's staff at headquarters in Philadelphia, the victory also brought tangible relief. Schultz, who was still nominally the campaign manager, was finally able to relax his hold on the purse strings.

"I swear to God, the night of South Carolina," a senior Biden campaign staffer recalled, "it's two in the morning and everybody's all fucked up and drinking and shooting champagne and whatever and Greg just goes: 'We're getting the water cooler!'"

───

MARCH 2, 2020, WAS THE FIRST DAY BACK AT WORK FOR THE BIDEN campaign after the primary victory in South Carolina. But they weren't in the office long. Sometime that morning in Center City, Philadelphia's business district, a strong odor of natural gas began permeating the streets.

The mysterious smell—whose cause was never officially identified—prompted widespread evacuations. Biden's headquarters, located in a nondescript office tower across from the ornate, nineteenth-century City Hall building, cleared out. Staffers of all ranks, including the campaign's new de facto chief, Anita Dunn, poured out onto Philadelphia's streets on foot, looking for a new place to set up shop.

It was a critical time to be without a real working headquarters. The following day was Super Tuesday, when fourteen states and the territory of American Samoa would hold their primaries. There was also the special "Democrats Abroad" vote for ex-pats. In total, there were 1,357 pledged delegates up for grabs in twenty-four hours.

It was the election day that was going to be Bloomberg's Waterloo. And, with a little push, Biden's team hoped it might be the end for Sanders too.

The Biden campaign, at that point, was feeling the pinch. Before South Carolina, fundraising had slowed down. The obscurity that had enabled their attack on Bloomberg had also left them out of the earned media sweepstakes. The campaign's war chest, never robust in the Schultz era, was exhausted. Biden had been unable to lay the groundwork in the Super Tuesday states, and if his showing was weak, he would likely have to drop out of the race.

"We spent a thousand dollars on Super Tuesday," a senior campaign aide confided. "The campaign was broke, b-r-o-k-e, broke. There was no money left in the banana stand at all."

Perhaps the aide was exaggerating, but the statement pointed towards a major cash flow problem. At the start of February 2020, according to reports filed with the FEC, the Biden campaign had $7.1 million on hand. Its burn rate was high. They would spend nearly twice that during the month. If it wasn't for an influx of cash that came after the victory in South Carolina, Biden's operation would have been in the red. As it stood, they were coming into an expensive contest that spanned a large swath of the country essentially living check to check.

Flushed from her office by the strange smell, Dunn still managed a maneuver that essentially won the nomination for Biden. It was a coup de grâce orchestrated on the fly.

"Anita was with us the whole day," a Biden campaign operative who was caught up in the evacuation recalled. "That was the weirdest part."

The group ended up camping out in the common area of a staffer's apartment building. Dunn was, the aide recalled, "basically creating this entire show that would go on later that evening."

Dunn and her lieutenants had begun hearing from candidates who were dropping out, Pete Buttigieg and Minnesota senator Amy Klobuchar, as well as one who had long since left the race but hadn't yet endorsed, Beto O'Rourke. Dunn and her team viewed the moment as a make-or-break chance to cement Biden's status as a unifying figure, the only option to beat Trump and save the party.

As they walked through the city, Dunn worked the phones. And she wasn't alone. Dunn called upon her most powerful ally, Barack Obama. Multiple sources confirmed the former president played a part in convincing Biden's rivals to back him. According to two senior staffers, "Obama was involved" that day working to put "things in perspective for candidates."

The precise details of Obama's involvement have mostly remained a closely guarded secret. It was exactly the kind of backroom power play that Sanders and progressives might see as corrupt. After all, a convention floor fight nearly broke out in 2016 over much lower-level party officials being caught playing favorites when the hacked emails were released. This was something far bigger, the party's most beloved figure working to end the primary and stop the progressive revolution. Almost no one would touch the subject in interviews.

"I have no comment. I'll get destroyed by one side or the other," explained Cody Keenan, the former Obama speechwriter, when asked about his former boss's role.

Keenan had a two-word explanation for his reluctance to talk: "Self-preservation."

Greg Schultz wasn't privy to everything Dunn was doing, but he was told she worked with Obama.

"I heard that as well," Schultz said when asked to confirm this reporting.

A source close to Barack Obama explained that understanding his role in the consolidation that effectively ended the primary "requires a level of nuance."

"It is true that Obama spoke with Pete Buttigieg and Amy [Klobuchar]," this source said.

He had laid the foundation for this key moment of the race months before.

"Obama had spoken with these people when they launched their campaigns too, and all of them came to him looking for guidance and maybe kissing the ring, whatever," the source said.

The memory of the bitter, protracted primary fight between Sanders and Clinton was still fresh for Obama. According to the source, Obama was convinced "the rift that stayed with the party after Hillary was nominated" had "arguably led to our downfall in '16." With that in mind, at the beginning of the new campaign, the source said Obama "had decided very intentionally" that he had a "role . . . to play at the end" of the process, "which was to help unite the party and help fill any gaps that were needed once we had a nominee." He would be the closer.

In those early conversations with the various candidates, the source said Obama had stressed "the existential threat that a Trump reelection poses." Then, Obama offered a mixture of encouragement and a gentle warning about when they might hear from him next.

"Go do this. Give it your best shot," Obama told them. "I'm not going to be partial in this primary, because I believe the most important role I can provide and the most value I provide is helping to consolidate at the end."

With Biden on the edge of victory and Dunn working the phones, the other candidates heard from Obama a second time. Thanks to his groundwork, Obama's message was clear: This was the end. They needed to come together to take on Trump.

"So when he does the calls with Buttigieg and Klobuchar . . . when they're dropping out, that comes up again," the source said. "He is reiterating how important it is to be unified going into the fall. That doesn't mean he's telling Pete, 'You need to drop out and endorse Joe Biden.' . . . He's more nuanced in—not a hammer like that. . . . It's stressing the importance of unity and being on as strong as possible footing going into November."

Four years and change after Obama had gently nudged Biden out of the 2016 race and let him know time was up, the former president was giving Biden's rivals the same treatment and pushing his old running mate across the finish line.

With the help of Biden's old White House boss, Dunn and her team managed to negotiate having Buttigieg, Klobuchar, and O'Rourke officially endorse Biden at two events that same Monday night in Dallas, Texas, the second-biggest of the states where voters would go to the polls on Super Tuesday. Biden and his new alliance dominated the airwaves.

At the two rallies, all three endorsers framed Biden as the best choice to unite a nation that was divided by Trump and facing the unprecedented pandemic threat.

"At a time that this country is so polarized, so deeply divided, we need somebody who can bring us together and heal us," O'Rourke said of Biden.

While none of them mentioned Sanders, the spectacle of the former rivals standing together was an implicit rebuke of the socialist who was Biden's strongest opponent. It was a powerful demonstration of moderate unity and exactly the type of coordinated attack Sanders's team had been expecting.

That night, Sanders appeared on CNN. Of his newly unified rivals, Sanders would only say: "It is no surprise they do not want me to become president."

―――

JUST AS BIDEN WAS GAINING FRIENDS, SANDERS LOST ONE OF HIS biggest advantages.

On February 25, 2020, three days after the Nevada primary, Nancy Messonnier, the director of the Centers for Disease Control and Prevention's National Center for Immunization and Respiratory Diseases, delivered the first clear warning to Americans that the "novel coronavirus" was going to change life as we knew it. Even as other Trump administration officials downplayed the threat, Messonnier made clear the virus was on its way to being officially declared a pandemic.

"Ultimately, we expect we will see community spread in this country," Messonnier said on a conference call with reporters. "It's not so much a question of if this will happen anymore but rather more a question of exactly when this will happen and how many people in this country will have severe illness."

The outbreak cast a pall of uncertainty over the remainder of the primary. Would voters be able to make it to the polls? Was Trump up to the task of a global pandemic? Most importantly for Sanders, the coronavirus threatened to shut down the large events and intense ground game that were key drivers of his campaign.

Barely twenty-four hours after Dunn's coup de grâce, Sanders, who had spent the past few weeks beginning his stump speeches with mock surprise at the huge crowds he was drawing, found himself in a small campaign office addressing about a dozen reporters after losing in ten of the fourteen states on the calendar.

A downcast Sanders pointed to the "delegate count," including the haul he expected from California, to argue he and Biden would "go forward basically neck and neck." Of course, that assessment ignored Biden's growing momentum and the increasingly unfavorable polling of the upcoming campaign calendar. When pressed by the reporters, Sanders admitted he wasn't thrilled with the Super Tuesday results.

"Of course I'm disappointed," he said. "What we are trying to do is unprecedented. We are talking about a political revolution."

There was just a week in between Super Tuesday and its sequel when six states were up for grabs. Sanders spent that period focused on Michigan. His campaign canceled events in other states. Michigan was psychically important. Sanders had won a massive upset there in 2016. It was also the biggest prize of "Super Tuesday II" and, as a result, Sanders's best shot at making up his growing delegate deficit.

At a rally in Detroit on March 6, Cornel West, the Harvard professor and one of Sanders's most high-profile surrogates, laid out the stakes.

"We need all hands on deck," West said. "We got our backs against the wall."

But Biden had already opened up a wide lead in Michigan, according to polls. He didn't even bother to campaign there, instead sending surrogates—including Klobuchar. Sanders's last-ditch effort failed to shift the momentum.

Biden won five of the six states on Super Tuesday II, including Michigan. The one place where Sanders did notch a victory, North Dakota, didn't have a complete count by Wednesday morning.

"In Minnesota we went from getting—we were going to get no delegates—to getting almost all the delegates. Klobuchar does not get enough credit for those votes in Minnesota," Schultz said.

A week later, Sanders suffered losses in all three states that were on the calendar. By mid-March, Sanders's chance of victory was mathematically slim and his senior aides were giving background quotes to reporters encouraging him to face reality and make the "hard" choice to drop out.

It was easy to see why Sanders might be in denial. It had all happened so fast. Less than a month earlier, he was arguably the front-runner, and even some on Biden's team had expected him to win.

"By the time we got to January, I was convinced it was going to be Bernie," one senior Biden aide said.

According to the aide, heading into South Carolina, some Biden campaign staffers were setting up job interviews and planning to leave Philadelphia. Some of them even began contemplating joining forces with Sanders for the general election. For moderate Democrats, this was a tough pill to swallow.

"I was like, 'Oh my God, do I want to go work for Bernie Sanders?'" the aide recalled. "I don't fucking know, you know?"

Many Democratic operatives felt some degree of personal affinity for Sanders's politics, but they hadn't reconciled themselves to continuing their careers under his rule. As the aide put it, staffers were, on average, younger and "more progressive than many of the mainstream candidates they work for." But Sanders represented an unknown. After all, the people who worked in Democratic politics had come up in the establishment. They had a deep faith in the system and many shared their bosses' view that Sanders had electability issues. That was an especially scary prospect in a world where taking a gamble and losing meant getting Trump.

Biden's win in South Carolina, the dramatic consolidation of his rivals, and the pandemic speeding up the end of the primary campaign largely ended the clandestine job searches. Biden staffers now had a general election campaign to plan.

Sanders ultimately gave up on April 8, a day after voters in Wisconsin came out to vote despite long lines and the presence of ununiformed

National Guardsmen who had to be called in to replace poll workers who refused to show up for work on account of the contagion. Voters and poll workers alike wore masks, goggles, and the elaborate protective gear that was de rigueur during the first weeks of the pandemic when it was unclear how exactly the virus spread.

Bowing out during the greatest health crisis in a century was especially painful for Sanders, a candidate who—after losing his mother to illness as a teenager—had made expanded access to health care the cornerstone of his career. Sanders was losing the race just as the world was facing a challenge that he felt deeply validated the core of his political platform.

"This current horrific crisis that we are now in has exposed for all to see how absurd our current employer-based health insurance system is," Sanders said.

Sanders's choice to step aside even as he felt his core argument was proving unmistakably correct was the formal beginning of a truce between progressives and the Democratic establishment that would last through Biden's first term. As the left rallied behind Biden, they were putting the bitterness of 2016 behind them—at least temporarily. And, in his endorsement of Biden, Sanders explained the reason for the cease-fire.

In 2020, the pandemic wasn't the only danger facing the Democrats and Americans more broadly. As the virus raged, Sanders and his allies feared another threat so significant that it was perhaps the predominant reason he and Biden's other rivals were so quick to fall in line.

"Today, I congratulate Joe Biden, a very decent man who I will work with to move our progressive ideas forward," Sanders said. "Together, standing united, we will go forward to defeat Donald Trump, the most dangerous president in modern American history."

Chapter 9

THE INSIDE-OUTSIDE GAME

I N EARLY 2019, WHEN THE FOUR MEMBERS OF "THE SQUAD" WERE sworn into Congress, all eyes were on them.

Their insurgent primary victories were a media magnet. And on Capitol Hill, where attention is the coin of the realm, the spotlight inspired attacks from Donald Trump and the right along with resentment from their own colleagues.

In an interview for this book, Ilhan Omar, one of the Squad members from Minnesota, recalled the pressure as being "both internal and external." As the group, which also included New York's Alexandria Ocasio-Cortez, Ayanna Pressley of Massachusetts, and Rashida Tlaib of Michigan, arrived for their freshmen orientation and met with their colleagues in the Congressional Progressive Caucus, Omar said they were greeted with mixed emotions.

"We were battling an extremist, fascist, racist former TV star president and you sort of had, I think, this burst of energy and excitement around a growing progressive movement," Omar said, adding, "There was . . . an equal level of excitement and an equal level of annoyance at the amount of attention that was gravitating towards us."

In Trump's Washington, their progressive fame meant enduring a constant stream of abuse and threats. Right-wing rage was to be expected. But almost as soon as they reached Capitol Hill they also began to feel a current of envy from some Democratic colleagues who had arrived in DC in prior cycles and with less fanfare. Ocasio-Cortez was just twenty-nine years old and had barely worked in politics. The other three women were more experienced, but they were all new to Washington. The level of scrutiny, pressure, and frustration at their presence was virtually unprecedented. It was a lot to take.

"I think a lot of us would have liked to figure out where the door to the bathroom is, and how do you get to your office, and pick committees before you get swarmed and followed around by endless cameras," Omar said. "It also, you know, created tension with some of our colleagues because a lot of them felt like, 'OK, they just got here . . . why do they have this outsized attention and interest? And why are people asking them about their opinions on this and that when there are all of these people who are either in leadership or seasoned that could be asked to have their input and opinions about policy debates?'"

Fellow Democrats in Congress, accustomed to prominence deriving from seniority, may have resented the attention being paid to the new members. But the base was looking to counter Trump and—as outspoken progressives and as women of color—the Squad repudiated everything Trump stood for. Despite the pressure, Ocasio-Cortez, Tlaib, Omar, and Pressley initially leaned into this role. Their unusual prominence was driven by a mixture of timing, political skill, agility talking about policy, and social media savvy. And, with neither side of the aisle exactly offering them a warm welcome to Washington, they had nothing to lose.

The group used their high profile and large online platforms to challenge the status quo—including within the Democratic Party.

"Being a progressive to me has always been pretty simple. It's about pushing for progress—forward," Omar said. "You know, when I first ran for office, I ran against a forty-four-year-old incumbent and I used to say being liberal is being open to ideas. Being progressive was pushing for action on those ideas, and I still see it that way."

Omar had been fighting her whole life. She was born in Somalia and was forced to flee the country as a little girl when civil war broke out. After four years living as refugees in Kenya, Omar and her family obtained asylum in the United States and settled in Minnesota. Her grandfather—a former Somali civil servant—inspired her to get involved in politics as a teenager. Omar got her first taste of American government by accompanying her grandfather and translating for him at local events. Her interest was strong enough that she studied political science in college before getting involved in her local city council and being elected to the state legislature.

Omar had firsthand experience with the rough and tumble of street-level American politics. In 2014, she suffered a concussion when a brawl broke out at a local event where she was supporting the challenger to a sitting state representative. While that bid did not succeed, Omar would go on to wrest the seat from the incumbent herself two years later. When she made it to Congress, the rules had to be changed so Omar, one of the first Muslims on Capitol Hill, could vote on the House floor in her headscarf.

Omar recognizes that her activist approach will always lead to friction between more moderate Democrats and the left, which has a "fundamentally different" approach.

"Many of us view this work as grassroots work. We organize our politics and organize around politics the way in which we would organize around issues," Omar said. "It's kind of, I think, our brand as progressives."

Elected leadership rooted in activism—what progressives have recently termed the "inside-outside game"—is a key part of how the Squad pursues their purpose in Congress. During their first few months in 2019, along with facing off against Trump, running that game meant taking on members of their own party, particularly House Speaker Nancy Pelosi.

Pelosi's role leading the Democratic caucus for over fifteen years made her a divisive figure. While many credited her with shepherding through key legislation—notably President Obama's Affordable Care Act—she was also the symbol of an aging leadership that had refused to yield to a new generation. And, by virtue of her role, Pelosi had to forge compromises between the party's moderates and left wing that often dissatisfied progressives. Omar had admired Pelosi, who had helped shepherd the rule change that allowed her religious headwear on the floor. She pointed out the Speaker was an example of a more main-stream Democrat who had some roots in activism and deeply valued her own progressive identity.

"There are folks who are considered establishment today, like for-mer Speaker Pelosi, who started out, I think, seeing political organizing with that sort of lens," Omar said.

One of the first major issues the Squad confronted with their inside-outside game was immigration. During the first months of 2019, just as they were attempting to settle into Capitol Hill, it was becoming clear that the Trump administration had separated thousands more migrant children from their families at the southern border than was previously known. At the same time, border security legislation was making its way through Congress. For immigration hawks who backed Trump's proposed wall and draconian treatment of migrants, the legislative push was an opportunity to secure funding for enforcement. Progressives saw their need for cash as a chance to demand safeguards and improved conditions for migrants.

Trump's child-separation policy had already provoked a national outcry, but the news kept getting worse. By June, a series of reports began to emerge detailing horrific conditions for migrants at detention centers including cramped facilities that lacked adequate food or sanitation and children allegedly being kept for hours in vans as they baked in the desert.

The next month, Ocasio-Cortez, Tlaib, and Pressley joined a delegation from the Congressional Hispanic Caucus that traveled to see the conditions firsthand. At a pair of detention facilities near El Paso, they met with migrants and clashed with border guards, turning their experience into headlines. The trip was a vivid example of their activist approach to politics, their personal solidarity, and the intense opposition they—and their uncompromising progressive views—faced from all sides in Washington.

Ocasio-Cortez described the visits in an interview that night for Yahoo News with one of the authors of this book. Her full comments from that conversation have not previously been published.

As they touched down in Texas, the group knew they were surrounded by enemies. On the morning of their visit, the news broke that thousands of current and former Border Patrol members were part of a secret Facebook group where some had mocked a teenager who died in custody. Members of the group discussed the planned visit and hurled racist insults at Ocasio-Cortez and another Latina congresswoman who was part of the delegation. They were particularly focused on Ocasio-Cortez and posted a series of vile, vulgar messages about her.

When she arrived at one of the facilities, Ocasio-Cortez demanded to be with the women who were held there. "I'm going in this cell right now and I don't want to be with CBP officers inside this cell," she said. According to Ocasio-Cortez, the border guards insisted they needed to accompany her for "safety."

Ocasio-Cortez rocked back and forth as she replayed the experience hours later. Her words reverberated with indignation.

"I said, I trust these women more than I trust you," Ocasio-Cortez recalled. "These women are not a threat to me. Let me inside right now." Ocasio-Cortez pushed inside the cell, which was crowded with women. It was a scene that floored her, literally; she knelt to get on the women's level.

"They were almost like talking over each other, trying to tell me everything," recounted Ocasio-Cortez before rattling off the stories she heard from the women: " 'I've been here twenty-two days.' 'I've been here sixty days.' 'I've been here fifty-something days.' This one was like, 'I'm fifty-eight years old. I haven't seen my daughter. My two kids were taken from me. I don't know where they are.' 'My hair is falling out.' 'We would go fifteen days without a shower.' "

These were women who looked like Ocasio-Cortez and her Puerto Rican family. They had no easy way to speak up for themselves. Ocasio-Cortez had let their words sear themselves onto her brain and now it was all pouring out of her.

For Ocasio-Cortez, the experience was "overwhelming." One woman spoke Spanish to her and described the treatment as "psychological war."

"There was, like, this kind of outpouring and then they just started sobbing. All of them. . . . Every single woman in that cell just started sobbing. . . . Completely and utterly traumatized," Ocasio-Cortez recalled. "They said, 'Please help us. We're not criminals. We didn't hurt anyone.' "

Pressley was sitting on the floor with Ocasio-Cortez. Pressley would later tell *Vanity Fair* she had to "physically remove" Ocasio-Cortez from the cell when it was time for the delegation to depart.

Despite the emotion of the moment, Ocasio-Cortez said she did not cry herself. She was focused on committing the women's stories to memory so that she could use her platform to share their stories. Ocasio-Cortez was going to play the inside-outside game.

"I kind of had this assessment earlier on where I'm coming in, I'm a freshman, no seniority, no one cares about what freshmen think, no one incorporates freshman feedback into anything, let alone if you come from a safe district. The only freshmen they'll listen to are swing district freshmen so that they can keep the majority," Ocasio-Cortez said a few hours after leaving the detention center. "Coming in with that little functional structural power, how do I influence outcomes? And in the inside-outside game, the less leverage you have on the inside, the more leverage you try to build on the outside. Which is why I tried to use today as an opportunity to really expose this to the public."

When they left the facility, the lawmakers participated in a press conference. They were greeted by a crowd of pro-Trump protesters who jeered and screamed at Ocasio-Cortez as she stepped up to speak. She and her fellow Squad members would later tell *Vanity Fair* they placed their hands on each others' backs for comfort during the tense faceoff.

"Hopefully we're able to get through this," Ocasio-Cortez said, before placing a hand on her chest and raising her voice. "What we saw today was unconscionable. No child should ever be separated from their parent. . . . They should be given water. They should be given basic access to human rights. And it is a false notion—the idea that we have to choose between people is a false notion. No child ever has to suffer for the benefit of another."

After staring down the angry crowd, the Squad members returned to a standoff of a different sort in DC. Five days after the congresswomen made their trip to the border, *New York Times* columnist and veteran chronicler of the Washington cocktail circuit Maureen Dowd published an interview with Pelosi where the speaker mocked the Squad members for their opposition to the border-funding legislation.

"All these people have their public whatever and their Twitter world," Pelosi said. "But they didn't have any following. They're four people and that's how many votes they got."

Ocasio-Cortez fired back on Twitter, where she suggested Pelosi lacked an appreciation for the inside-outside game. "That public 'whatever' is called public sentiment," she wrote. "And wielding the power to shift it is how we actually achieve meaningful change in this country."

The high-profile spat was accompanied by reports that Pelosi was freezing out the congresswomen behind the scenes. And, just over a week later, Trump jumped into the fray with a series of racist attacks posted to Twitter.

"So interesting to see 'Progressive' Democrat Congresswomen, who originally came from countries whose governments are a complete and total catastrophe, the worst, most corrupt and inept anywhere in the world (if they even have a functioning government at all), now loudly . . . and viciously telling the people of the United States, the greatest and most powerful Nation on earth, how our government is to be run," Trump wrote. "Why don't they go back and help fix the totally broken and crime infested places from which they came."

Of course, other than Omar, all of the women were born in the United States. Trump's comment was an unmistakable attack on Omar and Tlaib's immigrant roots, Ocasio-Cortez's Puerto Rican heritage, and Pressley's Blackness.

Trump's jabs at the Squad escalated from rabble-rousing tweets to a prepared speech on the South Lawn of the White House where—standing at a lectern behind the Seal of the President of the United States—he offered his opinion that the four women hated the country and invited them to leave it. The formality of setting did not match the crudeness of the racist message, but it telegraphed that Trump's salvo was deliberate—another calculated appeal to the nativist and anti-socialist elements of the Republican base in the early days of his reelection campaign.

In a tweet later that day, Trump reiterated the attack in all caps, writing, "We will never be a Socialist or Communist Country. IF YOU ARE NOT HAPPY HERE, YOU CAN LEAVE! It is your choice, and your choice alone. This is about love for America. Certain people HATE our Country."

The following day, Ocasio-Cortez, Omar, Tlaib, and Pressley conducted a joint interview with CBS host Gayle King in a darkened House hearing room belonging to the Oversight Committee. Reflecting on the appearance many months later, Corbin Trent, who worked with Ocasio-Cortez at the time, said, "That interview, I think, personifies their relationship."

King opened with a truly jarring question.

"According to the president yesterday, you all are people who hate our country with a passion, you hate Jewish people, and you love enemies like Al-Qaeda. You hear those statements coming from the president of the United States to describe you all, and you are all lumped together, and you think what?"

It was a quintessential moment in the politics and media of the Trump era. The president had said something false, outrageous, and demeaning—and as usual, he'd said it first on Twitter—and a broadcast news production team had risen to the bait, gathering his targets to confront them with the president's words and demand a response. The appearance also lingers as a snapshot of the four progressive congresswomen, under siege from all directions, defending themselves, each other, and their collective right to pursue their own agenda in Congress. It also displayed their distinctive personalities. Looking back on the interview years later, their vulnerability and defiance in that moment stands in marked contrast to the sense of acceptance and influence they would accrue during the Biden administration.

Sitting side by side with her fellow Squad members in the well of the Oversight Committee room, Ocasio-Cortez was the first to answer. She offered a vision of American patriotism rooted in the historic struggle for civil rights, implicitly drawing a contrast with Trump's appeals to a racial form of nationalism.

The American story, Ocasio-Cortez said, had always been about the "triumph of people who fight for everyone" over those who seek to secure special advantages to a select group. She invoked Ruby Bridges, one of the first Black children to integrate an elementary school in the Deep South—which she had done alone at the age of six years old surrounded by a guard of US marshals. Ocasio-Cortez said she had learned about Bridges's courage in her own elementary school and reflected on how civil rights activists had also faced "vitriol" and been labeled as "anti-American." The implication was clear: Ocasio-Cortez saw the struggles of the Squad during the Trump era in similar terms.

Omar and Pressley spoke next, and both objected to the idea of dignifying Trump's hateful remarks with a response. Pressley noted that, on the day before the interview, news reports had emerged that Trump's attorney general, Bill Barr, personally decided not to bring federal charges against the police officers responsible for the death of a Black man named Eric Garner. Garner had died in 2014 as a result of a brutal chokehold arrest by NYPD officers who suspected him of selling loose cigarettes on a Staten Island sidewalk. His last words, repeated gasps of "I can't breathe," had become an enduring refrain of the Black Lives Matter movement.

"This is a distraction from the corruption, the chaos, and the callousness of this administration," Pressley said, reminding King that Trump's attack had flowed out of a policy debate over immigration and drawing a chorus of affirmative murmurs from the other congresswomen. "That's why we're here."

Tlaib, a Palestinian American who represented a district with a large Muslim population, turned to her own experience to emphasize solidarity with the communities targeted by Trump.

"I wanted that little girl that was inspired by all of us, in looking to all of us, young people just saying 'thank you so much for running because I can see myself in you,'" she said. "I wanted them to know that we're unwavering. We're not going to back down."

The later parts of the interview pivoted from Trump to the underlying conflict with Pelosi. King asked Ocasio-Cortez whether it was a problem that she wasn't on the same page with the leader of her caucus. As Ocasio-Cortez sought to downplay the issue and stressed that the political system welcomes necessary disagreements, Tlaib repeatedly cut in to defend her colleague and criticize Pelosi's handling of the situation.

"I'm very protective," Tlaib said, as King tried to fend her off.

"Alexandria," King said pointedly after several exchanges with Tlaib, "are you interested in having a conversation face-to-face with Nancy Pelosi?"

"Oh, absolutely—" Ocasio-Cortez began.

"Why wouldn't she sit down with her?" Tlaib said, interrupting again.

Next it was Pressley who cut in and attempted to cool the temperature of the discussion by emphasizing the fact that, as members of

Congress, their obligation is to voters in their district. As a result, she suggested every member should stand alone rather than criticize their colleagues. It was a delicate, diplomatic rebuke of Pelosi.

Over the course of about half an hour with King, the congress-women demonstrated their distinctly different styles. Pressley is a disciplined politician, aspiring to lofty rhetoric and aphorism but mindful of the blocking and tackling of coalition building. Tlaib is a rhetorical brawler, quick on her feet and unafraid to throw a haymaker. Omar's answers were careful, cerebral, and confident.

Omar had responded to Trump's attacks the day before her sit-down with King by calling for his impeachment for "human rights abuses at the border" and a series of "racist" comments that culminated in his assault on the four women. Asked about the utility of pressing for Trump's impeachment when it then didn't appear to have popular support, Omar began to reel off polling statistics from the 1970s from memory, showing how much public opinion changed on impeachment within ten months.

Her analysis would prove to be prescient, in a way. Trump was impeached just about five months later in mid-December 2019 over allegations he withheld aid from Ukraine in exchange for political favors. He would be impeached an unprecedented second time in 2021 after fomenting the attack on the Capitol—and it was Omar who helped lead that charge.

At the time, however, King did not draw out Omar or the other Squad members on the subject of impeachment. She chose instead to press Ocasio-Cortez about whether she ought to keep her head down and learn the ways of Washington, being "new here." Ocasio-Cortez laughed.

"The entire freshman class, I would argue, regardless of ideology, was sent here because Americans are sick of how Washington works," she said. "So why would I learn a broken playbook? ... Why would we operate business as usual when business as usual is not serving the public?"

═══

IN THE INTERVIEW WITH GAYLE KING, RASHIDA TLAIB SAID SOMETHING that should have been shocking: "Some of us are getting death threats." In prior media and political eras, such threats would have been front-page news. But they had become commonplace in a world where every woman with a public profile struggles against a relentless undertow of poisonous misogyny online, where people of color often face overwhelming double standards and dehumanizing rhetoric, and where the demonization of Democratic figures by right-wing media has led to multiple, violent, real-world attacks. As the distillation of the progressive bloc, the Squad drew vitriolic hatred from the moment they arrived in Washington in 2019 right through the second half of the Trump administration.

During the interview in El Paso, Ocasio-Cortez noted that, unlike Pelosi and members of leadership, she had no official security, and acknowledged she was pushing through while facing risks every day.

"It's just the faith in the morning," she said.

Six months after their sit-down with Gayle King, that faith would be tested. On January 6, 2021, the group found themselves literally under siege when thousands of Trump supporters swarmed into the Capitol building to prevent Congress from certifying his loss to Joe Biden. During the riot, the outsized attention on the Squad added to the danger.

Due to the volume of death threats that had been made against her, Capitol Police evacuated Omar to a secure location with the congressional leadership. As the crowds raged through the halls, she immediately began drafting the articles of impeachment that would later be filed against Trump. Omar discussed the potential impeachment with House Majority Leader Steny Hoyer, Speaker Nancy Pelosi's right-hand man, in that secure room.

"Go for it," Hoyer said.

Ocasio-Cortez was not evacuated with Congressional leadership that day. She could have gone to a room with other lawmakers, but she was afraid some of her Pro-Trump colleagues might betray her location to the horde.

"I did not go to the secure location because I feared other members of Congress that . . . would have allowed harm to me," Ocasio-Cortez said during a town hall meeting. "So I was not in the secure location that day. I was almost never in a secure location that day."

Ocasio-Cortez found herself with a sole staffer and she faced a close call that she has, thus far, declined to describe in detail. She was alarmed at the seemingly lax response of some Capitol Police officers and the fact "the National Guard didn't come right away."

"One of the scariest parts is . . . just the lack of trust in our institutions and the people that are, you know, supposed to keep us safe," she said.

During the chaos, Ocasio-Cortez said she was in "active communication" with Omar about the articles of impeachment.

The planning for the second impeachment push—and the fact that leadership and every voting Democrat ultimately got behind it— showed the Squad's inside-outside game had earned them real leverage in their party and in Congress. Where once they had been agitators on the party's flank, they now found common cause with Democratic colleagues of all stripes.

By 2023, the Squad had nearly doubled in size. And the dark clouds of isolation and vilification that the original members endured in their early days in Congress had lifted in a number of ways. Trump had been banished to Mar-a-Lago. Omar herself had become the deputy chair of the Congressional Progressive Caucus, ascending to the number-two position in one of the largest organizations of lawmakers on the Hill.

The Squad has found a place among more moderate Democrats in Washington in part because much of the establishment has shifted in their direction ideologically. The Biden administration spent its early years being remarkably friendly to progressive activists. This rapprochement culminated in Joe Biden's 2023 State of the Union address, a speech that leaned hard on progressive policy priorities from promoting organized labor to getting a handle on police violence.

"Mr. President, that was awesome—that was awesome!" Representative Jamaal Bowman of New York, a new Squad member, shouted across the House chamber afterward, drawing out the final syllable with dramatic effect, as Biden chatted with amused but tight-lipped members of the Joint Chiefs of Staff. Bowman also reportedly hollered to Bernie Sanders, the Squad's inspiration and Biden's erstwhile rival, "Did you write that speech?"

Senator Ed Markey of Massachusetts had remarked, according to Representative Omar, that "Bernie might have lost the election, but he won the speech."

For her own part, Omar marveled at the way public policy had moved in a progressive direction over her relatively brief career. Omar spoke to us shortly after Biden's speech.

"We're talking about things like addressing the climate, talking about actual investments in environmental justice," Omar said, riffing on Biden's address. "We're talking about taxing the rich and making billionaires pay. . . . All of these things that you have being part of a State of the Union address by a president that was essentially proud of the image that he crafted as a centrist and a moderate Democrat, [and who is now] repeating the policy positions of Bernie Sanders, who was once his opponent and considered someone who, because of these policies, could not get elected. And now those policies are the policies that the Democratic Party is united behind, they're coalescing around, and are actually proud to be out there and campaign on."

Omar also pointed to student debt cancellation. While it only earned one brief mention in the State of the Union, Biden had already acted on what progressives saw as a critical issue facing the American people. Citing the pandemic as a qualifying "national emergency," he issued an executive order before the midterms in 2022 to cancel a swath of student loans estimated to total about $400 billion. Both the Trump and Biden administrations had used this approach to pause repayments and interest on these loans during the COVID pandemic. Biden pushed it a step further despite misgivings among other Democrats who were concerned both about the legality of the action and its impact on inflation, according to a senior aide to a more mainstream member on the Hill. As of this writing, Republican opponents had tied up the order in court, claiming it was beyond his authority, setting the issue up for the Supreme Court's review.

Omar marveled at Biden's willingness to take on the fight.

"Things like student debt cancellation—that was fringe when I ran for the Minnesota House in 2016 and was crafting my campaign platform in '15. Everybody was like, 'You have to take out student debt cancellation,' Omar said. "And now you have the president of the United States championing that issue."

All the potential difficulties of student debt reform serve to underline Omar's point. It was an example of Biden taking a substantial risk as president to push forward a progressive agenda item—an idea that had been considered unacceptable only a few years ago and that the Democratic establishment probably would have preferred that he leave to the backbenchers and to future Congresses, but now were obliged to support. By acting from the White House, Biden pushed the whole party in the progressives' direction.

Omar gives the credit for these developments to Bernie Sanders and Elizabeth Warren, who she says "fuel" the progressive movement. Her appreciation for Biden's early agenda seemed to show a convergence of the trajectories of progressives and the establishment. On so many policy fronts, Biden seemed to be bridging the great divide between the center and the left that emerged in 2016.

Still, even as she expressed excitement about unifying elements of Biden's agenda, Omar predicted "tension will probably always sort of exist" between more moderate Democrats and progressives who are drawn to the activist approach. Indeed, even within the Congressional Progressive Caucus, where she currently has a leadership position, Omar said the Squad sees themselves as dedicated to playing the inside-outside game and encouraging even more leftward colleagues to do the same.

"I think the Squad's role within the Progressive Caucus is to utilize the oversized presence and connection that we have to a growing young base, to an ever-growing and existing social media platform, to create the urgency for some of the things that are being talked about and negotiated," Omar said. "Much of our success as a Progressive Caucus has always been to not only do the inside organizing work in Congress or in positions of power, but to also have an outside game and be able to mobilize grassroots organizations and individuals to be in lockstep and to create the urgency and be able to throw down when it's necessary."

From that tense first term to their growing presence on the Hill, as they make their accommodations and choose their battles with the establishment, the Squad members have the same network of support they relied upon in their most fraught moment at the border—each other.

"It's one thing... to survive it alone, as I did the two years prior to coming to Congress," Omar said. "And it's another to go through it with... other women that you not only politically and ideologically identify with, but women who also share the challenges that you've gone through in growing up in society. We've developed a bond outside of just being colleagues."

Chapter 10

THE BRIDGE

THE TWIN TRAUMAS OF 2016 HAUNTED THE DEMOCRATS AS BIDEN wrapped up the nomination four years later.

That election had split the party and brought on four years of Trump. In March 2020, Democratic leaders were desperate for a different outcome. They knew the party would need to be united to defeat Trump. Forging a peace between Biden and Sanders was vital.

Sanders did his part by making a relatively quick, painless exit from the primary and immediately calling on his troops to rally behind Biden. Once that race was over, Biden repaid the favor by working to bring Sanders and the left into the fold. The ambitious agenda from Biden's first years in office that drew praise from Ilhan Omar and other progressives was the product of a sustained effort to reach out to Sanders and his cohort and give them input on shaping a policy platform that Biden carried from the campaign into the White House. Those peace talks began with Barack Obama.

A source who was involved in the process explained that the former president was fixated on the bitter battles of 2016—and on not repeating them when faced with the threat of Trump.

"Obama, it's fair to say he was obsessed with the unity aspect of this, having learned the lesson of '16," the source explained.

That race had ended with Sanders accusing the party establishment of corruption and with his supporters protesting at the convention and, more importantly, not turning out in force for the general election. In 2020, the party establishment that once thwarted Sanders worked to court him.

Privately, Obama spoke with Sanders and the other major progressive candidate, Elizabeth Warren. He wanted to ensure the two factions of the party could build a solid alliance to take on Trump.

"He had multiple conversations with Senator Sanders and with Senator Warren, knowing the context of '16," said the source, "making sure that the unity building behind Biden was more heartfelt and authentic and stronger and robust than it was around Hillary in '16."

As part of those conversations, according to the source who was involved, Obama suggested that the policy teams of the Sanders and Biden campaigns could begin to work together. It was the kernel of an idea that eventually grew into official "unity task forces." As of this writing, Obama's key role in the process has not been reported.

The task forces gave progressives real input on Biden's platform. That didn't prevent disagreements—including from Sanders himself—during Biden's first term. However, even though some on the left would criticize Biden for being insufficiently aggressive, the most consequential opposition to his agenda would ultimately come from the center.

Sanders initially jumped on board with the unity task force plan, and his campaign manager, Faiz Shakir, made a crucial stipulation: The Sanders and Biden campaigns would have to agree to each other's appointments.

When the task forces were announced in May 2020, the members included multiple former Obama administration officials; Conor Lamb, the outspokenly moderate congressman from Pennsylvania; Congressional Progressive Caucus Chairwoman Pramila Jayapal; and Alexandria Ocasio-Cortez. The representatives of both teams met and produced 110 pages of recommendations for the Democrats to include in their platform at the convention.

With their help, Biden faced off against Trump in the general election with what Waleed Shahid—the communications director for Justice Democrats and former campaign aide to Ocasio-Cortez—described to us as "the most progressive platform of any Democratic nominee in the modern history of the party." To be sure, Biden didn't produce a Green New Deal or Medicare for All. Nevertheless, as Shahid said, Biden's plans were well to the left of anything Hillary Clinton or Barack Obama had ever proposed.

The formation of the task forces also showed the pitfalls Biden faced as he embraced progressives. As soon as the members of the groups were announced, the Republican National Committee pounced on Ocasio-Cortez's presence and released a statement declaring that it should serve as a warning to the "American people that there isn't a far left policy [Biden] is not hellbent on advancing."

Biden was undeterred. The task forces had a distinct impact on the campaign trail. Many progressive operatives marveled at the way Biden applied his pragmatic moderate branding on a far more left-wing set of policy prescriptions than the Democratic Party had ever offered to the country. As the campaign accelerated towards election day in November 2020, Biden's stump speech became increasingly dominated by progressive promises to tax the rich, build up organized labor, abolish the death penalty, and tackle climate change.

In an interview, Congresswoman Pramila Jayapal of Washington State, who is the head of the Congressional Progressive Caucus on the Hill, reflected that the task forces "did two things."

"It actually allowed us to do a lot of planning and kind of outline the agenda that we wanted, so we actually had some time to do that work together," Jayapal said. "And it held the president accountable."

Overall, Jayapal, who credited Sanders with seizing upon the idea, said the task forces "forced a joining of the progressive movement and the Biden administration."

The policy exercise resulted in lasting relationships and that synergy persisted after Biden stepped into the White House.

"I'm still very close with some of the people on that task force, and some of the president's picks on that task force," Jayapal said, before rattling off the names of specific Biden advisers. "Faiz insisting on [the campaigns] approving each other's picks was actually important because it meant that we worked better together."

Jayapal would emerge as a crucial figure in that partnership.

AFTER HE DEFEATED DONALD TRUMP, BIDEN FACED THE DUAL CRISES OF a once-in-a-lifetime public health disaster and a volatile predecessor who had no intention to accept defeat or physically quit the White House.

Every previous president had enjoyed a peaceful transfer of power. Not Joe Biden. He watched Trump call a mob to DC and dispatch them to sack the Capitol in an effort to prevent the certification of his election.

Every previous president had sworn the oath of office with his face proudly uncovered. Joe Biden wore a mask to his own inauguration.

"A once-in-a-century virus silently stalks the country," he said in his address. "It's taken as many lives in one year as America lost in all of World War II."

To answer those challenges, Biden turned to the veteran Democratic operative Ron Klain, naming him chief of staff the week after the election was called. Klain had run Biden's vice presidential office, so he was firmly ensconced in the newly elected president's inner circle. He also had experience that was relevant to the two raging crises Biden was confronted with as he took office.

In 2014, Obama put Klain in charge of the administration's response to an Ebola outbreak. His stint as "Ebola czar" had given Klain the authority to become a harsh critic of the Trump administration's approach to the coronavirus pandemic. Biden's campaign produced a series of videos of Klain in front of a whiteboard criticizing Trump's handling of the crisis. He also had a unique experience navigating the murky waters of contested elections. In the nervous fall of 2000, Klain had been candidate Al Gore's commander on the ground during the Florida recount effort.

But Biden had given Klain another assignment as they transitioned from the campaign trail to the West Wing: tending to the relationship with progressives in Congress. A familiar face in the executive branch, Klain was less well known on the Hill, where he hadn't worked since the 1990s, and he threw himself into the task of making new connections. Jayapal became one of his regular contacts.

Jayapal had arrived in Congress in 2017, two years before "the Squad," with her own ideas about disrupting business as usual. Born in India, she came to the US as a teenager to attend college. After an improbable start as a financial analyst, she became a civil rights activist focused on immigrant advocacy. That work gave her an appreciation for the inside-outside game, which led her to set her sights on politics.

"I never wanted to be in elected office," Jayapal said, "but it occurred to me that you could organize on the inside, and that in order to organize on the inside, you actually had to have some structures to do that."

With Biden in office, Jayapal's inside-outside game had made it deep within the West Wing. She was in consistent contact with Klain throughout the start of the administration.

"I didn't know Ron when he came in, and we really built that relationship," Jayapal said. "Every text was answered immediately."

While Klain wasn't necessarily a familiar face to the progressives he was reaching out to, he did know the ropes. Starting on Capitol Hill as an aide for then-Representative and now-Senator Ed Markey in 1983, Klain had built a life within the institutions of the Democratic Party and the federal government. He'd started his career working with more liberal members, like Markey, but had also managed solidly centrist endeavors. Klain had staffed both of Bill Clinton's presidential campaigns and run the triangulation-focused Democratic Leadership Conference during the mid-'90s. He'd also been chief of staff to Attorney General Janet Reno and Vice President Al Gore, which is why Gore tapped him to lead his recount effort in 2000.

The world had changed drastically since 2000, of course, and especially since 2016 when Klain had last worked for the executive branch. Progressives had new prominence, particularly on social media. Klain's job was to build bridges with the left, and social media was where he found them—for better or worse.

"Ron is a bit of a mad genius," a senior White House aide said. "He's so smart, so, so, so, so, so smart, but he's very frenetic and I think a little reactive and has a bit of an old-fashioned sensibility, which I think is kind of funny. He's been working in this [business] for long enough and he knows the tricks and he's got his bag of tricks and that's what he does, but he is informed a lot by Twitter."

Klain's fastidious attention to the fast-paced discourse on Twitter helped—literally—bring activists into the White House.

A senior Hill aide recalled an early Biden-era experience of encountering Melissa Byrne, a progressive known for her relentless push for student debt relief, on a "message call" set up by the Biden campaign. The White House regularly schedules such calls to inform House and Senate offices and "outside validators," as the aide put it, of what they're doing, why, and how they will "message" it to the general public. This one was being held in the buildup to the president's August 2022 executive order forgiving a broad swath of student loans. Normally, this would have been a fairly staid affair where the administration hands off talking points to reliable cheerleaders. But in this case, the activist Byrne was on the line, and she was peppering the Biden team with "hard questions about student debt," the aide said, marveling that she maintained her influence despite the lack of decorum. "She kept pounding. But also, Ron Klain would retweet her. Like, she had their ear."

Byrne would later go on to defend Biden online even as other activists pointed out his policies fell well short of her longtime mantra: "Cancel student debt." While the administration wasn't giving rabble-rousers everything they wanted, it was soothing tensions by making them feel heard.

"The White House has been very attentive and very listening," Byrne said in an interview, while declining to say whom she had spoken with in the West Wing. "I definitely trust them, and I think they are genuinely engaged."

COMING INTO THE WHITE HOUSE, BIDEN'S TEAM WAS NOT EXPECTING a normal transition.

"We were prepared for it to be the most difficult" in American history, said Jen Psaki, who ran Biden's transition "war room" before the inauguration and became his first White House press secretary.

"That's how we were approaching it," she continued. "I mean, Trump was clear before the election, and certainly right after the election, that he was going to challenge the outcome, and that they wouldn't operate as a normal transition. Even pre–January 6th, they weren't sharing information. There were all sorts of challenges even before January 6th."

But there was an upside—the harrowing times made many Democrats eager to help Biden. In fact, Psaki said, the administration attracted a lot of staffers from the Obama era back to government service. She was one of them.

"If Hillary Clinton had won," Psaki mused, "we maybe wouldn't have gotten involved again, because it was time for another group of people to do it. But this was, 'if there's a way I can be helpful—' And everybody who works in government has an element of this; there's a pull of public service. . . . You're thinking: 'Maybe if there's any little thing I could do to help get us out of the last four years.'"

While the Biden team was groping towards normalcy, Trump was denying Biden everything: an acknowledgment of his victory, meetings with cabinet departments, vital information, and even—for an extended period—the transition office space due to Biden under federal law.

"I've been part of two transitions before this one," Psaki recalled, "You're preparing to govern the country. So, it's actually more of a time for any president—it should be: we'll put Trump aside—[to] make clear that though you didn't get everyone's votes, you're going to govern for everyone. That involves bringing your party together, and anyone who you may not have been the first choice for, but also making clear to the country that you're going to govern with the vision of trying to make people's lives better."

As he presented his vision, Biden wasn't casting himself as a member of any of the factions that had emerged within the party. Psaki framed this as a return to the way things were before 2016.

"It's less about positioning yourself as the leader of any particular wing, because most people in the country don't think like that," Psaki explained. "Most people in the country are not like, 'Are you a Blue Dog, or are you a member of the Squad?' The transition for him, but also for Obama, was more about saying, 'I know you didn't vote for me, but I'm here because I want to govern to make your life better.' And that's really what it's about."

The idea of appealing to and governing for all the people, even those who supported the other guy, is an old one, and it's central to American democracy. But the concept sat awkwardly next to the reality of 2020, in which a vast number of Americans had set aside their commitment to democracy, considered Biden's leadership illegitimate, and wanted an authoritarian installed in his place. It's one thing to transcend partisanship and occupy the lofty rhetorical space of a president for all Americans if your disagreements boil down to tax policy or social issues, but what happens when the other side is willing to violently assault the Capitol to prevent you from taking office?

Psaki acknowledged that tension and noted Biden "gave entire speeches on authoritarianism" and made efforts to repudiate the anger of the Trump era. However, it was also something he tried to transcend.

"At the same time," she said, Biden "made a point not to make it about an ongoing campaign with Trump, because he didn't feel that was what the American people wanted, or needed, or desired at that point in time."

But as he tried to move beyond the chaos of the Trump administration, Biden would need to deal with his razor-thin majorities in Congress and the enduring splits within his party.

NATIONAL UNITY WAS PERHAPS A CHIMERICAL GOAL IN THE IMMEDIATE aftermath of January 6.

The Republican Party, after a brief flirtation with respectability after the Capitol attack, plunged ahead with a defense of Trump against his second impeachment trial and a campaign of resistance to the COVID vaccines, which Biden's administration had put at the center of his pandemic policy.

Unity among Democrats, however, appeared within reach, and Biden's aides put together a team to lock it down. With the success of the unity task forces during the campaign, the Biden team found itself in extraordinarily close alignment with progressives.

"We were very deliberate when we started putting things together at the beginning of the administration," one senior White House official said.

With the various divisions on Capitol Hill, the official said Biden's team was focused on "taking a big picture" approach.

"There are cliques, caucuses, groups, committees, and we looked at everything and tried to make sure that basically we were going to have a representative from every quadrant that was going to be on our team," the White House official explained. "We knew that we were going to need that as we came into this with really high expectations and a great deal of excitement about Biden and about Democrats kind of running the tables."

That energy stemmed from the fact that, as Biden took office, for the first time since 2011, the Democrats had an edge in both houses of Congress. Voters who had poured their hearts into the effort to unseat Trump and retake the Senate expected dramatic changes, but Biden's margins were beyond slim.

In the House, the Democrats had a single-digit edge and, in the Senate, it was evenly split. Thanks to Bernie Sanders and Maine's Angus King, two independents who caucused with the Democrats, they had fifty senators—the same number as the GOP. With Biden in the White House, that positioned Kamala Harris to serve as the chamber's tiebreaker—a role she would need to fulfill more often during the first two years of their term than any other vice president in history. This tight dynamic meant that, for Biden to have any chance of passing a substantial agenda, which would not have Republican support, Democrats had to remain virtually in lockstep. For Biden, the trouble came from the center.

The Blue Dogs are a famously conservative group of Democrats, probably the closest to the Republicans in Congress. In late 2020, as Biden was preparing to take over, the group sent him a letter urging him to pursue "bipartisan priorities" in his first hundred days. The Blue Dogs listed out five potential policy focus areas: COVID relief, job creation, government reform, holding foreign adversaries accountable, and fiscal responsibility. With the exception of COVID relief, the long list of progressive policy priorities that Biden had campaigned on was absent from the Blue Dogs' letter.

While the Blue Dogs were firing warning shots, the Jayapal-led Congressional Progressive Caucus had, by contrast, made a key choice to embrace Biden as tightly as they could.

"It started very early on with a very strategic decision that we made to call this the president's agenda," Jayapal said. "Giving him credit early on and making him the focus of our work was really important because then it wasn't that we were fighting for a progressive agenda, which maybe some big portion of even Democrats don't identify with, but we were fighting for the president's agenda."

Biden's team knew that, as one White House official put it, the

Blue Dogs "had a big footprint" on Capitol Hill. With Congress as narrowly divided as it has ever been in living memory, for its first major legislative push, the Biden administration chose to prioritize a version of pandemic relief, known as the American Rescue Plan, followed by an effort to reform and strengthen ballot access and America's election systems. That meant deferring other essential agenda items, like infrastructure, industrial policy, and climate, to later in the administration, a time when victories come far less easily.

Biden's decision to put COVID relief before everything else was consequential and controversial. It would force the president to take a second pass in order to enact other aspects of his platform and some progressives—notably Sanders—would later express frustration that Biden didn't use his initial mandate more aggressively.

Asked about this critique, a senior Biden administration official invited us to think back to "where we were when we came in . . . and remember what this was like."

"We weren't even going up to the Hill. We were in lockdown. . . . It was crazy town," the official recalled.

The Coronavirus Aid, Relief, and Economic Security (CARES) Act, which had passed on a bipartisan basis under the Trump administration in the early days of the pandemic was "clearly not meeting the moment," this person said. Vaccines had yet to roll out, the economy was flailing, and people were suffering.

The Biden administration's challenge, the official said, was to get members of Congress "in a new environment and thinking more ambitiously about this as opposed to honestly, and this isn't disrespectful, everyone kind of being in a fetal position." Amid the chaos and danger of Biden's first months in office, the official said it was imperative he get some measure of pandemic relief passed quickly.

"We had to get people out of a fetal position, [and] get everybody aligned on where we needed to be," the official explained.

In these circumstances, the official argued Biden's American Rescue Plan actually seemed ambitious to most Democrats.

Bernie Sanders didn't think so. He had prepared an outline for the stimulus bill that included authorizing Medicare to negotiate drug prices, free preschool and childcare for working families, guaranteed paid family and medical leave for every worker in America, and student debt cancellation, according to one of his books. Sanders, in other words, wanted to wrap as much of the Democrats' agenda as he could into the COVID relief package. He thought that the $1.9 trillion American Rescue Plan should have been far bigger if it was going to occupy the precious political space of a new president's first major legislative push. Democratic leaders, he wrote, wanted to postpone the debate over those issues.

In Sanders's view, Biden should have used the momentum from his win and the emergency of the outbreak to enact many of the transformative policy goals that were agreed upon by the unity task force. To Biden's team, the urgency—and the hard reality of the numbers in Congress—made that approach unrealistic.

In the face of Sanders's criticism, Biden aides made certain to remain diplomatic. "I think, without commenting on whether I agree or disagree with Senator Sanders, because he's got views on this that are well thought out and well researched . . . ," a senior administration official began, before disagreeing rather strongly with the senator's analysis.

"The COVID situation was so dire, not only in terms of material conditions in the country but also in terms of the mindset in Washington, that everything else had to take a back seat," the official said.

The Biden administration official argued it was far easier for Sanders to nitpick when he sat down to write memoirs months later than it was to have an immediate impact in the midst of an unfolding crisis.

"I understand," the official said, "that maybe in a perfect world, in a sort of Monday morning quarterback, we could have done differently, but people have to understand the kind of clock we were under and what people were . . . like, our friends, our family, the people that we went to high school and college with, what they were living with at that time—It was nuts."

In light of the immense challenges and the nearly split Congress, the official argued it was "extraordinary that Biden managed to do as much as he did."

After the American Rescue Plan passed and the election reforms failed, when it came time to pursue the rest of Biden's initial agenda— his signature domestic spending measures and tax reforms—the administration still found itself allied with progressives. They may have had issues with some of his approach, but Biden's efforts to build relationships on the left had clearly earned him some support and trust. However, Biden would find that his prioritization of COVID relief over the more ambitious, progressive aspects of his agenda had not brought much bipartisan agreement, or even earned any appreciable warmth or goodwill from the Blue Dogs. National unity and party unity, as the first hundred days came to a close, remained tantalizingly out of reach.

As Biden navigated the rest of his first two years, it must have seemed like people were lining up to hang albatrosses around his neck. His signature domestic spending legislation twisted in the wind for a year and a half while centrist Democrats on the Hill extracted concession after concession. Arrests boomed along the US southern border. His initiative to end America's longest war in Afghanistan became a bloody catastrophe when the government that the United States had

spent two decades supporting with blood and treasure collapsed over-
night. Russia massed its troops and assailed Ukraine, starting a war on
NATO's borders.

A major falling out with progressives, however, hadn't been one of
Biden's burdens. The Democratic left had cause to complain, of course.
But, thanks to the lines of communication Biden had opened, when
they had issues they took them directly to the White House and were
far more muted in public. And, at the times when the Biden administration overruled the progressive argument and steered federal policy
away from their preferences, they didn't seek to impose any significant
political cost on the president.

Jayapal and her leadership of the progressive caucus was a major
force ensuring Biden didn't face attacks from his left flank.

"I made a commitment early on that we wouldn't always agree on
everything," Jayapal said, "but if we were going to do something and it
was going to be critical of the president, or the administration, that we
would notify them, that we would tell them, that he would never get,
or be, surprised by something we did."

That decision came from Jayapal's close relationship with the
administration, which was the result of Biden's sustained focus on outreach to progressives. Jayapal said she had "very deep engagement with
the White House from the very beginning."

"And that was at the highest level," she added. "It was with the chief
of staff. It was with the president himself."

There were times, Jayapal said, when she would hear from Biden
almost out of the blue.

"Ron understood and, most importantly, the president understood
that the biggest part of his base was progressives in Congress," Jayapal
said. "There were a number of times where the president has completely
surprised me by calling me because he saw me on TV—and I know he

has done this for other people too—and he really appreciated that we were pushing for his agenda."

Jayapal said these conversations with Biden made progressives "partners in the fight" and described the talks as being built on mutual trust and respect.

"There were things that we discussed that were not to be spread and they could trust me on that, and I needed to be able to trust them too," she said, "And so that really was the relationship we had. It was very consultative."

According to Jayapal, her admiration for Biden was "cemented" in interactions that were facilitated by Klain, including a breakfast where the president took her through pieces of his agenda in detail.

"I do think that breakfast was kind of a really incredible time, because he was so engaged on the policy and so was I," Jayapal said, adding, "He was asking me what I thought, and we were going back and forth, and it was just really great, it was a terrific interaction."

Klain's close work with progressives was so essential that, when he decided to leave after two years in February 2023, it created an awkward gap in Biden's bridge to the left. The exit heightened the risk that Biden's delicate truce, which was forged with the unity task forces and sustained by Klain's outreach, could fall apart.

A senior Biden administration official acknowledged that Klain's departure was disruptive, saying it was like when you "shake the globe and you're letting the snow fall again." But they were quick to downplay the problem, noting that Klain wasn't the only conduit to progressives.

But Jayapal said losing Klain worried her. Despite not knowing Klain beforehand, Jayapal had come to believe that his appointment as chief of staff "really helped" the progressive caucus. She reacted to his resignation with dismay.

"When I found out he was leaving—and I found out before it went public—I just, I said, 'What are we going to do?! What are we going to do without you there?" Jayapal recalled.

But Klain, as Jayapal recounted, set her mind at ease. "Don't forget, Congresswoman," he said, "the president's agenda is still the president's agenda. He still wants to get this done."

When progressives expressed skepticism about Klain's successor, Jeff Zients—thanks, in part, due to his past work as a corporate consultant—Klain urged Jayapal to work with him.

"Give Jeff a chance the way you gave me a chance," Klain said, according to Jayapal.

Jayapal followed Klain's lead and so did Zients. In the early part of 2023, Jayapal said she continued having regular calls with the new chief of staff and having visits at the White House. About a month after Klain's departure, Jayapal confirmed the truce was still in place and that progressives' inside-outside game was still being played all the way up to the West Wing.

"Jeff has called me. Actually, he dropped in on a meeting I had today at the White House," Jayapal said. "Jeff seems like a great guy. . . . I hope I can build the same kind of relationship that I had with Ron."

Chapter 11

FILIBUSTER

THE RULE THAT TORPEDOED MUCH OF PRESIDENT BIDEN'S FIRST-term agenda exists thanks to one of the most infamous villains in early American history.

A relic of a misbegotten edit to the Senate's rules that Aaron Burr proposed in the early nineteenth century, the filibuster has survived down the years as one of a minority party's most powerful checks on the will of the majority. As it is currently written, the filibuster rule requires sixty votes to call a halt to debate on a bill in the Senate. Stopping debate is a necessary preliminary step to passing a bill, because Senate procedures otherwise allow for unlimited discussion.

The unlimited-debate rule, which allows for the traditional filibuster practice of talking a bill to death, has a murky and ignoble history. Its creation was, more or less, a mistake no one noticed at the time.

America's Founding Fathers were preoccupied with the question of minority rights. Most of the founders you've heard of—James Madison, Alexander Hamilton, Thomas Jefferson—tended to believe when push came to shove, the majority should rule. Madison called this "the republican principle."

Madison and his allies, however, were hard-pressed by small states, like Delaware, who feared being dominated by the larger ones, like Virginia. Those small states threatened the unity of the Constitutional Convention, and their reservations about this issue delayed its work for weeks. The creation of the Senate itself was the resolution of this conflict; known as "the Great Compromise," the founders hit upon the idea of a bicameral legislature, with the House apportioned based on population and the Senate where each state would have equal representation, no matter its size.

Nowhere was it suggested that the Senate should have unlimited debate, or that a supermajority should be required to pass legislation. It was not in the debates at the Constitutional Convention, not in the correspondence of the founding generation, not in the famous *Federalist Papers* authored by Madison, Hamilton, and John Jay selling the new Constitution to the American public, and not in the text of the Constitution itself.

Madison himself clearly believed that the Constitution provided for most big issues to be resolved by simple majorities.

"If a faction consists of less than a majority, relief is supplied by the republican principle, which enables the majority to defeat its sinister views by regular vote," Madison wrote in *Federalist* No. 10. "It may clog the administration, it may convulse the society; but it will be unable to execute and mask its violence under the forms of the Constitution."

In the beginning, the Senate had normal parliamentary rules similar to those found in the House. These rules contained a number of mechanisms for ending debate on a particular measure, the most salient of which was the "previous question" motion. Though not commonly used this way at the turn of the nineteenth century, the previous

question rule allowed a simple majority to end debate on any given subject. The House resolved its own filibuster crisis with this rule during a
debate over the early stages of the War of 1812. The Senate might have
used the rule in the same way, but the founding generation's famous
scoundrel, Aaron Burr, had already done his work.

As Thomas Jefferson's vice president, Burr served as president of the
Senate from 1801 to 1805. It was a tumultuous time in Burr's life. By
the last month of Jefferson's first term in office, Burr had been dropped
from the Democratic-Republican ticket for Jefferson's reelection, lost
a race for governor of New York, and been indicted twice for killing
Alexander Hamilton—whom he blamed for his loss—in a duel. Rather
than face justice in New Jersey and New York, where warrants had been
issued for his arrest, Burr would soon flee to Georgia. From there, he
became involved in dubious conspiracies to carve a new country out
of the West.

But, in February and March 1805, Burr was still doing his job
in Washington and presiding over the Senate's particularly thorny
impeachment trial of Supreme Court Justice Samuel Chase for excessive partisanship. The justice was safely acquitted, and Burr's conduct of
the trial was widely praised in Washington. He acted, according to an
official Senate history, "with the dignity and impartiality of an angel,
but with the rigor of a devil." After a few days' work, Burr took the occasion to deliver a farewell oration.

Burr's words were clearly stirring. Though the full text of his speech
has been lost to history, a few quotes have come down to us including a
reporter's account of the speech.

"This House is a sanctuary," Burr said. "A citadel of law, of order,
and of liberty, and it is here—it is here, in this exalted refuge; here, if
anywhere, will resistance be made to the storms of political phrensy
and the silent arts of corruption; and if the Constitution be destined

ever to perish by the sacrilegious hands of the demagogue or the usurper, which God avert, its expiring agonies will be witnessed on this floor."

Beyond that lofty rhetoric, which sounds prophetic in light of January 6, Burr made some concrete recommendations.

Sarah Binder, a historian at George Washington University and a senior fellow at the Brookings Institution, found an entry in future president John Quincy Adams's diary describing Burr's speech and his recommendations in more detail.

"He mentioned one or two of the rules which appeared to him to need a revisal, and recommended abolition of that respecting the previous question, which he said had in the four years [of Burr's vice presidency] been only once taken, and that was upon an amendment," Adams wrote of Burr. "This was a proof that it could not be necessary, and all its purposes were certainly much better answered by the question of indefinite postponement."

Burr was held in such high regard—notwithstanding his indictments for slaying another Founding Father—that the change was made with no apparent difficulty at the next rules revision. For years, no one noticed a difference. But with the coming of the slavery crisis, senators grew to learn that without the previous question motion they could hold the floor as long as they wanted to prevent a vote, and no one had the power to stop them. Indefinite postponement of the measure under consideration, Burr's recommended alternative, supplied no remedy at all; in fact, it was exactly what most senators who used the filibuster typically wanted to achieve.

Allowing one lawmaker to hold up proceedings forever was untenable, but nevertheless, the senators were not inclined to give up their newfound privilege entirely and submit to Madison's "republican principle." Instead, the Senate created a cloture rule allowing for debate to end only with a supermajority vote. The Senate had accidentally invented, and then intentionally embraced, a greater check on the will of the majority than the founders ever intended.

Throughout the twentieth century, the filibuster's most common use was to torpedo civil rights bills. The procedure has been used to stop laws protecting the rights of Black Americans for a hundred years. Before the partisan realignments of the 1960s, the filibuster was the favored tool of the racist Southern Democrats to preserve Jim Crow racial codes. Since Nixon's Southern Strategy essentially flipped the two parties' positions on race, it has been the preferred method Republicans use to suppress minority turnout and oppose voting reforms.

Within the past two decades, the filibuster increasingly became a tool of massive obstruction—stopping ordinary legislation, blocking judicial nominations from going forward, and even preventing new presidents from staffing the federal government with executive appointees whose jobs require Senate confirmation.

The procedure's overuse in recent years has led to a pair of majority revolts that eliminated the supermajority filibuster rule for nominations. That process began in November 2013 with the Democrats, who were frustrated by years-long Republican filibusters of Obama's executive-branch and judicial nominees. In response, then Majority Leader Harry Reid employed a maneuver widely dubbed the "nuclear option."

Reid raised a point of order asserting—contrary to the then-applicable rules—that cloture could be invoked for all nominees other than nominations to the Supreme Court by a simple majority vote. When this point of order was denied, Reid appealed to the full Senate, and a simple majority vote sustained his new, whittled-down version of the filibuster.

. Another revolt, this time by Republicans, resolved the conflict that erupted following the sudden death of Supreme Court Justice Antonin Scalia in February 2016. At the time, with eleven months to go in Barack Obama's term, Republican leaders refused to consider or even hold a hearing for his nominee to replace Scalia, Merrick Garland—who threatened to bring an end to conservatives' 5–4 majority on the court. When Donald Trump took office in January 2017 and submitted his own nominee, Neil Gorsuch, aggrieved Democrats filibustered. In April 2017, McConnell invoked the same procedure Reid had used to break their filibuster. His point of order and subsequent appeal eliminated the exception for Supreme Court nominations. Republicans confirmed Gorsuch by a simple majority vote, 54–45.

Reid and McConnell's dueling maneuvers illustrated why many senators were reluctant to touch the filibuster. Any changes could be quickly followed by aggressive gains for the party in power.

Following these court fights, the only remaining use of the filibuster's supermajority requirement was to permanently stall ordinary legislation.

—————

CONVENTIONAL WISDOM HOLDS THAT EACH NEW PRESIDENT GETS A "honeymoon." It's a period of a hundred days or so when it's simply easier to get things done. Your mandate is fresh; your popularity is high; your party in Congress is behind you; your enemies are demoralized; your scandals—should they exist—have yet to emerge. It's a good time to get a big bill passed.

But even in his "honeymoon" phase, victories on Capitol Hill never came particularly easily for President Joe Biden. It quickly became apparent that all fifty Democrats in the Senate were not fully on board with his planned agenda. The first cracks in the Senate coalition began on an issue that Biden had deliberately tried to avoid—filibuster reform.

In early 2021, with Biden newly in office, progressives were eager to get rid of the filibuster altogether in order to pass the agenda crafted by the unity task forces. They were also hoping to enact transformational policies that would confront some of the lack of campaign finance regulations and gerrymandering that helped lead to Trump.

"I think it's on a lot of people's minds because the dark money problem and the voting rights problem are of such concern and the pathway to solutions there is obstructed by the cloture rule," Senator Sheldon Whitehouse said about the prospect of filibuster reform in a 2021 interview, "but I don't think we have consensus yet on what the strategy should be to try to solve that."

They were trying to ensure the party's future. Abolishing the filibuster could be the decisive first step to both give Biden legislative accomplishments to run for reelection on and to shape a fairer environment for him to run in. While senators weren't sure they were going to confront the filibuster, for some Democrats, the imperative to get it done was quite obvious.

"They have to get rid of the filibuster. They just have to," Obama's speechwriter Cody Keenan fumed, also in a 2021 interview. "It's really, really frustrating."

While Whitehouse and others were concerned about Senate norms and the reluctant colleagues who wanted to defend them, Keenan simply pointed to the stakes of the fight. He feared the party was sabotaging itself with excessive deference to congressional traditions.

"I guarantee you most of the pissed off people out there do not give a fuck about parliamentary procedure and the ins and outs of the filibuster fight," Keenan said. "Unless they get rid of it and do big shit in the next two years, then we're just doomed in 2022 and beyond."

Republican Minority Leader Mitch McConnell saw the looming fight in 2021 and moved early to head the progressives off. With the Senate split 50–50 in the first months of Biden's term, McConnell and Democratic Majority Leader Chuck Schumer were hashing out a power-sharing agreement. McConnell stalled the process and said he would not move forward without a promise from Schumer to preserve the filibuster.

In a memo to his Republican colleagues, McConnell suggested they needed to protect the filibuster quickly before its opponents managed to tie the issue to some great moral cause or piece of popular legislation. He characterized the effort to preserve the filibuster as a fight to save the Senate from destruction.

"I believe the time is ripe to address this issue head on before the passions of one particular issue or another arise," McConnell wrote. "We will need unity and the support of each of you as this may take time to work through."

Schumer rejected McConnell's demand that he commit to keeping the filibuster on general principle.

"We are not letting McConnell dictate how the Senate operates," Schumer declared.

But after a few days of the standoff, two Democratic senators— Joe Manchin of West Virginia and Kyrsten Sinema of Arizona—broke ranks. The pair sided with the Republicans and vowed they would never vote to kill the filibuster.

In winning the filibuster debate, McConnell had also succeeded in detaching two Democratic senators from the rest of their party. No policy, nor any great social cause, had been much discussed. That was exactly the way McConnell had wanted it. And this two-member crack in the Democrats' coalition would gradually grow to threaten Biden's agenda and shape the principal political dramas of his first two years in office.

HAVING LEARNED THAT McCONNELL WOULD NEVER COMPROMISE ON any legislation, the administration designed the pandemic relief bill known as the American Rescue Plan Act of 2021 to avoid the filibuster and pass by an alternative process known as budget reconciliation. This maneuver eliminated the prospect of a Republican filibuster in the Senate, limited the bill's potential scope, and subjected it to an arcane and time-consuming procedure that afforded every senator the opportunity to offer amendments.

Reconciliation allows legislation to bypass the filibuster as long as it affects the budget—and does so without adding to the deficit. The process is enforced by the Senate parliamentarian, an unelected legislative-branch employee, who typically determines whether a given provision fits within the proper scope of the process. The parliamentarian quickly became an obstacle to Biden's agenda.

One of Biden's proposed features of the bill was hiking the federal minimum wage to $15 per hour—a cherished progressive goal—but the parliamentarian ruled it couldn't be included, an outcome Biden had predicted. This set up one of the first flashpoints between progressives and moderates in the Senate.

Seeking to force a vote, Senator Bernie Sanders offered an amendment to reinsert the minimum-wage provision, and when the parliamentarian again ruled it out of order, he moved to appeal the ruling. In the ensuing vote, seven Democrats and the independent senator from Maine, Angus King, voted along with all the Republicans to sustain the parliamentarian's decision. Senator Kyrsten Sinema of Arizona stole the show with a theatrically exaggerated thumbs-down gesture. Turning on her heel, she strode out of the chamber and into progressives' pantheon of villains.

Sinema's star turn somewhat obscured the names of the other seven Democratic senators opposed to moving forward with raising the minimum wage. For the record, they were: Manchin; Tom Carper and Chris Coons of Delaware; Jon Tester of Montana; and Maggie Hassan and Jeanne Shaheen of New Hampshire.

While there weren't enough Democratic votes to move the $15 minimum wage as a standalone amendment, many progressives were confident it would have passed if the parliamentarian had allowed Biden to include it as part of the larger reconciliation bill. This suggested another path for Majority Leader Schumer: Fire the parliamentarian. It was a step progressives were eager to see him take.

"We should have been willing to get rid of the parliamentarian to get a $15 wage," Representative Ro Khanna of California said in an interview for this book conducted months after the fight.

Schumer opted to follow the more standard operating procedure. When it reached the final votes, in late February and early March 2021, the American Rescue Plan passed with slender margins—50–49 in the evenly divided Senate and 219–212 in the closely split House. In the lower chamber, two Democrats joined Republicans in voting against it.

The American Rescue Plan was an impactful piece of legislation, even if many key parts of it did not last beyond 2021. Perhaps no aspect had a greater effect than its expanded Child Tax Credit.

The credit served as an example of how meaningful even a relatively small legislative change could be. But it also became an example of how resistant Manchin and Sinema were to change and how their whims could dictate outcomes for Biden and progressives.

A brainchild of Democratic senators Michael Bennet of Colorado, Sherrod Brown of Ohio, and Cory Booker of New Jersey, the provision built on a long-standing $2,000 per child federal tax benefit. For lower-income and some middle-class families, the ARP expanded that credit to $3,600 per child under the age of six and $3,000 per child between the ages of six and seventeen. Crucially, for the first time it made the credit fully refundable—meaning that very low-income families could claim the full benefit in cash, $300 paid monthly, even if their tax liability was less than the total.

The effect was dramatic. Expansion of the tax credit kept six million American children out of poverty in the first month of its implementation in 2021, according to one study. However, the change was not a permanent one.

Because the American Rescue Plan, which passed in March 2021, was an emergency COVID measure, many of its provisions, including the Child Tax Credit, were set to expire at the end of that year. Progressives—including Sanders—scrambled to save the tax credit. They were overruled. The Biden administration promised that a permanent provision would be included in the flagship spending bill they planned to introduce next, in April or May 2021. Yet, once again, Biden and progressives would find their priorities thwarted by Manchin and Sinema.

AFTER THE SLIMMED-DOWN VERSION OF BIDEN'S COVID RELIEF PACK-age passed, a pair of voting rights and election reform bills that progressives had yearned for, which were the Democrats' next priority for 2021, passed the House and got filibustered into oblivion in the Senate. Even though Manchin and Sinema supported the measures, they both said that the goal of making American elections fairer and more accessible was superseded by their desire to preserve the filibuster and prevent the majority from ruling without wider consensus.

That early fight set the tone for Biden's first two years in office. The legislative filibuster was alive and well. With no votes in the Senate to spare, any Democratic senator could in theory kill any bill or nomination, barring an unlikely epiphany from a Republican senator (or eleven of them together, in the case of non-reconciliation legislation). Manchin and Sinema, radical centrists, were the most likely to kill any given bill. Everything had to go through them.

Because Manchin and Sinema were often in dissent together on major pieces of legislation, they were often spoken of in the same sentence. However, the White House worked to learn their idiosyncrasies—and cater to them. It was vital if Biden hoped to get anything done.

"They're different politicians; they have different equities; they come from different states," one senior White House official said of the pair. "While they get sort of get lumped together . . . we think they're very different, and we try to take an approach that is tailor-made for each one of them."

In the spring of 2021, with the American Rescue Plan enacted, the Biden team turned towards the signature domestic spending legislation he had campaigned on—the one he had promised progressives would include the expanded Child Tax Credit and so much more. The work on the Hill began in March 2021 on a reconciliation bill styled the Build Back Better Act, or BBB—a direct reference to Biden's 2020 campaign slogan.

The fight that developed over BBB saw the centrist Democratic resistance to Joe Biden—or at least their resistance to the progressive set of ideas he had campaigned on—take on its full scope and compass.

Biden may have hoped that he'd get his signature domestic policies enacted by a united Democratic Party at the tail end of his honeymoon. What ensued was a torturous seventeen-month journey in which the project seemed to die multiple deaths.

The long saga of intrigues and disappointments would include, among other things, multiple alliances between centrist Democrats and Republicans, a bipartisan infrastructure package that appears to have been intended to spoil the pitch for BBB, and the writing and rewriting of Joe Biden's political obituary.

In perhaps the clearest sign of how much power the radical centrists were wielding over the president, along the way the legislation lost the name of Biden's campaign slogan. It was reborn with a name that Manchin chose: the Inflation Reduction Act, or IRA.

As 2021 dragged on and Biden's agenda twisted in the wind, the White House was gripped by fear and frustration. Their poll numbers and prospects for the coming midterm elections were gloomy. Staffers who had been there since the campaign were feeling drained and defeated.

"The vibes are bad," a senior White House aide told us in the middle of those dark days. "A lot of the people in this generation are people who have been working straight through since the primary. You think about it, these are people who have not taken a vacation since January of 2019. People are fucking fried, the news is bad, the numbers are bad, the midterm looks like it's not going to be awesome. I truly don't think it's too late to turn it around, but we're losing daylight, and it's not the most fun."

Like a latter-day moderate version of the Boston Tea Party, the rebellion in the Democratic ranks was all about taxes. Shortly after the plan was introduced, a group of centrist Northeastern Democrats large enough to scuttle any bill in the narrowly divided House issued a demand that the next major legislative package include a repeal of the cap on SALT, the federal tax deduction for state and local taxes.

The cap had been imposed during the Trump administration as a cost-saving measure, but it was also widely seen as a vindictive swipe at the "coastal elites" and liberal jurisdictions that tend to have higher tax levels and lower levels of support for Republicans. It was an ironic piece of policymaking because the cap was a progressive tax reform, the kind typically favored by Democrats, but it also happened to serve Trump-era Republicans' overriding interest in culture war and revenge.

The group included Tom Suozzi of New York and Bill Pascrell, Mikie Sherrill, and Josh Gottheimer of New Jersey. The cap they wanted to lift by its nature mostly affected wealthier families—people who generally paid a lot of state income and property taxes, but the advocates for repeal nevertheless cast it as a middle-class issue. They had a point; homeowners who didn't consider themselves inordinately rich were paying higher state taxes and feeling the burden.

A full repeal of the SALT cap would be expensive and regressive, eating up around $475 billion in five years, with $400 billion of that going to the top 5 percent of households, according to one nonpartisan estimate. It would also be supremely popular in high-tax blue states, and both Republicans and Democrats who represented areas that would see relief from a repeal could expect to be strongly pressured by their constituents to support it.

The four Democrats who made the demand soon had backup. More blue-state Democrats rallied to their side. They teamed up with a group of Republicans and christened themselves the SALT caucus. The coalition was led on the Democratic side by Josh Gottheimer. A stocky Harvard-trained lawyer, Gottheimer won election to the House in 2016 in a New Jersey district spread across several prosperous New York City suburbs. He had quickly become a villain in the eyes of many progressives.

Gottheimer's pedigree was almost perfectly designed to provoke the left's ire. Before Congress, he worked for years in close proximity to the Democratic operative Mark Penn, who was one of the chief strategists from Hillary Clinton's 2008 campaign against Barack Obama. Gottheimer followed Penn from the PR firm Burson-Marsteller to various campaign posts and to a strategy job at Microsoft. He is often described as Penn's protégé. In Congress, Gottheimer co-chairs the Problem Solvers Caucus, which is closely aligned with the centrist advocacy group No Labels, which is run by Nancy Jacobson—who just so happens to be Penn's wife.

The Problem Solvers' stock-in-trade is across-the-aisle compromise. However, progressives contend that the Problem Solvers use their bipartisan branding mainly to subvert progressive policy.

"Josh Gottheimer . . . is definitely the number-one official on the Hill who's working to sabotage Joe Biden," one progressive activist said.

In addition to the SALT gambit, Gottheimer and the Problem Solvers also crafted a plan in the summer of 2021 to push their own bipartisan infrastructure bill, which could be passed quickly. They proposed removing a pillar of the BBB framework—urgently needed infrastructure spending—and passing that popular measure first as a separate bill. Doing so would sap popularity from the BBB package while also shoving it onto the back burner.

While the plan clearly threatened Biden's signature legislation, the president's team decided to take a win where they could easily get one. The White House embraced the bipartisan infrastructure deal, which swiftly passed in the Senate. Although it wasn't everything Biden wanted, all the measure needed was House approval and he could sign a second major piece of legislation before his first autumn in office.

Now, it was the progressives' turn to throw their weight around. They fought to keep the BBB bill off the back burner. Progressives would gladly sign off on the bipartisan infrastructure bill in the House, just as soon as the Senate had finished passing Build Back Better—all of it.

It was only natural that the progressives were the fiercest defenders of Biden's original agenda. After all, they had worked closely with his team to craft it. Congressional Progressive Caucus Chairwoman Pramila Jayapal found herself putting her foot down with the West Wing.

"We made it very clear to the White House that we were not going to pass the infrastructure bill without the Build Back Better Act in the House," Jayapal said, "And there were people, I think, that were worried that that was going to lead to not passing the infrastructure bill, but I knew that if we could just hold the line—and we did a lot of work with our members to keep everyone together on that—and if we could just insist that we had to pass both of them through the House, that that would give us the momentum that we needed."

A series of caucus meetings followed. Democrats were split between the progressives, who wanted to seize the opportunity of full government control to pursue long-held progressive goals, and the Problem Solvers with their more centrist allies, who preferred the immediate benefits of the infrastructure bill.

Abigail Spanberger, a moderate Democrat from Virginia, was frustrated. She waved around a handful of papers summarizing the infrastructure bill's benefits for her district as she vented to reporters on Capitol Hill following a meeting with Biden and other congressional Democrats.

"So, I guess we'll just wait, because evidently failing roads and bridges can just wait in the minds of some people," Spanberger declared.

The progressive side understood that impatience gave them negotiating leverage. The infrastructure bill came with shovel-ready spending, and many members were eager to see that money flow to their districts.

Conditioning the release of that infrastructure money on the passage of the rest of Build Back Better was a powerful incentive to make moderates vote for Biden's larger agenda. Jayapal and other progressives were certain the moderates would be highly unlikely to pass the rest of BBB if the infrastructure money was already on its way.

But Biden wanted to get a deal done. He made a pilgrimage to the Hill to meet with progressives. This broke the logjam. The progressives relented, passing the Senate-passed infrastructure bill in the House in late November. The House, led by the progressive caucus, passed the BBB package a few days later and sent it off into an uncertain future in the Senate.

Manchin had indicated he would support Build Back Better as long as the House passed the bipartisan infrastructure bill. However, as the bill hit the Senate floor, there was what Jayapal described as a "breakdown."

"Then he decided, as you know, not to support Build Back Better," she said of Manchin.

At least part of that discord came because the Senate was not impressed with the House's work. "The bill that passed in the House was a mess," said a former Democratic Senate aide who was familiar with the process. "You had a panoply of programs stuck in there, and some would go on for two years, some would be for four years, some would be for six years. Everything was set to expire at different points. And nothing, except the climate spending, was permanent."

The radical centrists began sharpening their pencils.

"There was just this very weird dynamic where it seemed like Schumer was just waiting for Manchin and Sinema to tell him what they were going to cut," the former aide said.

Understanding their leverage, Manchin and Sinema took their time. They also took very different approaches to the process. "Joe Manchin ended up just picking the programs he wanted to do," the former aide said, noting that Manchin selected reforms to the Affordable Care Act, the energy package, and the Internal Revenue Service.

The former aide credited Manchin with choosing popular, broadly acceptable initiatives that would reflect well on Biden upon passage. However, they also argued Schumer and the White House should have exerted more control over the process by doing more to dictate the proposals from House progressives.

"Joe Manchin shouldn't have been the one doing that. And I think we would've avoided a lot of that mess in the fall," the aide explained.

It was the radical centrists who ended up controlling much of Biden's agenda in his first year, and, the former aide added, Manchin was a better, more canny bill editor than Sinema. According to the former aide, Sinema wanted to make the prescription drug price negotiation program less progressive. She also refused to consider changes to the carried interest exception that gave preferential tax rates to hedge fund and private equity managers. Sinema was effectively standing up for the wealthiest investors rather than senior citizens.

"Nothing she did made that bill more popular or better, whereas [Manchin], I think, was the reverse," the former aide concluded.

For progressives and the White House, the radical centrists' editing of the Biden agenda was a bitter pill to swallow. A particularly painful loss was the Child Tax Credit, which had such a proven positive impact on families. According to a source who was involved in the negotiations, Manchin was the lone holdout on that front. The source said other Democratic senators repeatedly pressed Manchin with data points about how much the credit helped people and demonstrably alleviated child poverty.

"I had more conversations with Joe Manchin than I care to think about," Senator Cory Booker of New Jersey, one of the architects of the tax credit, recalled in an interview for this book.

Manchin, a millionaire who made his fortune in coal and lived on a yacht when he was in Washington, was unmoved. He would fire back with vague concerns about poor people using their tax refunds to buy drugs. According to the source, a good chunk of the Democratic caucus refused to keep dealing with Manchin.

"There's ten to twenty of them that are just so angry at him," the source said of the Senate Democrats.

With Manchin increasingly digging in and his fellow Democratic senators giving up, some lawmakers wanted Biden to step in.

"Manchin was not with us and the way to do this was to take him away to Camp David and just pound this out, get an agreement from him," the source said.

In December 2021, Manchin decided he was done talking, picked a fight with the White House over a press office statement naming him as a continued holdout, and then went on Fox News to torpedo BBB for good. It took several months for Schumer's staff to find a way to re-engage with him.

Few on either the House or Senate side had much good to say about the White House's negotiating efforts, and some offered blistering criticism.

"You just don't need the smartest policy person to do these kind of things," the former Senate aide observed. "You need someone who knows Joe Manchin and what he gives a shit about and has a relationship with him and has known him for years."

The consequences of failing to bring Manchin along were apparent to all. Midterm elections were fast approaching. Those races are normally a bloodbath for a first-term president's party and Biden risked heading into them having few legislative accomplishments to show for his first years in office.

When Schumer's office finally brought Manchin back to the table, he agreed to let a bill proceed. But it was no longer BBB. It was renamed the Inflation Reduction Act and it was limited to the programs that Manchin was willing to entertain.

Biden ran for president as a staunch moderate. However, after his efforts to connect with progressives, they proved to be far better allies for him than the centrists in his party.

For her part, Jayapal argued it was the progressive caucus's defense of Biden that ensured even a reduced version of his agenda had passed. "I would argue that the Inflation Reduction Act would never have happened had we not passed Build Back Better in the House," Jayapal said.

A senior House aide explained that Jayapal deserved "a ton of credit" for managing to keep her caucus together and willing to back Biden even as the centrists carved progressive priorities out of his legislation. "It took a lot of discipline to keep people focused on the end goal—climate, lowering prescription drug costs," the House aide said. "Jayapal was strong there."

Former White House press secretary Jen Psaki put things more in the president's court. In an interview for this book, Psaki argued that—whatever issues there may have been with the process—Biden knew exactly what he was doing all along.

"Biden has negotiated a lot of deals," Psaki said about the process of passing the Inflation Reduction Act into law. "Sometimes, as somebody who recognizes you need to plant the seeds and water and let things grow for a while, it's not always it's going to happen this moment, tomorrow. Sometimes things take a while to grow, and sometimes things need to happen behind the scenes, and he recognized that from having struck a lot of deals, and I think now people see that."

Chapter 12

EMPIRE STATE

URING THE BRUTAL PUSH AND PULL THAT WHITTLED AWAY AT much of Biden's agenda, the midterm elections of 2022 were fast approaching. Democrats understood the stakes: the Republican recapture of either chamber of Congress could effectively end even the limited ability the Biden administration had to pass meaningful legislation. Losing the majority also threatened to spawn a swarm of vexatious partisan investigations, and provoke crises like a government shutdown or standoff over the debt ceiling.

The poll numbers looked bleak and losses in the midterms had obvious implications for Biden's presidency and prospects of reelection. The tough landscape also posed problems for progressives as they sought to build their footprint in Washington.

Alessandra Biaggi and Yuh-Line Niou, two of Alexandria Ocasio-Cortez's closest allies in New York, exemplified the shocking victories some insurgents scored against the Big Dem establishment during the Trump administration. Their stories showed how—as Bernie Sanders and "the Squad" gained steam in Washington—progressives were also expanding their influence at the local level. In time, their roller-coaster trajectory also revealed the limitations of this new generation. Within three short years, the pair managed to help topple three entrenched political machines before failing in their quest to reach Capitol Hill as the Empire State proved to be ground zero for Biden's issues in the midterms.

Niou and Biaggi, who are both in their thirties and participated in a series of interviews for this book, tend to describe themselves as sisters. However, their backgrounds could not be more different. Niou is the daughter of Taiwanese immigrants who came to the US with almost nothing. Her mother and father moved Niou and her two siblings from state to state—Idaho, Texas, Washington, Oregon—as the parents built careers as a hospital administrator and an engineer.

Biaggi, who grew up in the suburbs just north of the five boroughs, was an insider. Her grandfather was a Democratic congressman, Mario Biaggi.

The elder Biaggi, whose parents came from Italy, was a decorated New York City police officer before he won a House seat in 1968. His story was emblematic of the old-school urban Democratic Party machines which drew support from working-class European immigrants. Decades later, his granddaughter would see how the heirs to those machines retained power and resisted reform.

From these disparate roots, Niou and Biaggi both blazed a path to Albany, the state capital, after battling powerful incumbents.

Niou cut her teeth working for anti-poverty advocacy organizations and as a campaign staffer for state assembly member Ron Kim. She set her sights on the legislature after the shocking fall of one of New York's most infamous Democratic Party bosses, Sheldon Silver.

Silver, who came out of the historically Orthodox Jewish community on Manhattan's Lower East Side, was a power broker who plied his trade in back rooms. He first entered the assembly in 1977. That same year, a Republican named Joe Bruno was elected to the state senate. Both men became leaders of their respective chambers in 1994. For the next fourteen years, Silver and Bruno were the two permanent members of the triumvirate whose dealmaking defined New York's government, the so-called "three men in a room." The third member of this unholy trinity was the governor. This arrangement spanned the terms of four governors from both parties. Silver's and Bruno's power lasted through them all.

In 2008, Bruno stepped aside amid a federal corruption investigation. Silver was hit with an indictment of his own in 2015 for a series of schemes that netted him millions and benefitted connected real estate developers. He died behind bars in early 2022.

Despite Silver's fall from grace, his powerful allies were still able to control the selection of his initial replacement in 2016. With the incumbent abruptly out of the picture, there was no Democratic primary. Instead, that February, party leaders met to pick the nominee. It was a smaller-scale version of the backroom process that helped Joe Crowley come to power in Queens. Once again, the choice was largely being snatched from the voters by the smooth operation of the political machine. But this time, Niou decided to spoil the festivities.

Several candidates had put their names forward to succeed Silver. The likely favorite was Alice Cancel, who was dubbed Silver's "crony" and "handpicked successor" by some local press. While only the members of the New York County Committee for the Sixty-Fifth Assembly District could vote, the meeting was public and each candidate was given five minutes to speak. Niou used her time to denounce the insider-run proceedings and withdraw herself from the running.

"Let's be honest here," Niou said. "This process is the problem."

Despite Niou's protestations, the committee overwhelmingly chose Cancel to represent Democrats in the general election.

Niou felt confident bucking the party because she had a way to circumvent the machine. The week before, Niou had secured the nomination of the Working Families Party, an organization founded in New York City in 1998 by a coalition of advocacy groups and unions. The WFP was tailor-made to provide voters in the five boroughs an alternative to the Democratic establishment.

New York has long been a breeding ground for third parties, in large part because of a unique legal quirk: fusion voting, which allows one candidate to run on multiple party lines. If a party can get enough votes on their line, they get guaranteed access to the ballot in subsequent elections. The system means smaller parties seeking to establish themselves can work with politicians from either of the two major outfits. The mainstream candidate gains coalition members, the upstart party gains legitimacy, and the dominance of the two-party system is a little bit lessened.

In 1998, fusion voting meant the newly formed Working Families Party didn't have to directly confront the city's network of Democratic Party clubs, many of which were remnants of the infamous Tammany Hall machine. Instead, they made a tactical choice to back Peter Vallone, the Democratic Speaker of the New York City Council, as he ran for governor against the incumbent George Pataki, a Republican. This gave voters an option to signal their desire to push the party left by supporting Vallone on the WFP line while still backing a main-line Democrat who had a good chance to win. And if Vallone attracted 50,000 votes to the Working Families Party line around the state, the organization would cement its place on the ballot in the next elections.

Even in that first year there was also clear foreshadowing of an issue that would remain a major thorn in the side of the WFP and other

modern progressive groups—the labor movement that formed the core
of the progressive coalition was not united. Some of the city's unions were
reluctant to cross Pataki and stayed neutral. And while the nascent WFP
backed Vallone and a candidate for state attorney general, they refrained
from jumping into other races that year—like the marquee race for US
Senate—because, as the New York Times put it, "leaders of the various
unions could not agree on one" candidate. Staying out of that race that
year meant the WFP played no role as Chuck Schumer, a man who would
go on to become majority leader and one of the most powerful figures in
Washington, first ascended to the Senate.

Despite these issues and Vallone's eventual defeat by a more than
twenty-point margin, that first campaign ended victoriously for the
WFP. Vallone earned 51,325 of his votes on the party's line. That was
only about 3 percent of his total, but it was just over the 50,000-vote
threshold needed to ensure the party's continued relevance.

The Working Families Party would go on to rack up more meaningful wins, including the 2013 election of Mayor Bill de Blasio, a
WFP ally. In his first term, de Blasio pushed through several of WFP's
top priorities including paid sick leave, universal pre-kindergarten,
and a guaranteed $15 minimum wage. Following the race, the party's
national director, Dan Cantor, promoted an ambitious plan to expand
to multiple new states around the country.

As the Working Families Party grew in size and stature, New
York—and specifically the five boroughs—remained the organization's
base. And, in 2016, the party helped Niou win her first election.

It wasn't a straight path. Niou fell 1,219 votes short of beating Alice
Cancel in the April 2016 special election to replace Silver. However,
that race helped Niou build a brand. The regularly scheduled election
took place a few months later. This time, Niou reversed the margin and
defeated Cancel in the Democratic primary by nearly 1,700 votes.

Niou might have taken down Silver's machine in Manhattan, but in the state capital, the tradition of backroom wheeling and dealing remained strong.

"It was just toxic from top down," Niou said about the political culture in Albany in an interview for this book. "People accept these things as the status quo and I never understood that. . . . It's only status quo if you let it be."

Niou found a kindred spirit in Biaggi, who was elected in 2019 after her own battle with one of the city's entrenched machine leaders.

Alessandra Biaggi got her start in politics with her grandfather, Mario, the congressman. She spent weekends with him and credits that time with sparking her interest in legislative work.

"Growing up at the time that I did, there weren't young people in politics, there weren't young women in politics," Biaggi said in an interview. "I still felt like my voice mattered and I belonged because of him."

After college and law school, Biaggi continued on the inside track. Her first major political work came as a staffer on Hillary Clinton's 2016 presidential campaign. She credits the experience of going house to house for Clinton in New Hampshire with deepening her desire to get involved and defining her approach. Her brief stint on the trail also left Biaggi wondering why "the Democratic Party doesn't obsess about organizing and do it off cycle and all the time."

"That is where you learn what people feel," she said. "It's where you learn what people are suffering from."

After that race, Biaggi caught the political bug—and she wasn't the only one.

Following Clinton's defeat and the rise of Trump, there was a newly energized Democratic "resistance." Biaggi capitalized on the anti-Trump momentum and worked with some of the organizations that popped up in the aftermath of his win. She came up with a "curriculum" focused on local government and started going house to house again.

"I taught civics in peoples' living rooms for like four months," Biaggi said, adding, "Then, I was like, 'Oh shit . . . I need to actually get a job.'"

She landed a gig in the counsel's office of Governor Andrew Cuomo. Cuomo was the son of former governor Mario Cuomo and a veteran of President Bill Clinton's cabinet. With his credentials, inborn fluency in retail politics, and calm confidence, Cuomo, who had been in office since 2011, was a popular figure with the state's Democratic voters. Those same attributes would carry him to national stardom during the dark early months of the COVID pandemic—but the reality of Cuomo's approach to governance was often at odds with the person he played on TV.

During his time in office, Cuomo elevated Albany's opaque deal-making to an art form. The governor was known, to close observers of politics, for an iron-fisted leadership style characterized by foul-mouthed lieutenants who doled out intense retribution for the smallest of slights.

Cuomo's many progressive critics accused him of aiding Republicans by empowering a breakaway group in his own party, the Independent Democratic Conference. The IDC, which formed shortly after Cuomo took office in 2011, caucused with GOP lawmakers in exchange for committee chairmanships. The arrangement dashed Democrats' hopes of a senate majority.

Cuomo always implausibly denied supporting the IDC even though there was ample evidence he encouraged their rise. And he was clearly sympathetic towards their position. In a 2022 interview for this book, Cuomo defended the IDC and suggested it served an important political purpose defending Democrats' frontline districts in the state.

Most New York City legislators, he said, can vote for "crazy" and "far-left" policies "because there's no Republican opponent" to run against them. IDC members, on the other hand, couldn't "vote for crazy" and keep their seats.

"They all happened to be from the moderate districts that could go Republican," Cuomo said of the IDC.

The IDC offered many advantages for Cuomo. The faction relieved his administration of significant pressure from the left. Republicans were also weakened by their dependence on the conference, with their cherished leadership positions and chairmen's gavels subject to the continued support of opposition party members beholden to the Democratic governor. Thanks to this unique arrangement, the old tradition of "three men in a room" had started to look a lot more like one man's reign.

Biaggi was aware of Cuomo's aggressive reputation when she joined his administration.

"I had very clear eyes about who this guy was, but I also knew being inside was my best bet of helping," Biaggi said. She stayed in Cuomo's counsel's office from April through December of 2017. It was a baptism by fire.

"The worst thing that Andrew Cuomo could have ever done was literally hire me in his office," explained Biaggi. "It gave me a front row seat to the worst show on Earth, which was behind the scenes in Albany."

Years later, Biaggi's voice still grew sharp as she rattled off a litany of alleged outrages. She described a "toxic" culture where staff was "incessantly berated and yelled at." Biaggi was particularly alarmed that, with Trump ascendant, New York had not codified abortion protections.

During his first years in office, Cuomo had repeatedly expressed support for a plan that would codify *Roe v. Wade*, the Supreme Court ruling allowing abortion, at the state level. However, he stood by as the

IDC blocked passage of the legislation for years. (Abortion protections would only become state law in 2019.)

Along with getting an inkling of Cuomo's leadership style, Biaggi began learning about the intricacies of the IDC. She came to blame them—and by extension the governor—for blocking a slew of progressive reforms.

In the summer of 2017, Biaggi was approached by the IDC's nemesis, State Senator Mike Gianaris, a legislator who was working on a plan to oust the eight rogue Republican-aligned Democrats.

"We were the victims of Cuomo's centrism," Gianaris said in an interview. "He wanted a Republican senate and actively opposed our efforts to take the majority. . . . That ultimately culminated in the creation of the IDC, which he supported."

Gianaris asked Biaggi if she might be interested in taking on the leader of the breakaway conference, Jeff Klein.

After hearing the proposition, Biaggi sought advice from Bill Mulrow, a veteran political hand. Mulrow had served as a secretary to Cuomo in between stints at a private equity firm. A powerful businessman and operative might seem like an odd adviser to a young reform-minded staffer, but he was close with Biaggi's grandfather.

"Bill Mulrow was my mentor," Biaggi said. "He was really important to me."

Her mentor didn't encourage Biaggi to run for office. Instead, she said Mulrow urged her to notify Cuomo's chief counsel, Alphonso David. The experience led Biaggi to see her grandfather, who left office in 1988 after two corruption convictions, in a whole new light.

"I didn't realize it even until a little bit later, like, 'Oh, my grandpa was like part of the machine,'" said Biaggi.

David's handling of Biaggi went off the rails. She has a vivid sensory recollection of the scene in his office where the governor's top lawyer was "eating pistachios" as they spoke. "The noise of, like, the nut cracking was so crazy," she said. "He kept putting the shells in the drawer and I was like, 'Oh my God.'" The meeting was the first of many searing experiences that converted Biaggi from Cuomo's staffer to his sworn enemy.

After telling David that she had been approached about challenging Klein, Biaggi said he pressed her to print her emails and to recount every detail of her interactions with Gianaris, the Democratic senator who presented the idea.

On October 2, 2017, the *New York Daily News* published a story detailing Gianaris's effort to convince Biaggi to take on Klein. The paper's piece quoted one of the emails Gianaris sent her proposing plans for the race. It closed with a quote from Cuomo framing challenges to the IDC leadership as "ego" and "petty politics" getting in the way of Democratic Party unity.

It seemed to Biaggi that everything she'd told David in confidence was being used to plant a "trash story" in the press attacking potential IDC challengers.

"These fuckers," Biaggi thought to herself. "They placed the story in the fucking paper."

When she went into work that morning, Biaggi said David called the counsel's staff in for a meeting. He began by discussing the article with the team.

"I had a conversation with Alessandra and she fully appreciates and understands the severity of this," David said, according to Biaggi's recollection, before adding a distinct Cuomonian flourish, "The governor thanks her for her loyalty." (David did not respond to a request for comment.) Then, Biaggi claimed, David threw his head back, burst out laughing, and said, "It's not like we think she could win."

The public belittling put Biaggi over the edge. Her voice still quakes with anger when she recalls the moment.

"In that moment, in that room, I was like, 'I don't care what happens to me. I'm running against Jeff Klein and I am going to literally do everything in my being to expose what is going on here,'" she said. "Laughing at me in front of all the counsels was one of the most demeaning, degrading moments I've ever had in my life. It just sparked complete rage in me and that was it."

———

BIAGGI'S CAMPAIGN FOCUSED ON KLEIN'S ROLE IN THE IDC. SHE FRAMED him as someone who enabled the GOP and blocked progressive policies in order to benefit himself and his allies.

"What I was saying was like, 'There are fake Democrats in office who are empowering Trump Republicans.'"

The message was a simple one, but the race was still an uphill battle. Amid pressure from progressive groups ahead of the primaries, Cuomo finally presided over a deal to dissolve the IDC in April 2018. Klein was given a powerful legislative post, deputy minority leader, as a consolation prize.

That leadership position enabled Klein to dole out discretionary dollars to pet projects and key leaders in his district. He also had a substantial personal fundraising machine. Klein piled up about $3 million to spend on the race compared to roughly $300,000 for Biaggi. Outspent ten-to-one, Biaggi turned back to her affinity for door knocking and focused on running an aggressive ground game.

"We organized the shit out of the district," said Biaggi.

Biaggi also had support from progressive allies including the Working Families Party and Alexandria Ocasio-Cortez, who was just a few months removed from her own shocking primary victory.

Ocasio-Cortez's story, which had made national headlines, dovetailed nicely with Biaggi's campaign and helped galvanize voters around the idea of young women taking on powerful insiders. One local paper, the *Journal News*, even dubbed Biaggi "The Next Ocasio-Cortez."

The race was also when Biaggi joined forces with Niou, who brought in groups of young volunteers who'd joined her during the insurgency on the Lower East Side.

After the polls closed on September 13, 2018, Biaggi was driving to her election-night event when news broke on the radio that she won the primary. "My sister almost crashed the car into a pole," she said. "Everyone was screaming at the top of their lungs."

And Biaggi wasn't the only winner. Five other challengers won their primaries against the IDC incumbents. The *Riverdale Press*, a local paper in Biaggi's district, dubbed the campaign cycle a "progressive guillotine."

Klein made one final effort to avoid the chopping block. Taking advantage of the same fusion laws that enabled the rise of the WFP, he remained in the general election against Biaggi on the ballot line of the relatively obscure Independence Party. His move was a failure. The district Klein had used to block a Democratic majority was, in the end, staunchly Democratic. He only netted about 7 percent of the final vote.

Biaggi was headed to Albany as part of a growing progressive faction that included Niou and the other IDC challengers. One of the insurgents, State Senator Julia Salazar, was a member of the Democratic Socialists of America, which brought their ranks in the legislature up to three. That number would more than double by 2021.

Gianaris, the lawmaker who helped orchestrate some of the challenges to the IDC, said in an interview for this book that defeating the breakaway conference allowed the legislature to "be a lot more muscularly progressive." The new lawmakers supported measures like police reform, added protections for renters, expanding public education, and environmental initiatives. They also chafed against Albany's traditional ways of doing business.

Albany didn't necessarily like them, either. Shortly after her victory, Biaggi said she met with her assembly counterpart, Mike Benedetto, at a diner in the overlapping Bronx portion of their districts. Benedetto, who was a close ally of Klein's, allegedly was seething because Niou had campaigned for Biaggi in his territory.

"Yuh-Line, she came to my district," Benedetto said, according to Biaggi. "When her bills come through the committee, I'm gonna stop them. . . . When I see her, I'm gonna rip out her throat."

Reached on the phone, Benedetto said he was "shocked" and had "no memory" of making the threatening remark—unless it was in jest. "I never had any reason to have any dealings with Ms. Niou that I would get annoyed with her or mad at her," Benedetto said. "I remember the breakfast meeting I had with Ms. Biaggi. . . . I can't think of why that would be the case that I would say something like that unless I was just making a joke or something."

Either way, the disputed threat was just the beginning of the hostilities between Cuomo, his cronies, and the new lawmakers.

———

THE RANCOR PARTICULARLY ACCELERATED AT THE START OF THE pandemic—a moment when Cuomo had more power than ever.

In March 2020, when New York City emerged as the epicenter of America's first COVID outbreaks, the state legislature granted Cuomo broad emergency powers that expanded his ability to issue executive orders without approval from lawmakers. Cuomo was also enjoying a newfound national spotlight. His daily COVID briefings were being carried live on cable news and Democrats eagerly embraced the governor as a calming counterpart to President Trump's shambolic pandemic denialism. There was even an emerging Twitter subculture of "Cuomo-sexuals" whose appreciation of the governor's leadership amid the outbreak had turned romantic.

Cuomo previously experienced the national spotlight alongside his father, the late New York governor Mario Cuomo, who was considered a viable presidential candidate in both 1988 and 1992, though he never launched a campaign. That second time around, the elder Cuomo came particularly close. The *Washington Post* described it as "a sometimes bizarre, two-month odyssey" of indecision. Mario even had a plane waiting to take him to New Hampshire on December 12, 1991, the filing deadline for that year's primary. However, shortly before that cutoff, he walked out before the assembled press at the state capitol and announced he wouldn't run for the White House after all.

While Mario attributed his decision not to enter the race to delays with that year's budget process in Albany, there has long been speculation about what really happened. In an interview for this book, his son, Andrew, who was one of his top advisers, explained that his father's heart simply wasn't in it.

"At the end of the day, he didn't want it bad enough," the younger Governor Cuomo said. "He did not want it bad enough and that was the bottom line. . . . I said, 'That's the end of the conversation, because, if you don't want it like you want oxygen, you're going to lose.'"

Andrew Cuomo also flirted with a presidential run in 2020. A source close to Cuomo said he abandoned that bid after a phone call and meeting with Joe Biden. According to the source, Biden appealed to Cuomo's concerns about the ascendant progressives. The source recounted Biden's words to Cuomo: "Do me a favor, you and I will be going after the same vote and some nut on the left will win. You're young, you have time. Support me, otherwise we're going to have some nut.'"

According to the source, Cuomo was swayed by Biden's prediction that his candidacy would lead to the rise of a leftist "nut." He stayed out of the race. It was yet another example of the effective coordination among more moderate Democrats that helped Biden consolidate support to fend off the left and win the 2020 primary.

Back in Albany, there was much less cooperation between Cuomo and progressives in the legislature. As always, the annual budget proved to be a flashpoint. Lockdowns caused by the pandemic were expected to cost the state billions in lost taxes. These revenue shortfalls were paired with the urgent need to buy supplies like ventilators for the sick people pouring into the hospitals and masks for essential workers.

Cuomo proposed drastic cuts to the budget, and most Democrats were ready to follow his lead. The progressive faction was up in arms. Niou voiced her fellow progressives' frustrations in an impassioned speech on April 2, 2020.

Niou cut a striking figure in the assembly chamber. Wearing a coat with a black-and-white splatter print, she stood out against the staid maroon carpet and high leather-backed chairs as she explained her vote against the governor's budget proposal.

The subject of Niou's remarks was decidedly bleak. Manhattan's Chinatown, the core of her district, saw a steep drop-off in business amid a wave of discrimination and hate crimes based on the coronavirus's initial emergence in Asia. In the days before the budget vote, the number of COVID cases and deaths in New York City had increased exponentially. Some patients in emergency rooms who were gasping for breath could not be placed on ventilators due to short supply. Refrigerated morgue trucks appeared outside city hospitals to accommodate the flood of corpses. Unclaimed bodies were piled into mass graves on Hart Island, the public cemetery and potter's field.

Niou blamed the grisly scenes on "decades of shortfalls" in social spending. She expressed shock that the legislature was being asked to respond by "cutting more" during an escalating crisis.

"This virus has laid bare just how weak our institutions have become in a time when we need them to be strong," Niou continued, with evident pain in her voice. "People are literally dying in the halls of our public hospitals because they simply don't have the capacity."

While Niou's remarks addressed the specifics of the pandemic, they were also essentially a progressive manifesto in favor of taxing the rich to fund social programs and health care.

"Are we choosing to cut our social safety net when the needs have never been greater?" she asked incredulously. "Are we making deep, devastating cuts to our basic needs while protecting tax credit programs for big businesses?"

Niou, who is outspoken about being on the autism spectrum, speaks with quiet, forceful deliberation. Biaggi is more rapid-fire, drawing listeners in with enthusiasm and broad hand gestures that she attributes to her Italian ancestry. But both are thirtysomethings with native millennial fluency in social media. They used those skills to mount a full-scale PR blitz against Cuomo in the first half of 2020.

With the world around them locked down, Biaggi and Niou relentlessly criticized the governor on Twitter, taking shots at everything from the budget process, to his enabling of the IDC, and New York's lack of automatic voter registration. They also honed in on the governor and his team's reputation for targeting enemies with abusive language and political retaliation.

Taking on Cuomo, especially at the height of his pandemic popularity, was a risky move that could have led to their legislation being stalled, discretionary funds frozen, and even primary challenges. But they both had managed to push past serious political machinery to be seated in Albany. Now that they were there, the pair had no qualms about attacking the biggest machine of them all.

"It was born out of rage," Biaggi said of their anti-Cuomo offensive. "I started to realize the evil—that's really what it is—in him, and that overtook me."

As the pandemic progressed, real questions began to emerge about the governor's handling of the crisis and his efforts to promote himself as a hero of the outbreak. In late March 2020, two weeks after COVID-19 was officially declared a global pandemic, Cuomo used his expanded powers to order nursing homes to accept people returning from hospitals with active COVID infections. The directive mandated that COVID patients who were still contagious be reintroduced into facilities filled with the people most vulnerable to contracting severe disease—the elderly and immunocompromised. Mortality rates at facilities subject to the policy spiked dramatically.

Cuomo argued that it was a catastrophe that stemmed from necessity. At the time, New York was ground zero for the virus in the United States. Hospitals around the state were slammed and needed their beds for the most severe cases. However, to critics, Cuomo's sin wasn't only the order, it was an attempt to cover up the fallout.

For months during 2020, Democrats in the legislature pushed the Cuomo administration for precise figures showing the number of people who died in nursing homes after they began accepting COVID patients. Cuomo's team worked to downplay and obscure the numbers.

At the same time, it would later emerge that Cuomo was pitching a book about his leadership during the crisis that would ultimately sell for an advance over $5 million. In it, he cast himself as the most accomplished governor "in modern history." The book, which was published in October 2020, dismissed criticism of the nursing home deaths as a "truly despicable" right-wing smear campaign.

Cuomo's state health department initially released data showing over 6,000 people died in nursing homes during 2020. The following January, a scathing report released by Attorney General Letitia James determined that figure "may have been undercounted by as much as 50 percent." James's claim turned out to be an understatement, too. Following the report, Cuomo's administration made multiple updates to the data. There are now known to have been over 15,000 deaths in nursing homes during the first year of the pandemic.

On February 10, 2021, during a videoconference with Democratic lawmakers, Cuomo's top aide, Melissa DeRosa, apologized and essentially admitted they withheld the data for political reasons. DeRosa said the governor and his team "froze" and feared the numbers would be "used against us" by enemies in Albany or by Trump, including as a pretext to a federal investigation.

The following day, Assembly Member Ron Kim, Niou's mentor, spoke to the *New York Post* about the admission and argued that the rationale was essentially "that they were trying to dodge having any incriminating evidence that might put the administration . . . in further trouble with the Department of Justice."

Kim, whose uncle died in a nursing home from a presumed case of COVID in 2020, had been one of Cuomo's loudest critics on the issue. Hours after the article came out, Kim said he got a phone call from the governor himself. Kim recounted Cuomo's call in an interview and accused the governor of yelling for about ten minutes, questioning his honor, and threatening to "destroy" him.

Kim's allegations went viral. Cuomo responded at a news conference with an approximately twenty-minute tirade against Kim.

"If you attack my integrity and my administration's integrity, am I going to fail to respond? No. No," Cuomo sniffed.

The governor's outburst was fresh ammunition for Niou and Biaggi. They spent their nights on audio chat apps trashing the governor to anyone who would listen. The pair also filmed a YouTube series in which they outlined Cuomo's expanded emergency powers, the nursing home scandal, and what they framed as a generally toxic atmosphere in the state capitol. Along with Kim, they became Cuomo's most vocal opponents, steadily slamming the governor.

And then, the floodgates broke open. On February 24, 2021, Lindsey Boylan, a former Cuomo aide, alleged in an essay on the self-publishing platform Medium that the governor had made sexual advances towards her during her time working in the executive chamber. Three days later, another former Cuomo aide came forward and accused him of making inappropriate and explicit comments. By March 9, two more ex-aides and a current Cuomo staffer had levied more harassment accusations.

As the scandal grew, more than a dozen current and former staffers from Cuomo's office also spoke to reporters about a work environment they called brutal and traumatizing. James, the attorney general, began mounting an investigation into the alleged harassment. Calls for the governor to resign turned into a cacophony that included most of New York's congressional delegation.

Even with federal firepower arrayed against him, Cuomo saw Niou and Biaggi as two of the driving forces behind the cascading controversies. In his interview for this book, Cuomo accused them of "plotting" his demise along with his accusers.

"Biaggi and Yuh-Line Niou on Twitter were talking about how to get rid of me," Cuomo said. "They were planning it because they were part of the new left and they were the real lefties. . . . They literally were plotting it."

Cuomo also offered a harsh assessment of the pair's record in Albany. "What I'd say to them when I see them is: Name one thing that you accomplished. Name one thing that you got done," Cuomo said. "A 'new progressive?' Really? What did you get done?"

Biaggi shares Cuomo's belief that she and Niou helped amplify the accusations against the governor, though she had a decidedly different take on the matter. In her view, the years she and Niou spent going after Albany's culture of "three men in a room" helped break the fear and silence that came along with it.

"Consistently banging the drum meant that we basically took an iron clad shut door and we held it open like a little—like a centimeter— just enough where people saw an opening that they could also say other things," Biaggi said.

In an interview, Lindsey Boylan stressed that she chose to come forward with her allegations of sexual harassment by the governor on her own and had been raising the issue on social media for months before her Medium post; however, she noted "all of us together made each other safer."

On August 3, 2021, Attorney General James released a report detailing claims Cuomo had harassed eleven different women.

"I got calls when the [attorney general's] report came out from all kinds of elected [officials]," Boylan said. "The only person whose call I answered that day was Alessandra. And I texted Yuh-Line back, because I had formed a sisterhood with them."

President Joe Biden, who had reportedly considered appointing Cuomo as his attorney general in 2020, responded by calling on the governor to resign.

Despite the pressure, Cuomo fought back. The governor had

initially apologized for having "offended" anyone and said his "customary way of greeting" was to kiss and embrace people. But it wasn't all hugs. Cuomo retained an aggressive legal team that attempted to poke holes in James's report and cast it as a politically motivated attack. Although that fight would go on for months and Cuomo denied the most serious wrongdoing, he announced a decision to step down one week after the publication of James's report. The two young lawmakers who had beaten local party bosses had now helped topple the most powerful man in New York.

"I'm still shocked by it. I really am. I really, really am," Biaggi said over a year later. "It's unbelievable."

After the battles that brought them to Albany and brought down the governor, Biaggi and Niou set their sights on Congress. They found themselves in the worst state for Democrats in the midterm elections. This time, the pair would be unable to beat the odds, leaving Boylan and others suggesting two important voices for transparency and reform had been shut down.

"Look how they're both not in office right now," Boylan said. "I wonder who's served by that."

Chapter 13

THUNDERDOME

NOVEMBER 8, 2022, WAS A SURPRISINGLY GOOD NIGHT FOR Democrats—but it would have been an extraordinary triumph were it not for what happened in New York.

Midterm elections are typically rough for the party that holds the presidency. That conventional wisdom, combined with Biden's anemic approval rating and the races that were on the calendar, led to dire forecasts for Democrats.

Throughout the year, pundits predicted a "red wave" would sweep through the House. The Center for Politics at the University of Virginia reported signs the GOP could "build its biggest majority since the Great Depression." The Democrats' Senate majority, already balanced on a razor's edge, was in doubt despite a favorable map and key GOP senators retiring in North Carolina and Pennsylvania. CNN's Chris Cillizza published multiple columns projecting Republican wins, including one that declared, "The real question, at this point, is how big the red wave will be."

When the votes were counted, the Democrats vaulted over that abysmally low bar. They held onto the Senate, expanding their thread-bare majority by one crucial seat, and Republicans were left with a smaller than expected nine-vote edge in the House.

The midterm results represented a surprising triumph for Biden. However, on a national map filled with tenacious defensive stands, New York—normally a blue-state stalwart—stood out as the place where Democratic lines broke. The losses there cost the Democrats four critical seats.

It was an embarrassing bloodbath. One of the Republican winners was George Santos, a man with a fabricated résumé and questionable campaign finances. And one of the Democrats who went down was Sean Patrick Maloney, who, as chairman of the Democratic Congres-sional Campaign Committee, had been the man responsible for secur-ing the House majority.

Yuh-Line Niou and Alessandra Biaggi both fell victim to New York's midterm chaos. Making it to Washington proved far more difficult than any of the fights the pair had previously taken on. They were not able to repeat the success they enjoyed locally when faced with the twin engines of Big Dem power—big money and the party establishment.

Yet, even as their campaigns exposed the limitations of progres-sive insurgents, those same races showed the weaknesses of the moder-ate party machinery. The situation in the state illuminated the factors that have conspired to keep Democrats from winning despite popular support for their policies—including internecine disputes, influxes of Republican megadonor cash, and the steady barrage of right-leaning media machinery.

Timing also played a role. Niou and Biaggi made their plays to join New York's congressional delegation in a year when the existing mem-bers had been forced into a last-minute game of musical chairs. The scramble was set in motion in 2020 when the state fell short in the once-a-decade US Census count.

While the census is conducted by a federal bureau, governors play a role in funding, promoting, and planning for the effort in their states. Leading up to the count, which determines the apportionment of seats in the US House of Representatives, some progressives expressed concerns that New York's governor, Andrew Cuomo, wasn't doing enough to run up the numbers. They criticized the governor, one of the powerful officials supported by the donors and the establishment, for failing to provide sufficient resources for the benefit of the broader party. It was an important cause for Democrats at the national level, since their House majority runs through the two biggest, bluest states; New York and California.

When the 2020 census was done, New York lost one of its House seats by the slimmest margin in modern history. If the state had counted eighty-nine more people in a population of more than twenty million, its footprint in Washington would not have diminished. Leaders in New York City, the state's largest population center, had aggressively tried to encourage residents to participate. After losing the seat, they pointed the finger at Cuomo for not doing more.

"The state was simply M.I.A.," New York City Census Director Julie Menin told the *New York Times*. "The governor and the state simply did not want to prioritize the census."

The blame game was just beginning. The midterms turned the state's Democratic Party into a thicket of finger-pointing.

After the census debacle, with the encouragement of nervous Democratic leaders in Washington, the party's lawmakers in Albany advanced a plan to make up the difference. During Cuomo's administration and at his insistence, New York had passed constitutional changes that created an independent commission charged with proposing new district lines to the legislature. Following the census, that commission redistricting process had broken down, the legislature had rejected the first set of maps the commission had proposed, and the commissioners had declared themselves unable to submit any more proposals for the legislators to consider. Each party blamed the other for throwing a wrench in the gears. Many progressives blamed Cuomo all over again for the flawed design of the redistricting commission.

In January 2022, Democratic state lawmakers seized the initiative. They passed an aggressive map that would have left Republicans with only four solidly red districts. Overall, the new map would have likely cost Republicans three seats and delivered them to the Democratic delegation.

The map was an ambitious project that gave Democrats a glimmer of hope amid the predicted Republican House gains. The data wonks at the website FiveThirtyEight described it as "heavily biased" and "ruthlessly efficient." It was a partisan gerrymander with every line drawn to maximize the number of Democratic voters in each district.

However, by overriding the independent redistricting commission process, the legislature created a risk that its map could be thrown out by the courts. And by attempting such an egregious gerrymander rather than mounting a more subtle effort to shore up seats, they almost certainly increased the likelihood of a judicial backlash.

In other words, if the state's Democrats had just sought to grab one extra seat rather than three, they might have avoided a showdown. Instead, they proposed a map that was almost asking for a legal fight.

Ultimately, tactically astute Republicans petitioned a judge in rural Steuben County, a deep-red region five hours from Manhattan, to review the redistricting process. The judge pounced on the Democratic plan. He ordered the maps redrawn and appointed a "special master," Jonathan Cervas, an academic who specializes in preparing remedial district maps, to draw new lines.

The impending release of Cervas's maps produced a breathless moment in professional politics, with operatives and candidates on tenterhooks. When the new lines came out in May 2022, they sent shock waves through the state's political system.

Cervas's map erased the advantage Democrats hoped to have over their Republican rivals. It also set incumbents up to challenge each other. Two veteran committee chairs in the House, Jerry Nadler and Carolyn Maloney, woke up to find themselves in the same district, and they resolved to battle it out.

The fight over the map also pushed the primary date into late August, the dog days of summer when many New York residents—especially in the city—decamp to more genial climates. Midterm primaries are never high-turnout affairs, but this race, a dauntingly complex jumble of personalities and ideologies, would concentrate the turnout and enthusiasm problem like few contests before it.

One of the House members upended by Cervas's map was Sean Patrick Maloney, the head of the national Democratic Congressional Campaign Committee. Maloney, whose mission at DCCC was fighting for the House majority, had tried to score extra points on his home turf and was one of the Democratic leaders who put forward aggressively partisan maps.

A top New York Democrat who was involved in the process blamed the overambitious map on Maloney and Mike Gianaris, the party's deputy majority leader in the state senate who had previously encouraged Biaggi to run and had helped take out the IDC.

"They wrote stupid lines, Maloney and Gianaris. They were pigs," the Democrat said. "They were *pigs*."

Gianaris and the legislature had crafted the lines. Maloney and the DCCC submitted their own aggressive proposal through a public comment process.

Gianaris, for his part, blamed Cuomo's past efforts to weaken the Democratic majorities in the legislature and consolidate his own power. The governor had left the state with a court system dominated by conservative judges and a redistricting commission that was designed to take authority away from lawmakers.

"Cuomo used every lever at his disposal to impose his rule on state government," Gianaris said in an interview for this book. "It's his negative influence. Like, we're still cleaning up the mess that he made."

Maloney described the state court system as a monstrosity and offered a verdict that would seem to apply to many of the issues Democrats faced as they stumbled through the midterms in New York.

"Democrats are really good at giving away our power, and Republicans are really good at using theirs," Maloney said in an interview for this book.

A raspy-voiced former aide to President Bill Clinton, Maloney had a closely cropped gray crew cut and a congressional career that began with taking out a Republican incumbent in 2012. In speeches, Maloney often leaned into the idea that his moderate platform was the common-sense approach needed to win in battleground districts. Despite highlighting his appeal with more conservative voters, Maloney also never tired of bringing up his identity as an openly gay "father of interracial kids" to burnish his liberal bona fides.

However, the home Maloney and his husband purchased in 2012 so that he could run in New York's Eighteenth District was suddenly about two and a quarter miles outside of it. Maloney now found himself living in a new Seventeenth District, three-quarters of which had been represented by Mondaire Jones, a Democrat who had been in office for just over a year.

For Maloney, this was a serious inconvenience, particularly since, as chair of the Democratic Congressional Campaign Committee, or

"D-Trip" as it was known to insiders, one of Maloney's major goals was protecting incumbents like Jones.

Even without moving again, Maloney would have been allowed to run in the district just next door. It would have been somewhat awkward, but he had represented most of the constituents in the Eighteenth District for about a decade. However, the Seventeenth District was seen by experts as a relatively safe seat, whereas the redrawn Eighteenth District now looked far more competitive.

Instead of letting Jones be and trying for the Eighteenth—or moving to a new house—Maloney decided to run in the Seventeenth. His choice meant going after Jones, but it was a shorter commute and a safer seat. Maloney disputed the analysts' ratings that labeled his new target safer for Democrats and insisted the decision was all about the location of his home.

Maloney's choice set up a generational and ideological clash. Both men were openly gay lawyers, but Maloney was a white man in his mid-fifties and had run as an unabashed centrist and Jones was a Black, thirtysomething ally of Ocasio-Cortez's "Squad" in Congress. The move also meant that Maloney, the man tasked with securing the Democrats' majority in Congress, had gone from using his incumbency and experience to hold onto a newly competitive district to almost certainly costing the party at least one member of Congress—either him or Jones. In the end, Jones sought to run in a crowded race in the city rather than take on Maloney.

Leading the DCCC requires striking that balance between protecting incumbents and trying to swing poachable districts. When he took the helm of the organization, Maloney argued the prior leadership was overly focused on taking out Republicans and insufficiently invested in protecting its own incumbents. He also faulted the left and argued calls to "defund the police" hampered the party's standing nationally.

Progressives had their own ideas about what was wrong with the party committee. Following the 2018 races that brought in Alexandria Ocasio-Cortez and the Squad, the DCCC made it official policy to refuse to work or even communicate with consultants that supported Democratic insurgents who mounted primary challenges against incumbents. Ocasio-Cortez and others argued this "blacklist" cut the party off from firms that were coming up with innovative ways to raise small-dollar donations and engage young and diverse voters. Despite his disdain for the left, it was actually Maloney who ended the "blacklist" policy when he took the reins of the committee in 2021.

His position leading the party's campaign arm also exposed Maloney to personal criticism. Along with concerns about his level of engagement in his own district, Maloney faced questions about having the DCCC invest in his race. Ocasio-Cortez, who had battled with the organization over her desire to challenge incumbents, also blasted Maloney for his decision to encroach on Jones's district. Speaking to reporters on Capitol Hill, she called it a "terrible," "hypocritical" move and said he should step down due to the "conflict of interest."

"I think it's ridiculous," Ocasio-Cortez said. "If he's going to enter in a primary and challenge another Democratic member, then he should step aside from his responsibilities."

Maloney insisted he had spoken with Jones, who was not interested in running the competitive suburban race.

"I think, if Mondaire was being honest, he would tell you that he had real concerns about running in a district that was more conservative and it was those concerns that led him to . . . ultimately run in the city," Maloney said. "I essentially offered to rethink the whole thing if he wanted to run in New York 17 and he told me not to worry about it."

Jones told a very different story. In an interview for this book, Jones said Maloney blindsided him when he decided to run in the Seventeenth.

"There was no...meaningful communication, when, as soon as—I think it had been twenty minutes after the maps came out—that he went on Twitter and said he was running in my district," Jones said.

As a progressive, Jones was not shocked to find himself on the wrong side of the party leadership.

"Perhaps in retrospect, it should not be surprising. When I ran in 2020, the establishment did not support me and that's because, while I do battle with people who want to overthrow our democracy, and tell women what to do with their bodies, and rig this economy for the super-rich, I also push members of my own party to do better for working families," said Jones. "That, it turns out, can create resentment among some Democratic elites."

While he denied surprising Jones with his decision to run in the district, Maloney conceded he made some mistakes.

"I'm sure he has some hard feelings against me," Maloney said of Jones. "I could have done things better, to be sure."

Maloney also admitted one of the things he could have done was call Jones when the lines came out to warn him of his decision.

"Sure. Sure. I could have done that," he said.

Maloney was right that Jones had hard feelings. In his interview for this book, Jones argued Maloney's handling of the situation was especially awful given his role leading the congressional campaign committee.

"The job of the D Triple-C chair is to keep and expand our majority," Jones said before noting that Maloney "lost the majority" and adding, "The essence of your job is to give candidates the resources to win tough fights. It sent a horrible message that he then would leave a district that was, by a few percentage points tougher, to have a better shot at remaining in Congress even if it meant, you know, screwing me in the process."

Maloney's decision sent Jones on a collision course with Yuh-Line Niou. And it put Maloney into the ring with Alessandra Biaggi.

———

AFTER SUCCESSFULLY TAKING ON THE GOVERNOR, BIAGGI CAME INTO 2022 considering her next move. She eyed multiple different offices as the lines evolved and was initially prepared to run for a congressional seat that included parts of Long Island. When the new maps came out, Biaggi decided to stay close to her home just north of the city and take on Maloney. Biaggi was driven by his handling of the redistricting process and his treatment of Jones.

"I felt like this guy fucked up our congressional lines," Biaggi said of Maloney. "You have taken away our ability . . . for New York to have as many seats as possible because you got cute with the lines. That's fucked up."

The race had clear echoes of the battle that initially brought Biaggi to Albany. Once again she was challenging a member of leadership with a message that they were not doing enough to deliver progressive reforms. In their lone debate on August 5, 2022, Biaggi noted the similarities.

"I ran for the state senate for the exact same reasons that I am running for Congress today, because I was frustrated with corruption and corporate-backed politicians," Biaggi said.

Maloney countered by painting Biaggi as too far to the left for the upstate district. He highlighted the fact her state senate seat covered portions of New York City and dubbed her "the leading advocate for defunding the police in the state senate." While both Biaggi and Maloney were for police reform, Biaggi had used the divisive "defund" terminology, some of which she deleted from her prolific Twitter page as she prepared for the congressional campaign.

And, once again, Biaggi had to overcome the advantages incumbents and power players have at their disposal. Maloney raised over $4 million compared to about $800,000 for Biaggi.

Even though the new district did not include any part of the five boroughs, Maloney was also bolstered by about $410,000 from a political action committee affiliated with the Police Benevolent Association of the City of New York. The union and its longtime leader, Patrick Lynch, regularly sparred with progressives and had endorsed Trump in 2020. They funded a slew of ads attacking Biaggi in the last two weeks of the primary. Biaggi described the spending from outside the district as "dark money."

While Biaggi had been able to overcome a massive funding gap en route to Albany, she was unable to make lightning strike twice. The August 23, 2022, primary was a relatively low-turnout affair with approximately 37,000 of the more than 775,000 residents in the district coming out to vote. Roughly two-thirds of them voted for Maloney.

To Biaggi, the chaos with the maps was a major factor in her loss. The first time around, she defeated the remnants of the IDC machine by running a huge ground game. Even more organizing would be necessary in a race coming in the middle of summer when few people were accustomed to participating in elections. With the lines scrambled, all of this needed to be done in just three months.

"Ninety days is like no time at all, just to be fucking clear," Biaggi said.

Yet the ultimate factor was clearly cash. The experience convinced Biaggi fundraising was an issue the left would need to focus on more going forward to avoid similar defeats. She alluded to strong poll numbers for policies like expanded health care and public education.

"People actually find the message of what we're talking about as progressives really powerful, but it doesn't reach as many people as the moderate message reaches. What's the reason? Money," she said.

On election night, Biaggi held a small gathering for her supporters at an ale house where most of the patrons at the bar were watching the Yankees and completely unaware there had been a primary. She walked in shortly after the polls closed and stood on a chair to make a speech for the cameras. Biaggi struck an optimistic tone. She also urged her supporters to get behind Maloney for his general election fight against a Republican opponent.

"What we are doing is honestly transformational work and transformational work takes time. It takes time, it takes patience," she said, punctuating her words by bending down and clapping her hands, before adding, "This is the beginning of something bigger, but here's the reality. What is even bigger than that is November, because what we're up against in November is not a political party, it's fascism. . . . So, I understand the disappointment that we feel right now, but here's the deal, we have to show up in November and we have to come together."

The boilerplate call to unify around a man who, in Biaggi's view, had done more to damage the prospects of both progressives and Democrats than nearly any other official in the state rang a bit false. And, when November came around, amid questions about whether he had done enough to excite and engage voters in the district, Maloney became the first Democratic Congressional Campaign Committee chair to lose his own race in over forty years.

ROUGHLY FORTY MILES DOWNSTATE, YUH-LINE NIOU FACED A BATTLE of her own. When the lines came out, the newly cut Tenth District included all of her Lower Manhattan assembly district along with a swath of South Brooklyn that included the center of the borough's Asian community. She was instantly drawn to the race.

"First off, open seats don't happen very often. This was an open seat . . . a hundred percent of my district was inside of it . . . and it was, two Chinatowns basically, Brooklyn and Manhattan's," recounted Niou. "I just knew that it was really important for us to be able to have representation and we have very little representation and diversity inside of our congressional body."

However, with the maps in flux, the proposition wasn't nearly that simple. The heavily Democratic district also attracted an array of progressives who relished the chance to vie for the kind of uncompetitive seat that often translates to what is essentially a lifetime appointment. Along with Niou, the group included city council member Carlina Rivera, former mayor Bill de Blasio, and a variety of viable but noncompetitive supporting characters.

The district also attracted Mondaire Jones, who had opted not to defend his territory against Maloney. Instead, Jones left his suburban district, avoided the neighboring seat held by Bowman, skipped the Jerry Nadler versus Carolyn Maloney thunderdome that was playing out on both sides of Central Park, and moved to an apartment in Brooklyn to run in the Tenth.

Biaggi had been undone by one major progressive weakness—the fundraising gap. Niou was being stymied by campaign cash too, but she was also dealing with the perennial lack of unity on the left.

Niou, Rivera, Jones, and de Blasio were all staunch progressives who were clearly competing for some of the same votes. With a crowded left lane, the race also drew Daniel Goldman, heir to the Levi Strauss & Co. denim fortune, and the former House counsel who had taken a star turn during the 2019 presidential impeachment hearings.

In a race with an odd midsummer schedule that wasn't exactly designed to attract media attention, Goldman brought a unique asset to the contest: his massive bank account. Goldman spent approximately $4 million of his own money on the primary. Most importantly, Goldman stood out from the crowded field of progressives as a relative centrist who opposed some more left-wing policy priorities like Medicare for All and student debt cancellation.

De Blasio, who ended eight years in City Hall at the start of 2022 with low approval numbers, bowed out of the race in July. His team cited polling that made clear the former mayor didn't necessarily have a viable path to victory. De Blasio wasn't the only one whose cause looked lost, but the rest of the pack stayed in even as the polls increasingly indicated it was a race between Niou and Goldman.

As the campaign stretched on, some wondered why the progressives in the field could not consolidate and rally behind a single champion as more moderate Democrats had done for Biden at the presidential level. In an interview for this book, De Blasio, who did not endorse any of his rivals following his departure, offered a simple answer—progressives don't know how to do that: "That trick never works. Clearing the field or, you know, consolidating around a single progressive, I have seen that work so few times."

The ex-mayor recalled the 2020 presidential race where he was (very briefly) part of the Democratic field along with the progressive senators Bernie Sanders and Elizabeth Warren.

"What they failed to achieve . . . was that, if one or the other had not reached whatever milestone by X date, they would fold in," he said.

De Blasio couldn't imagine a scenario similar to the one former president Obama orchestrated among moderate candidates in 2020 unfolding on the progressive side. "I couldn't go to these other folks and say: 'Defer to me.' It wouldn't have made sense to them. If they said it to me, it wouldn't have made sense to me, and there was no other entity that could have mediated," he said.

In other words, part of the problem was that there was no leader of Obama's stature on the left who was willing to weigh in. Regarding the congressional race in the Tenth District, de Blasio suggested New York's progressives would have needed an "elder statesman" or an over-arching "single organization" to give the impetus to a consolidation, and observed that the Working Families Party evidently did not serve that function.

Rather than marshaling its resources effectively, the WFP had found itself paralyzed in the 2021 mayoral contest, the race to replace de Blasio. In that election, the WFP made a co-endorsement of two candidates before ultimately getting behind the top progressive contender. It left many activists wondering whether a more decisive approach could have prevented the subsequent victory of the eccentric centrist Eric Adams.

For his part, when asked why he didn't give way to Niou when he had no path, Jones suggested the Tenth District race was far more com-plicated than armchair pundits might have realized. Jones didn't see it as a simple question of progressives versus a moderate. His campaign's polling indicated voters in the district were either drawn to him and Goldman or Niou and Rivera. Jones believed this was because he and Goldman had the most federal experience.

"Voters don't behave as ideologically as people on Twitter . . . appear to think," Jones said. "People consider a candidate's record, the way the candidate presents, a candidate's story, and so many other things."

It was a similar view to the one Warren's allies offered when asked why she didn't consolidate behind Sanders. Warren and her campaign believed that—despite overlap in their platforms—she had a funda-mentally different base and brand than Sanders that meant her sup-porters might not have transitioned to him so easily.

One progressive who could have brought the left's voters together in the Tenth District was Ocasio-Cortez. She stayed out of the contest due to her relationships with both Niou and Jones, according to a senior staffer to Niou.

While Niou didn't have any harsh words for the allies who didn't come out for her, she was far more critical of Maloney's choice to run in the district that was a clear fit for Jones. "Like I get that he would've run in a place that would've been a little bit more challenging for him, but he's got millions of dollars at his disposal and he's the D-Trip chair," Niou said of Maloney.

Niou also had some criticism for Jones's decision to switch districts. "I also think Mondaire could have stayed and fought," she said.

In the end, when the votes were counted on August 23, Niou lost the primary to Goldman by just 1,306 votes out of more than 64,000 cast. In a sign of how hard-fought the race in the city had been, there were nearly twice as many votes cast in the Tenth District as there were in the Biaggi-Maloney contest in the Seventeenth. The two other progressive candidates were nowhere close to the front-runners, but they had more than enough votes to put Niou over the edge if they had managed to come together.

The WFP had ended up throwing its support behind Niou in late June. With the party's ballot line and the slim margin of her defeat, there was widespread speculation Niou could remain in the race and take on Goldman again in the general election on the WFP line. A move like that would have embarrassed the Democratic Party, forced it to devote resources to propping up Goldman in an otherwise deeply safe seat, and seriously strained relations between Democrats and the WFP across the state.

Niou nevertheless considered the play for two weeks, but on September 8, she posted a seven-minute video on Twitter announcing that she was conceding and would not be moving forward as a third-party candidate.

"We simply do not have the resources to fight all fights at the same time, and we must protect our democracy now," she said, seemingly near tears.

Later that month, as she reflected on the loss, Niou indicated there was some division among WFP leadership about whether she should have continued on the party's line, and she made clear that she had not been given free rein to break with the Democrats.

"So, that was a, you know, a co-governing decision by the WFP," she said, her voice catching. "I think that it's really tough to even discuss."

Progressives had failed to unite behind her twice in the same cycle.

The primary races in New York revealed how the left was hampered by a lack of unity and a fundraising gap as they faced off against incumbents. Maloney's ultimate defeat would show that the mainline Democratic establishment struggled with these exact same issues as they took on Republicans.

IT WAS THE NIGHT OF THE 2022 MIDTERM ELECTIONS, AND SEAN PATrick Maloney was supposed to be in four places at once.

Even as votes started to come in, the country and its political class were preparing for a Republican rout. According to one DCCC staffer, the campaign committee was looking at a map filled with "one- or two-point races." They could have broken either way, the staffer said, for reasons that were largely out of party control.

"It was going to depend on the price of gas, Donald Trump, if people still cared about abortion, and whether or not Joe Biden had, you know, taken a full senior moment by election day," the staffer said.

Maloney started his day in his district where he cast his vote. His

campaign planned an election-night reception with the Rockland
County Democratic Party. Ahead of that event, reporters were told it
was unclear whether or not Maloney would make an appearance. After
voting, Maloney had rushed down to Washington to join Speaker
Pelosi, who had her own election-night routine.

"She has a tradition of watching results at the D-Trip with her
family and some senior staffers . . . a few top top-tier donors, personal
friends," said a staffer at the DCCC. "It's a catered buffet dinner and
she's in her own war room."

But Pelosi, too, had been forced to scramble her plans for the day.
She had planned a celebratory dinner, but with the numbers looking
bleak, guests were turning down the invitation. Pelosi pivoted to a
lower-key meal.

"They changed it to a lunch, which obviously wasn't a great omen,"
the staffer said.

Even in the afternoon, before that evening's results could start
rolling in, DC power players were reluctant to dine with Pelosi. "They
invited K Street and didn't get a lot of lobbyist RSVPs, so they opened
it up to members," the DCCC staffer explained.

As head of the House's reelection efforts, Maloney had reason to
stay close to Pelosi on election night. According to the staffer, Maloney
was "going back and forth" between three locations in DC: Pelosi's
election-night buffet "to have a glass of wine with the speaker and some
donors," a space with DCCC staffers monitoring the national map, and
a "bunker" where his own campaign team was tracking results in the
Seventeenth District. He was everywhere and nowhere.

Maloney's experience spoke to criticism leveled by Ocasio-Cortez
and others, who had pushed for the party to have a professional operative leading its congressional campaign committee rather than a sitting

member—and certainly not one who needed to focus on a tough race in a frontline district.

As election night wore on, it became clear that Maloney wouldn't be making it to New York. His campaign team set up a television feed so he would be able to deliver remarks remotely to the crowd that was beginning to gather at the Nyack Seaport, a catering hall on the shores of the Hudson River.

In Maloney's absence, Rockland Democratic Party chairman John Gromada served as the event's main speaker. Gromada was a bespectacled Broadway composer and former DSA member who became more involved in politics as the founder of a "local resistance group" in 2016. While he wasn't a moderate himself, Gromada shared Maloney's view that only a centrist pitch could win the purple counties straddling New York's suburbs and more rural regions.

"I wanted to come into the party and help change the party," Gromada said. "We've got to meet people where they are . . . instead of trying to get people to move to where we are."

In between speeches at the election-night soirée, Gromada explained why he thought Maloney had been a better bet than a progressive like Biaggi.

"I saw Sean as more of a bridge to try to get back Democrats in Rockland County that haven't been voting for our party," Gromada explained. "He said he wanted to try to move those guys instead of always trying to throw rocks at them."

But Maloney and Gromada's theory would prove incorrect. With Maloney absent from his own election-night party, Gromada found himself emceeing as downcast Democratic candidates came up to deliver concession speeches for races in the state legislature and a local town council. Every conceding candidate stood across from a television showing live footage of the empty podium that was set up at the DCCC for Maloney to speak.

Gromada blamed the down-ballot failures on the cash spent to take out Maloney. Some reports calculated that $10 million had been raised to oust the DCCC chairman. "We really were the victim of dark money here," Gromada said with clear frustration. "We were the target of Republican PAC money from around the country that hurt all of our candidates."

Maloney conceded as well the next morning. In his interview for this book, he pointed out that—apart from New York—Democrats did well in a year when they faced "the universal expectation that we were going to get our ass kicked."

"I think the Republicans had an assumption that they would win based on historic trends and we had a plan," Maloney said. "It didn't work perfectly, but we won thirty-five of thirty-nine frontline races."

However, Maloney's home state and his own loss were black marks on the otherwise strong performance. Maloney noted that congressional Democrats outraised Republicans when it came to capped campaign contributions. But they were vastly outspent when it came to dark money PACs funded by major donors. Maloney suggested this was an area where Democrats might want to catch up.

"They definitely won the war of highly interested billionaires who gave north of $10 million bucks—and that's a real thing," Maloney said. "It might be somewhere where we want to have equally motivated, super-high-net-worth individuals helping us at that level."

The cash advantage helped Republicans put a target on Maloney's back, but his loss wasn't the only embarrassment for Democrats in New York. Republicans had a net gain of three seats in the state and, on Long Island, the DCCC had failed to expose George Santos, who won the Third District despite having a résumé full of brazen lies. DCCC staffers compiled an eighty-seven page "research memo" on Santos, but it largely focused on criticizing his policy positions and past work in the financial industry. Instead of digging into Santos's many fabrications—such as his claim to have been an asset manager at Citigroup, where he never worked—the DCCC simply listed "dates unknown" next to his periods of supposed employment and moved on.

Maloney believes the Democrats' congressional campaign organization "could have done a better job" and needs to make some strategic "tweaks." This includes the DCCC research operation, which he said "should be completely overhauled." Nevertheless, he was adamant that the ultimate blame for Santos lies with the Republican Party.

"Let's start with the Republicans who put up that asshole and who continue to defend him. So, let's just lay this at the right doorstep," Maloney said, criticizing the GOP for running "shithead candidates who lie about their résumés" and how "they stick with them nonetheless."

Maloney also pointed out that Rupert Murdoch's tabloid *New York Post* had hammered a narrative that Democrats had let crime in the Big Apple run wild. The coverage sent tremors of terror through the suburbs and rural upstate counties. Maloney blasted the content as "industrial-strength lies."

Even in loss, however, Maloney claimed a Pyrrhic victory. According to the DCCC staffer, Maloney gave a brief speech to the team on election night arguing that the $10 million Republicans spent on him had been wasted as it would have been more effective if it was doled out across a few more competitive districts.

"Those stupid motherfuckers spent millions of dollars trying to take me out," Maloney said, according to the staffer. "They, in the process, took other seats off the map for themselves."

Maloney denied cursing in front of staff, but he said the sentiment was correct. "The Republicans sometimes act like a bunch of drunk guys at a fraternity," he said. "Like, they think it's going to be really cool to beat the gay chair of the DCCC. And they became obsessed with it."

Maloney insisted he deliberately tried to "encourage" the GOP to use its cash on him, rather than more fragile frontline Democrats. He characterized himself as the GOP's "white whale." In this case—unlike the situation in *Moby-Dick*—for a relatively minor investment of time and money, the Republicans had indeed landed a big fish.

While Maloney and his home state underperformed relative to the party nationally, Democrats managed a better midterm performance than anyone expected. The DCCC staffer credited the overall success to a "dual-track" strategy that consisted of highlighting "positive" narratives about Democratic candidates and their plans to lower the cost of living while going "negative" on Republicans' opposition to abortion, which was a white-hot issue after the landmark June 2022 Supreme Court decision in *Dobbs v. Jackson Women's Health Organization* that overturned *Roe v. Wade* and ruled abortion was not protected by the Constitution. The White House—and particularly a barnstorming Vice President Harris—helped to bring the issue to the fore. Harris rallied the troops by holding events in multiple states with 200 local legislators and by beating the drum about reproductive rights in a series of campaign and media appearances. The focus paid off.

"Some Democrats wanted to make protecting democracy a thing and it didn't catch fire," the DCCC staffer said. "Abortion was something that voters latched on to where they were like, 'Shit, these guys don't respect bodily autonomy; they actually are the raging monsters Democrats have been saying they are.'"

This was an attack line for which Republicans had no answer. "Their committee did not have them prepared for how to deal with *Dobbs*," the staffer said. "It was a free-for-all on their side."

The intense battles between progressives and centrists in 2022 didn't exactly settle the debate of which might be the winning approach going forward. Nor did the results heal deep schisms that had formed.

Both Biaggi and Niou indicated they still might consider attempting to make a political comeback. And the pair clearly haven't lost their appetite for taking on the establishment.

"I think that Yuh-Line and I have done a number on lots of powerful people and interests in this state that they won't be able to recover from for like a generation," Biaggi said. "I feel pretty good about it actually."

Meanwhile, Jones, who gave up his district for Maloney, packed up the home he had moved to in Brooklyn. He headed back to the Seventeenth District and, in July 2023, launched a campaign to run against the Republican who had defeated Maloney and taken his old seat. As he announced, Jones declared that he was focused on both fighting the GOP as it tried to "overthrow our democracy" and on pushing his fellow Democrats "to fight harder for working people."

"I've never been Washington's choice," Jones wrote on Twitter, adding, "I'm running to finish the work I began."

Chapter 14

THE NEXT EPISODE

COMING OUT OF THE MIDTERMS, THERE SHOULD HAVE BEEN NO doubts about Joe Biden. He was an incumbent president whose party defied all expectations. And yet, as Biden headed into the final half of his first term, questions swirled about his future.

It was always this way for Biden. The doubts began from almost the moment he took office.

In the early days of his administration, some people assumed that there was no way Biden would stick around for a second term. An early episode involving Chief of Staff Ron Klain, the top-ranked official in the White House, showed just how much Biden's future was an object of intense curiosity—and uncertainty.

Klain was one of the more freewheeling tweeters in the West Wing. On February 7, 2021, just eighteen days after the president was sworn in, Klain stirred up a perfect storm of DC gossip when he hit "retweet" on a post involving Vice President Kamala Harris and Transportation Secretary Pete Buttigieg—the two officials who most often figured in early speculation about the president's future.

Buttigieg, still fairly fresh off his surprising star turn in the 2020 Democratic primary, had just done an appearance on one of the Sunday shows touting Biden's COVID relief package. Barely two years removed from serving as mayor of South Bend, Indiana's fourth-largest city, Buttigieg had become a national media darling, with natural appeal to independents, a gift for debating the enemy on Fox News, and oratory that drew comparisons to former president Barack Obama. All of those qualities were on display in Buttigieg's brief interview.

"You've seen economic advisers from the last four administrations— think about what that means, that's Clinton, Bush, Obama, and even Trump—saying that we need to do this," Buttigieg said. "You've got Moody's saying that we could have four million fewer jobs if we don't act now. And we're operating in a time of historically low interest rates. This is a moment where the greatest risk we could take, as the president has said, is not the risk of doing too much. It's the risk of doing too little."

Buttigieg somehow managed to be bipartisan, dramatic, and wonky all at once in his call for expanded pandemic spending. His appearance, as so many of them did, sent the pundit class into a swoon. Jennifer Rubin, a columnist at the *Washington Post* who changed her stripes from conservative to centrist Democrat during the Trump era, tweeted a video of Buttigieg on the show along with the caption "Harris-Buttigieg 2028."

Rubin's post was essentially innocuous speculation, the kind of Democratic Party fan fiction that tends to bubble up on Twitter feeds and off-hours cable panels during slow news days. But then Klain touched the retweet button under Rubin's post, and it became something more.

Klain quickly un-did the retweet, but it was too late. His post was screen-capped for posterity and it became, for the span of one rapid-fire, internet-addled news cycle, a retweet heard round the District. Klain's click kicked off a chorus of armchair analysis in the capital. Was he supporting the idea of the two as a joint ticket, or would he back either one individually? How significant was the "2028" part? Did Klain mean to signal that Biden planned to stay for eight years? Was he just mildly amused by Rubin?

Part of the reason the stray post from one of Biden's closest advisers generated so much interest was the fact that people—including some in the president's orbit—were already wondering about his plans and what role Harris and Buttigieg would play in them.

"There's a presumption that, if the president does not run for reelection, that Buttigieg could be a good potential vice presidential candidate for Harris," a former Biden campaign staffer explained in the days surrounding the episode.

Rubin and Klain weren't the only ones taking note of Buttigieg. The staffer said it seemed the transportation secretary was doing the "most press" out of Biden's cabinet. His post also appeared to put Buttigieg in a strong position. As transportation secretary, Buttigieg was set up to gain federal experience and to "make bipartisan deals" on infrastructure.

"Look at how much power this position gives him," the staffer said of Buttigieg. "That potentially opens more doors for him such as vice president. . . . I think people look at the situation and just put two and two together. . . . If Biden doesn't run for reelection, then Kamala runs and who is her VP?"

A former Buttigieg staffer described him as a perfect complement to Harris, who is the first Black woman to break the glass ceiling of the executive branch. They pointed out that, in addition to being a high-profile surrogate and former presidential candidate, Buttigieg is a veteran and the first openly gay man to win a presidential primary. And they noted that Harris has a "personal relationship with Pete in a way that she doesn't with other people."

"You get the double history with the gay thing, Midwest, white guy, perceived moderate. You can't say that he's not ready on day one," the former Buttigieg staffer said. "He has the name ID, he's good on TV, like a lot of it just clicks and makes sense."

There can be no understating how bizarre this all was. Klain's retweet had occurred just about three weeks after Biden had taken office. He was three months removed from defeating Donald Trump—a powerful, polarizing incumbent—and then facing down the assault on the Capitol by Trump's aggrieved supporters. And yet, Biden was still perceived as weak. Party insiders were already imagining future presidential tickets and moving around members of his administration like they were deck chairs on the *Titanic*.

Then again, the president was in his late seventies. Some Democrats whispered that he might not last the full four years. The COVID-enforced Zoom campaign of 2020, conducted mostly through remote video conferences, had spared Biden the intense travel of a traditional White House bid. For Biden, running for a second term would mean mounting a grueling, full-scale campaign at the age of eighty-one.

The weird episode encapsulated issues that would persist for Biden throughout his first term. Doubts constantly swirled around him. They were fueled by the inevitable frailty brought on by his advancing age and the general shakiness of a country coming out of the chaos of Trump and the pandemic. And then there was Biden's staff's tendency to make unforced errors, like that retweet.

As time went on, Biden had another issue as well: unpopularity. Averages of his personal approval numbers had hovered in the mid-fifties during the early days of his term, but they crashed down to the low forties during the crisis over the withdrawal of US troops from Afghanistan, and by the end of his first year in office they had not recovered. The next year, they sank even further, into the high thirties. The administration's legislative accomplishments and the Democratic party's stirring successes in the midterms only managed to pull Biden's personal approval ratings back up into the low forties. A president with numbers like that faces an uphill battle in a reelection campaign.

Biden never quite managed to overcome his naysayers. There were real reasons for all the questions about his ability to stay in office. And yet, despite similar doubts in 2020 and 2022, hadn't Biden managed to come out on top?

———

IOWA IS NORMALLY THE CENTER OF THE PRESIDENTIAL PRIMARY UNI- verse. In 2021 and 2022, Democrats began to drift in and out of the state, careful to avoid saying they were considering a potential primary challenge to Biden—or preparing a campaign in case the president decided not to run, or could not run.

Zach Wahls, the Democratic minority leader in Iowa's state senate, said in a September 2022 interview that he had heard some early rumblings around Des Moines. Labor Secretary Marty Walsh, the former mayor of Boston, had traveled to Iowa "a couple times," Wahls said. California congressman Ro Khanna, a prominent progressive Sanders supporter, had been spending time in Iowa "for a while."

Khanna "genuinely has . . . relationships with people across the state," Wahls said. "I think it comes from a place of understanding this kind of mutual symbiosis between heartland America, coastal America, and the need for those relationships to be better because there is real codependence in both directions."

Overall, Wahls said the state was "very quiet" from a pre-presidential

perspective, with big names like Harris and Buttigieg notably miss-
ing from the list of potential candidates who may have been testing
the waters.

"I haven't heard from her in a while," Wahls said offhandedly of
the vice president.

Harris wasn't the only one who was conspicuously absent from
the potential primary fray. While Wahls acknowledged there was still
speculation surrounding Biden's plans, the potential field seemed to be
giving the president a wide berth.

"Although there are questions about the president—'Is he going to
run for reelection?' [and] all that—I think the field is being very respectful," Wahls said. "I think very few people are coming to Iowa.... They
want to be respectful to the president and his team."

The fact potential rivals were giving Biden room to run was a testa-
ment to his status as a surprisingly and uniquely unifying figure in the
fractured party. As his second year in office drew to a close, Biden had
taken Democrats from intense infighting and the daily indignities of
the Trump administration to the White House and a surprisingly solid
showing in the midterms. The man who had run as a moderate had also
built real bridges to the left and—even as Biden suffered some defeats in
Congress—those connections had produced legislation that both the
White House and progressives were genuinely proud of.

There were still rifts between the left and center, but he'd earned
real goodwill. Under Biden, the Squad was no longer having daily
heated fights with the establishment and primary challenges were ending in quick, stirring calls for unity.

Of course, the party's newfound gains were delicate. Polls showed
a second coming of Trump was a real possibility.

And there were other worries. While Democrats were giving Biden
space to campaign without serious opposition in their 2024 primary,

a more outlandish scheme was being hatched for the general election. Throughout Biden's second year in office, the centrist advocacy group No Labels reportedly raised tens of millions of dollars from undisclosed donors for an initiative to try to get on the ballot as a full-fledged third party and put forward a candidate of their own in enough states to win the presidency. Their audacious plan looked like a threat to spoil the race that was mostly aimed at Biden, and some No Labels allies like Representative Josh Gottheimer disavowed it. But at least one Democrat gave the would-be third party a warm embrace. Senator Joe Manchin praised the No Labels initiative to reporters as "the only game in town that wants to bring people together" and pointedly declined to rule out potentially running as the No Labels presidential candidate. Once again, after years of tension with progressives, it seemed like the radical centrists were the clearest challenge to the Democratic Party agenda.

For Democrats, the persistent primary fights and periodic legislative spats made clear the foundational tension between the left and center had not been fully resolved. Biden had his issues, but he had stopped the bleeding. The party's desire to stick with him was indicative of fears there was no one else who could replicate his ability to build and sustain an anti-Trump coalition.

And, if Biden himself was hoping to step aside, that possibility was starting to seem increasingly fraught. Both of his likeliest heirs— Buttigieg and Harris—spent the start of his administration taking a series of stumbles that cooled all of the initial speculation about their futures.

The problems Harris and her team had experienced on her campaign had persisted during her time as vice president. Harris saw heavy staff turnover, with aides describing a toxic climate riven with factionalism and mismanagement. One source who worked for the vice

president declined to go on record or even discuss matters anonymously
due to the heated atmosphere around the office. They refused to characterize the experience of working for Harris apart from offering a three-
word assessment. It was, they said, "Game of Thrones."

Along with the turbulence behind the scenes, Harris's public profile had taken a hit. While Buttigieg had been set up for success with
his position as transportation secretary, the vice president, it seemed,
got all of the trickiest tasks.

In April 2021, Biden tapped Harris to tackle immigration. A long-
standing policy challenge, immigration had in recent years been made
even more difficult by an increasing flow of migrants escaping intolera-
ble conditions in Central America and seeking asylum on the southern
border. As the *Washington Post* put it in a report announcing the move,
Harris had been given "a politically perilous assignment."

A White House official pointed out that, as vice president,
Biden had played a high-profile role in the Obama administration's
failed immigration reform push. They suggested Harris wasn't fazed
by the job.

"Of course it was a difficult assignment," the official said. "But a lot
of the assignments she deals with are difficult."

Harris brought her analytical approach to the immigration issue
and focused much of her efforts on addressing the root causes leading
to the exodus from Central America. She traveled to the region and
brought together a public-private partnership that drove $4.2 billion in
investment to countries there. However, despite some signs of progress,
the topic remained fraught.

It was unclear why the White House would want to so closely tie
Biden's running mate and most natural successor to such a hot-button
issue. It overshadowed other initiatives Harris spearheaded that fit with
her longtime focus on families and economic opportunity. As Harris

led efforts to expand high-speed internet access, eliminate lead pipes, and promote maternal health care, immigration dominated the headlines. The assignment made Harris a frequent target on Fox News. In 2022, Republican Texas governor Greg Abbott began sending busloads of migrants to Washington DC in an attempt to make the point that the border states were disproportionately bearing the cost of national policy. He often directed the buses straight to Harris's official residence at the Naval Observatory.

Meanwhile, Buttigieg's cakewalk had turned into a tightrope. A series of significant infrastructure failures including a holiday travel meltdown at Southwest Airlines that left passengers stranded, an FAA systems outage that grounded planes around the country for ninety minutes, and a train derailment that spread hazardous material in East Palestine, Ohio, led to questions about his leadership and put him under pressure. His normally quiet cabinet post had, by virtue of intervening events, become a hot seat.

Biden's team had long said that he intended to run again, and there may never have been much reality to the idea of Biden—who had, after all, dreamed of inhabiting the presidency for decades—voluntarily forgoing the possibility of a second term. But as it happened, neither Harris nor Buttigieg inspired much confidence in their ability to quickly pick up the baton.

While it made sense that more establishment Democrats—particularly members of his own administration—would defer to Biden, progressives who might seem like natural challengers also kept their distance from the 2024 cycle.

Sanders, who is now in his eighties, repeatedly indicated he will support Biden if the current commander in chief runs for reelection. In an interview for this book, Sanders also urged his fellow progressives to focus on offices other than the presidency.

"If Joe runs, I will support him," Sanders said. "I see other people may have different points of view, but I think what our job right now is ... I think we've got to keep organizing at the grassroots level, both at the Congress, for the governor's races, for city council, school boards, whatever."

The next highest profile progressive, Alexandria Ocasio-Cortez, was just old enough—by a few weeks—to qualify for 2024. While she was technically eligible, in a mid-2023 interview for this book, her fellow "Squad" member, Minnesota congresswoman Ilhan Omar, noted Ocasio-Cortez had shown no interest in running for president.

"I think I would respect the fact that she has repeatedly said this is not something she thinks about and has not factored into the decisions that she's made about politics or policy," Omar said of Ocasio-Cortez, with an audible chuckle.

Omar, who was born in Somalia and is not eligible to run for president, suggested progressives overall were unlikely to touch the race.

"If I were to suspend my actual thoughts on this and just think politically, there could be nothing more damaging to Democrats' potential to win a presidential campaign in 2024 than having a Democratic sitting president be challenged in the primary," Omar said. "I think that would devastate our ability to win that election and I think it would undermine our ability to continue to talk about the headways that we've made in regards to policy, the achievements that we've been able to have in regards to policy and what we've actually been able to deliver to the American people."

"I cannot imagine," Omar continued, "without the president himself saying, 'I am stepping aside, I'm not running for reelection,' that it would be wise—politically wise—for anyone to say, 'I am going to primary a sitting Democratic president as a Democrat,' and not ruin and be responsible for ruining our chances of keeping the presidency."

Asked what her "actual thoughts on this" might be, the ones she "suspended" to "think politically," Omar declined to answer.

"I'm suspending it so you don't get to know it," Omar said with a laugh, later adding, "You were being sneaky."

———

WHILE THE BIGGEST PROGRESSIVE STARS STAYED OUT OF THE FRAY, there were some Democrats who lamented that progressives seemed to have agreed to the Biden truce as the president went into the second half of his first term.

Nina Turner, a former Ohio state senator who was a co-chair of Bernie Sanders's 2020 campaign, suggested her experiences watching that race convinced her Biden needed a progressive challenger. To that end, she praised the candidacy of Marianne Williamson, the bestselling New Age author and eccentric 2020 candidate, who kicked off a second long-shot White House bid in March 2023.

Biden, Turner explained in an early 2023 interview for this book, "was at a fundraiser, I think it was at somebody's home, but he was at a very-high-dollar fundraiser during the 2020 presidential election and was on record saying to that audience that nothing will fundamentally change for you. He is honoring that pledge that he gave to those ultra-wealthy donors. Nothing fundamentally has changed for the people who are in the one percent in this country, and nothing will fundamentally change for them as long as you have moderate Dems such as him—more moderate leaning and conservative in the White House."

Turner, in trial balloon mode for her own potential candidacy, went on to say that "the people need a champion. They need somebody, they need a freedom-fighting progressive populist out there." Turner explained that part of her decision-making included wanting to see the movement grow beyond presidential races.

"I will be out there front and center no matter who is running. I'm pushing as hard as I can and really trying to shake even the progressive movement that is somehow in a lull right now."

And while she was one of Sanders's most visible allies in the past two elections, part of Turner's eagerness to see a new progressive challenger emerge stemmed from a belief the left needs to move beyond him.

"Another challenge that I see for this progressive movement is that we were tethered—and I don't mean that in a negative way, right? To the persona of—of Senator Bernie Sanders during a presidential election cycle," Turner said.

It might have been easy to dismiss Turner's ambition to field a progressive primary challenger against an incumbent Democratic president as the normal operation of the ever-present discontent on the left-wing fringe. However, early 2023 polling showed sizeable majorities of Democrats and Democratic-leaning independents believed the party should nominate someone other than Biden to run in 2024. Those polls continued to reflect Biden's perennially low approval ratings, which were little affected in 2022 and early 2023 by the string of laws he's passed or the largely favorable results for Democrats in the midterm elections.

The lesson of the Democrats' experience in 2016, arguably, was that widespread discontent with the establishment's consensus nominee can be a potent force on the campaign trail. Any candidate who throws their hat in the ring, even an unlikely one like an aging socialist senator or a spiritualist author, may find themselves riding an unexpected wave of popularity.

And, as she contemplated the race and her own part in it, Turner noted the energy of a presidential campaign could be vital for the progressive movement.

"It's a whirlwind unlike anything you can create without having the imprimatur of running for president," Turner said. "The challenge is to figure out whether or not we can get that same kind of energy within our movement not attached to somebody running for president."

Turner's ambitions aside, more established progressives who have a position in DC seemed to be steering clear.

Ro Khanna, the California congressman who had laid initial groundwork in Iowa, said he was staying out of the way—for Biden or Sanders. "I'm supporting President Biden for 2024," he said in an interview for this book. "I fully expect him to run. If he didn't run, I would support Bernie Sanders."

Khanna did not see Biden as a fellow progressive; however, he called the president a bridge to a progressive future.

"He saw the energy . . . and adopted some of the good ideas of the progressive movement, particularly in Build Back Better, but I think we have to go further," Khanna said.

As he predicted that the party's two last leaders were still their most likely candidates, Khanna also suggested Harris was not going to be a factor. "I just don't think she'll be running in '24," he said. "I think Biden will be the nominee or, if not, I think Bernie will be."

For Khanna, it all traced back to Sanders.

"He is going to be seen as the father of the modern progressive era— and I do think that we will have a modern progressive era," Khanna said. "I hope it'll be as soon as possible, but it'll happen. And then when it happens, Bernie Sanders will be seen as the father of that movement."

While Khanna did not want to take on Biden or Sanders, he also clearly was not ruling out a potential run for president one day. In even a brief phone call, Khanna seemed to offer a clear glimpse at what the next generation of progressive candidate might look like. As he pushed for Medicare for All, free public college, and universal preschool, Khanna framed himself as a "progressive capitalist" and emphasized his roots. Khanna's comments sounded like the beginning of a stump speech.

"Coming from being born in Philadelphia in 1976, our bicentenary...I frame a lot of our economic policies as supporting a new economic patriotism," Khanna said. "I think [that] can be framed in very patriotic ways that help us get a majoritarian appeal for our progressive policy."

Chapter 15

SOFT LAUNCH

JOE BIDEN WAS DOING IT AGAIN.

In the year leading up to the 2024 election, Biden was repeating the same thing he had done eight years earlier, standing on the brink. He had a campaign in waiting, but he had not pulled the trigger and made an official announcement. The uncertainty had started to lead to bad headlines. Party insiders were increasingly antsy.

Biden's aides brushed off the speculation and concerns.

"Democrats are always worried," one staffer from Biden's 2020 campaign said in April 2023.

After all, this was not 2015. Biden was the sitting president of the United States and the leader of his party. Waiting was his prerogative. He had the ability to fly Air Force One and make appearances around the country without a campaign apparatus. All of his most serious potential primary challengers had fallen in line and the donors would too.

"He intends to run," the staffer said. "We've been clear. We're making preparations."

The staffer indicated Biden had "the space he needs, especially coming off the midterms. . . . We don't feel like we're in any rush."

But the pressure wasn't all coming from the press or anxious boosters. Trump was back, and Biden's own team had put him on a deadline.

Trump officially launched his comeback bid in November 2022 and reporters wanted to know when Biden would make an announcement of his own. Ron Klain, who was still Biden's chief of staff at the time, offered a real answer the following month. Klain said that he expected Biden to kick off his campaign after the holidays.

Yet the holidays came and went. Not just Christmas and New Year's, but Valentine's Day, St. Patrick's Day, and Easter too. Throughout early 2023, Biden hesitated to come out of the gate. As January passed, his team said the announcement would come after February's State of the Union address. By the time that speech was delivered, Biden's inner circle was again signaling something new—that the campaign would take off in April. As that month began and the flowers bloomed, Democrats who approached Biden aides looking for campaign work were told it would be even longer.

The president's waffling led to a swirl of doubts, rumors, and probing articles by respected reporters suggesting he could bow out. Other politicians who were deferring to Biden were quietly making their own Plan B preparations and fishing for gossip about the president's plans.

But for the expectation Klain had set, Biden's hesitancy might not have even been noticed. Barack Obama waited until April 2011 to officially kick off his second campaign. George W. Bush went in May. Indeed, when pressed about Biden's intentions, his aides would point to those two dates, which they had committed to memory.

Once again, drama unfolded around the president fueled by the public's almost reflexive doubts about Biden and his team. By late

February 2023, Politico joined the chorus of pundits speculating Biden might stay on the sidelines with a flashy article bylined by six reporters that suggested the president "may not run." Biden's aides dismissed it all as the DC press corps' obsession with the campaign horse race and insatiable need for content.

"Our view on the speculation on us is that it's like dumb and pointless," the campaign staffer said.

The president's aides knew he was plotting his campaign with an innermost circle of confidants who weren't talking to the press: his longtime advisers Mike Donilon, Steve Ricchetti, Anita Dunn, and Jen O'Malley Dillon.

The campaign staffer said they "wouldn't put any stock" in coverage suggesting Biden was waffling and cast it as the product of reporters feeding a need for content with the musings of gossipy figures in the president's outer orbit. "Especially Politico. . . . They just feel like they need to do things on this all the time and they're talking to people on the periphery."

But there were real concerns at play. There was work to be done; presidential races kick off in earnest the year before the election. Between the primaries and the general, the campaign goes on for months and, well before that, it takes time to build your machinery in the key states, hire staff, and raise the massive amounts of cash needed to pay for it all.

Biden ultimately pulled the trigger on April 25, 2023. During the months when the president bided his time, Trump was traveling the country, hosting rallies, and raising millions. Other Republicans, including former South Carolina governor Nikki Haley, were starting to do the same.

But Biden wasn't just standing still prior to his campaign launch. He had already put his stamp on the presidential primary.

━━━━━

AT THE DEMOCRATIC NATIONAL COMMITTEE'S WINTER MEETINGS IN February 2023, Biden pushed through a sweeping realignment of the party's primary process. The plan was designed to answer some of the tensions and frustration that emerged around Iowa's collapse three years earlier. The changes also gave Biden a smoother path to a second term. However, elements of the new system set the stage for major conflicts down the road.

On the surface, the reforms were part of efforts by Biden and top Democrats to make peace with progressives and address their concerns from 2016 and 2020. However, as it was enacted, Biden's vision sparked discontent from the left. It wasn't just about the next campaign. Aspects of the plan virtually guaranteed the primary calendar would be a focal point of feuds for years to come.

The modern primary process is the product of past tensions between the Democratic left and center. It dates back to 1972. Prior to that race, party nominees were chosen on the floor of the quadrennial conventions and, really, in smoke-filled back rooms during those conclaves. The old-school machines that controlled Democratic cities and counties around the country also had a hold on the presidential nomination. Early primary voting took place, but it was on a small scale and played little formal role in the final decision. A state's voters might elect their delegates to the convention, but the delegates' names were what appeared on the ballot, not the presidential candidate's. Once those elected delegates got to the convention, they could vote however they wished—or however they were told. Party bosses, not voters, held sway. For decades, true participatory democracy was just a token element of the Democratic Party. The infamous "Siege of Chicago" at the DNC's 1968 convention, when protesters from an array of anti-war and countercultural groups battled with police in the streets, helped pressure the bosses to make a change.

Following the riots, the party created a commission that was initially chaired by progressive senator George McGovern to review the delegate selection process. Following the recommendations produced by the commission, the votes conducted by state parties took on a much larger role in the presidential nomination. More than ever before, primary voters would choose the presidential candidate they preferred, and their collective choices would be given a binding effect at the nominating conventions.

States are generally supposed to hold their nominating contests between the first Tuesday of March and the second Tuesday of June, a period the DNC's bureaucracy refers to as "the window." However, a certain number of states are permitted a waiver to go earlier, in what's called the "pre-window period." Iowa and New Hampshire owned this early "pre-window period" for most of the modern primary era.

There are various stories about how Iowa ended up first on the calendar. According to one tale, the state party had a slow-moving mimeograph machine and they set an early date in order to have time to produce copies of the results in all the precincts.

The state's early caucus date garnered little attention at the time due to the overall novelty of the process. Because it was a caucus rather than a primary, it also sidestepped a potential clash with New Hampshire, which was immensely proud of its own "first-in-the-nation" primary that dates back to 1920.

New Hampshire's tradition went unchallenged during the decades when the voting was largely an afterthought in the nominating process. However, with the tensions of 1968, leaders in the Granite State mounted an effort to protect their status.

As the 1976 election approached, a bipartisan group of New

Hampshire lawmakers backed by the Republican governor (who was mulling his own presidential bid and eager to secure home field advantage) proposed a bill to forever enshrine the state's "first-in-the-nation" primary. The legislation allowed the secretary of state to schedule the primary "seven days or more immediately preceding the date on which any other state shall hold a similar election."

In an essay held in the secretary of state's archives, James Splaine, a Democratic former state senator who helped mastermind the plan, explained that the law was specifically designed to ensure New Hampshire stayed at the front of the line. Splaine and his allies realized they needed to give the secretary of state the authority to quickly change the date of the primary to avoid a game of hopscotch between states. Splaine made his case at a state senate committee hearing in March 1975.

"The bill you have before you was first introduced last December after I learned that a number of other states were trying to take the first-in-the-nation presidential primary away from New Hampshire," Splaine said. "There was an amendment tacked onto the bill. [It] guarantees that even if [there is a] concerted effort to get a regional primary [we] would still guarantee that ours will be first."

It took only ten minutes for the committee to approve the bill. The senate passed it that same day. Soon after New Hampshire enacted its primary law, Iowa adopted its own measure designed to keep its caucuses first.

Splaine's essay demonstrated the paradox at play in the efforts by the early states to guard their status. "In the Granite State, our presidential primary not only has stood the test of time, it is pure American democracy at its best," he wrote. Splaine and his fellow lawmakers had convinced themselves that an election process that granted them undue influence despite the protests of their countrymen was somehow uniquely fair.

Along with legal maneuvering, Iowa and New Hampshire managed to fend off various challenges from other states for decades with the help of national party leadership who saw the benefit of opening the primary campaign in relatively cheap media markets—and avoiding broader conflict.

For Democrats, increased pressure for diversity and the debacle during the 2020 Iowa caucus changed all that. Even Iowa's leaders began to realize the decades-old arrangement would have to change.

"I certainly don't think we're ever going to see the old, traditional caucus ever again," one high-level Democrat who worked in the state said in a 2022 interview for this book. "I think people are done with that. I think the counting fiasco was really what finally gave everyone the hook."

Iowa's Democratic establishment knew they had little defense for the overly complex, undemocratic nature of the game. One Democrat who'd served in various campaign and government roles in the state over several decades described coming to a reluctant conclusion that change was overdue.

"We all know you fundamentally don't really have a good answer for why this process leaves out all the people who can't show up at seven o'clock at the church hall or somebody's basement or wherever it is," this Democrat said.

"As someone who has spent a chunk of my career and life in Iowa, I nonetheless absolutely believe—and would have believed this whether or not the counting blew up in 2020—that the time has passed," they added. "When I first started working in Iowa, I probably didn't have the language to tell you that . . . a very old and very white state exerts an ideological influence in the way that I do now. . . . It becomes sort of hard to reconcile in your head."

The problems went beyond the caucus process and the vote count meltdown. Many Democrats—particularly former HUD secretary Julián Castro, who ran for president in 2020—had begun to raise concerns with the fact that over 60 percent of the state was white.

In April 2022, citing worries about diversity and the general election competitiveness of the early part of the primary calendar, the DNC's Rules and Bylaws Committee (RBC) expanded to five the number of states it expected to permit to hold contests during that crucial "pre-window" period and invited any state or territory that wanted an opportunity to go early to apply. For the first time, Iowa and New Hampshire would be at risk not only of having their first-in-the-nation status diluted, but of losing it entirely.

"We said, 'Let's throw the door open,'" observed 2022 RBC member and longtime Democratic operative Mo Elliethee in an interview for this book. "Let's just see who wants it. The current four can reapply."

Twenty states submitted their bids over the course of the summer. Even tiny Delaware, Biden's home state, put in an application to the committee.

The RBC was set to meet to discuss changes to the primary calendar on the first weekend of December 2022. That Friday, coming off the Democrats' reassuring performance in the November midterms, Biden sent a letter to the committee explaining how he wanted the process to look.

His letter listed a series of principles. First, Biden wrote, "We must ensure that voters of color have a voice in choosing our nominee much earlier in the process." Second, "Our party should no longer allow caucuses as part of our nominating process."

"We are a party dedicated to ensuring participation by all voters and for removing barriers to political participation," Biden wrote. "Caucuses—requiring voters to choose in public, to spend significant amounts of time to caucus, disadvantaging hourly workers and anyone who does not have the flexibility to go to a set location at a set time—are inherently anti-participatory. It should be our party's goal to rid the nominating process of restrictive, anti-worker caucuses."

Third, "the early states" on the calendar "must reflect the over-all diversity of our party and our nation—economically, geographically, demographically." Fourth, somewhat repetitively, "There should continue to be strong representation from urban, suburban, and rural America."

At the conclusion of the letter, Biden outlined the rationale behind his push for changes.

"I have made no secret of my conviction that diversity is a critical element for the Democratic Party to win elections AND to govern effectively," Biden wrote, later adding, "Just like my Administration, the Democratic Party has worked hard to reflect the diversity of America—but our nominating process does not. . . . I am committed to working with the DNC to get this done."

But there was a fifth principle as well. Biden specified that "the Rules and Bylaws Committee should review the calendar every four years." It was just a dozen words, but that simple idea is likely to detonate inside the party for years to come.

———

ALONG WITH OUTLINING HIS PRINCIPLES FOR THE PRIMARY PROCESS IN writing, Biden let it be known more discreetly the specific lineup of states he would prefer. Various comments made by party leaders during the RBC's meetings acknowledged that the new order had come down from the White House. The party followed Biden's recommendations precisely.

The plan officially passed at the DNC's winter meetings, which took place in Philadelphia in February 2022, two months after Biden sent his letter. On the night before the vote, Biden and Harris made a rare appearance to rally the troops in the hotel ballroom where the proceedings were set to take place.

A stage was set up in front of a bank of TV cameras with a lectern, a printed "Biden—Harris" backdrop, and a pair of risers where a couple dozen supporters could stand in tight knots behind the speakers holding signs that read "GO JOE" and "KAMALA."

Standing at the lectern beneath the hot lights, Harris cast the moment in heroic terms that were starkly at odds with the pair's actual standing.

"When someone asked me a few weeks ago for my one word to describe the new year, I said, 'momentum.' Momentum!" she declared.

A moment later, Harris seemed to admit that, despite her feeling they had "two years of good work" with "a lot of good material to show for it," the public was not necessarily sold.

"We have momentum, and now let's let the people know!" she said.

After Harris warmed up the crowd, Biden took the stage.

"Folks," he said. "I truly believe we're living in an inflection point in modern history, it comes along every four or five generations where what happens in a short period of time in a country or around the world has a fundamental effect for the next three to four decades."

Biden's assessment of the moment was dramatic, but it was also fundamentally optimistic. With his voice alternating between shouts and a stage whisper, Biden called it an "extraordinary opportunity to build America and a world that's more fair, and just, and more free." And, in the president's telling, he'd already made great strides on that front. As he ran through the dangers, including an ascendant China and increasingly extreme right wing, Biden also rattled off a laundry list of his own achievements including a rebounding economy, significant gun control, police reform legislation, and major steps to combat climate change.

The performance was vintage Diamond Joe. With all of the questions hanging in the air, the speeches, which were punctuated by chants of "Four more years!" felt like a clear answer. One DNC member in attendance aptly described it as "the soft launch" of their 2024 reelection run.

Without making much news, the event signaled to any loyal Democrat who had pondered the president's advancing age or the ticket's flagging popularity that it was time to put such thoughts aside. Biden and Harris remained a united ticket with the full support of the official organs of their party, and whatever their faults, the train was leaving the station.

The dress rehearsal the DNC held for the campaign was a simple and safe, if emphatic, exercise in practical politics. What came the following day was more audacious and far riskier.

When the DNC dignitaries gathered in the ballroom, they voted to move South Carolina to the front of the line. Along with resetting the location of the first vote, the DNC proposed scrambling the other early states on the schedule. According to the plan, three days after South Carolina's voters headed to the polls, New Hampshire and Nevada would simultaneously hold a second round of primaries. Georgia would go next and Michigan would be the last of the early states.

The basic intention behind the changes was clear. This lineup was a major injection of diversity into the process. According to census data, the new list of states brought over 3.1 million new voters of color into the first two rounds of the primary process. Swapping Iowa for Nevada and South Carolina meant the early primary electorate would be about 24 percent more diverse. Reordering the states also removed caucuses from the party's early primary calculus.

These moves followed all of Biden's recommendations. They also rewarded South Carolina, the state that propelled him to the nomination in 2020.

In elevating South Carolina, Biden also seemed to be dealing a blow to progressive insurgents—a notion that the allies of Bernie Sanders instantly seized upon. Faiz Shakir, Sanders's 2020 campaign manager, blasted the proposal. In a *New York Times* op-ed published shortly after Biden's letter was made public, Shakir argued that South Carolina's conservative political tradition, its hostility to organized labor, and its status as a staunchly red state in general elections made it undeserving of the special honor of going first. To him, the move was more about doing a favor for Biden's allies in the state, who helped him vault past Sanders in the primary.

"We all know why South Carolina got the nod," Shakir wrote. "President Biden, Representative Jim Clyburn and many of his top supporters were buoyed by their campaign's comeback in February 2020 when the state delivered Mr. Biden his first victory of the season—and a big one at that. . . . None of that story is a reason to put South Carolina first, however."

Nina Turner, the co-chair of Sanders's campaign in 2020 who was mulling her own potential presidential campaign, saw the move as an attempt to handicap her and others on the left.

"There is only one reason why they changed that, and that is to make sure that there's a higher hurdle for progressive candidates to jump," Turner told the online publication Semafor shortly after the DNC vote. "There are plenty of states with diverse electorates that they could select to be the first. But they pick South Carolina, deliberately, to try to thwart the chances of any progressive candidate. . . . It's not in service to Black voters, it's in service to artificially creating momentum for their status-quo candidates."

There is some truth to this interpretation. Both Biden and Hillary Clinton scored some of their biggest wins over Bernie Sanders in South Carolina. Accordingly, moving up South Carolina's primary might also be seen as a way to put obstacles in the path of any challenger to the incumbent president or—one day—to his anointed successor.

On the other hand, in 2008, Barack Obama bested Clinton and

John Edwards in South Carolina by a thumping margin as a progressive insurgent. Moreover, Edwards had won the South Carolina primary four years before that, balking John Kerry on his otherwise untroubled march to the nomination. If Biden chose South Carolina for its predictability, he might be disappointed.

The remainder of the new calendar also largely aligned with Biden's general election needs. It would spur Democrats to get a head start organizing the key battlegrounds of Nevada, Michigan, and Georgia, close contests in 2020 that were essential to Biden's electoral college victory.

Biden's slate stripped Iowa—a state which had gone for Trump in two straight elections—of power. However, New Hampshire, which Biden had won by seven points in 2020, was staying in the early window. And, according to Elleithee, an RBC member, it was Biden who saved their spot.

"It is because of President Biden that New Hampshire is being offered a waiver to stay second in the nation," Elleithee said.

Elleithee noted there was substantial support for pushing New Hampshire down the list.

"A lot of people were saying, 'Well, let's bump them. Let's maybe push them further back into the window. That might actually make more sense.' The president saved them," he explained.

With South Carolina going first, New Hampshire could no longer claim it was the "first-in-the-nation" primary. Sharing a date with Nevada also meant it was not alone as the second stop on the calendar. Still, Elleithee made the case that, practically speaking, this is where New Hampshire had always been—as the perennial second contest—and that the distinction of being the first-in-the-nation primary, rather than a caucus, was always a "fallacy."

"The committee was torn on whether or not New Hampshire should remain in the early window at all," Elleithee elaborated. "I think they made some very compelling arguments to stay in early window, not the least of which is they make the most sense [as the representative] from the East."

In his assessment of why the DNC kept New Hampshire among the early states, Elleithee touched on a few of the requirements the committee had as it evaluated the various applicants. Ideally, the DNC wanted states from the different major regions of the country. It also wanted to select states where candidates would be able to compete without massive budgets. This gave smaller states, which are easier and cheaper to barnstorm, an advantage in the selection process. It also meant locations with pricier media markets, like New Jersey—which is largely serviced by television stations in the major cities of New York and Philadelphia—were out.

"There were slim pickings among the Eastern states," Elleithee explained.

Delaware, which is the second smallest state by size and roughly a third non-white, would seem to fit the bill. However, in Delaware's case, its association with Biden proved damaging. A former DNC official asked to maintain anonymity when discussing Delaware due to the sensitivity of the matter.

"Let's stay on background on the Delaware question," the official said. "At least until Joe Biden leaves office."

According to this official, when the Delaware delegation came to the DNC, they were told in no uncertain terms that it would not work out by Elaine Kamarck, an RBC member and fiancée of Representative Steny Hoyer of Maryland, who was the Democrats' House majority whip at the time.

Kamarck saw Delaware as "the worst idea." She had two opposing concerns. Legitimate challengers might stay away and view the state as in the bag for Biden. Meanwhile, more left-field upstarts like Marianne

Williamson, the New Age author who entered the Democratic Primary in 2020 and was running again in 2024, could "wound" Biden if they decided to compete in Delaware and notched even 30 percent of the vote.

"There is literally no upside to having the home state of the incumbent president in the early window," Kamarck said, according to the staffer. "It becomes a wasted primary."

With few options in the East palatable to the RBC, New Hampshire would basically stay second on the calendar. Iowa received no such olive branches, and a wide range of voices pronounced the outcome just.

"Iowa failed the country," Shakir wrote in his op-ed. "It embarrassed a party that was trying to defeat Donald Trump by appealing to democratic foundations and principles. And most unfortunately, Iowa failed its own residents, who cycle after cycle had shown an incredible seriousness of purpose in fulfilling their unique role to choose a president."

While others may have rejoiced at Iowa's downfall, the decision left many in the state with raw feelings. Scott Brennan, Iowa's representative on the RBC, told a local newspaper, *The Courier*, that the move would help drive the state further right.

"Republicans in Iowa will seize this opportunity to double down on their caucuses and feed the narrative that Democrats have turned their back on Iowa," Brennan said. "We are creating a self-fulfilling prophecy of electoral failure and creating a Fox News bubble for our presidential candidates in which they have no opportunity or responsibility to meet and communicate with voters in red-leaning states."

There was bitterness from New Hampshire too. Brennan voted against the measure along with New Hampshire's RBC delegate Joanne Dowdell. "It is frustrating because the DNC is set to punish us despite the fact we don't have the ability to change state law," Dowdell said.

Her comment underscored a major potential problem with the DNC's plan. The party organization controls the nomination process and the delegates that are awarded based on the primary results, but it is not actually in charge of the primaries themselves. While the DNC voted to make changes to the primary calendar, it had no direct power to make that calendar a reality. Primaries are run by state governments and scheduled according to state law, and caucuses are generally run by the state-level political parties, which are not obliged to take orders from the DNC.

In New Hampshire's case, the law mandating the first-in-the-nation primary was bipartisan and applied to both the Democratic and Republican races. For its changes to be implemented, the DNC would need to rely on the good graces of New Hampshire's secretary of state or legislature. Iowa and its caucus law posed a similar problem—and, as of this writing—both states are led by Republicans who have little motivation to do any favors for the DNC.

There were similar problems elsewhere. While Georgia was theoretically being rewarded by the committee with an opportunity to move up its date, it had a Republican governor and secretary of state who control the calendar. As of this writing, both of these Republicans insist the date for the primary is already set at its normal place outside of the early window.

Republican power in Georgia meant the DNC's handling of its reforms gave the opposition the ability to create serious headaches for the Democrats. It also highlighted a simple fact: while the Democrats' primary process was mired in debate and uncertainty, the Republican National Committee and its constituents swiftly signed off on their 2024 schedule and were set to maintain their status quo. While the major establishment Democratic institutions may have been more unified than their progressive counterparts, they couldn't match the ruthless efficiency on the opposite side of the two-party system.

The DNC could not dictate the primary calendar outright, but its control of the nominating process gave it substantial leverage to enforce its will, and the Rules and Bylaws Committee sketched out a range of fairly stern penalties to that end. This enforcement mechanism was based on a precedent set in 2008, which was the last time the Democrats had a major fight over the primary calendar.

That cycle showed how difficult and dangerous it can be for the party to change the primary process. The problems in the 2008 race actually started in 2006 when, in a gesture at diversity, the DNC opened up the pre-window period to add South Carolina and Nevada for the 2008 primary. That last series of reforms to the calendar ended up putting the entire system through an intense stress test.

When the pre-window period was expanded to include Nevada and South Carolina for 2008, Florida and Michigan opted to jump the line. Each scheduled primaries before Iowa (and all the other early states) without obtaining a waiver. The DNC initially reacted harshly, stripping Florida and Michigan of all their delegates at the national convention and warning candidates not to campaign there.

This became a potent issue in the protracted contest between Barack Obama and Hillary Clinton. Obama had done as the DNC wished. He had taken his name off the Michigan ballot (it wasn't an option to do this in Florida) and he had refrained from campaigning in either of the two states. Most of the other candidates in the primary, including Biden, had done the same. Clinton had not; unlike the other candidates, she had kept her name on the Michigan ballot and had visited Florida again and again for fundraisers in the days leading up to its vote. Naturally, Clinton won the most votes in both Florida and Michigan. When the officially recognized primaries were over, Obama held an insurmountable lead in pledged delegates and he was set to become the nominee—*unless* you were to count the disqualified delegates from Florida and Michigan.

With the race down to the wire, the Clinton campaign and its supporters—hardened in opposition to Obama by months of campaign brawling—seized on the possibility of legitimizing the Florida and Michigan delegates, who, after all, were backed by the votes of millions of Americans, and just maybe snatching the nomination from Obama. It turned into a bruising battle, which featured a tumultuous protest by hard-core Clinton supporters on the outskirts of a decisive 2008 Rules and Bylaws Committee meeting at a Marriott hotel in Washington.

In the end, the RBC settled on a face-saving compromise: Florida and Michigan would each have half of their pledged delegates seated. It was not enough for Clinton to win or to throw the convention into chaos, but it was something. The rogue states were punished for their intransigence, and the nomination was settled, but the roughly two million Democrats who voted in Michigan's and Florida's primaries would at least have some voice at the convention.

That compromise served as the blueprint when the RBC met in late 2022 and outlined the penalty for states that refuse to comply with the DNC's 2024 primary calendar. The rules would automatically strip any state that held a nominating contest outside the window without a valid waiver of half its delegates. Moreover, any candidate that campaigned in such a state would lose all pledged delegates from that state.

During the 2022 RBC meeting, David McDonald, a committee member, elaborated: "The penalties [for non-compliant states] are automatic and don't require a vote of the DNC. You lose half your delegates without us taking any action. But in practice, we are highly likely to take away the rest of the delegates with an actual vote depending on the state. That's what happened in 2008. Because if a state is large enough, half of its delegates is still a big chunk of delegates. So for larger states, we might well take away the rest of the delegates [and] go beyond the automatic."

Of course, the enforcers of these rules on the RBC would confront a situation somewhat unlike 2008. Rather than policing up-jumped states who sought to disrupt the established order, the RBC would be trying to institute a new one. And their vision of enforcement gives color to the fears that the DNC's calendar reforms could go seriously awry. If New Hampshire scheduled a primary before South Carolina, as its long-standing law would require its secretary of state to do, Joe Biden's reelection campaign and any other campaigns in the field would face hard choices driven by New Hampshire's potential as a battle-ground state in a general election race.

If the state's leaders follow through on their threat to ignore the DNC's rulings, Biden would be forced to either boycott New Hamp-shire, which would mean devoting no early resources to the state, or to campaign there and open himself up to delegate penalties in a primary or charges of hypocrisy later on.

Biden entered the 2024 race as a powerful incumbent within his own party, but he won the White House in 2020 by fewer than 100,000 votes spread across several states. As his reelection bid began, Biden could much more easily afford to sacrifice New Hampshire's convention delegates than risk losing its electoral votes. State leaders potentially could exert considerable leverage on the Biden campaign by arguing that sitting out a noncompliant primary would cost him those electoral votes in the general. As of this writing and as the 2024 general election draws nearer, those pressures appear likely to build.

Biden's own calendar may have created land mines for him on the general election trail. But the delegate issue wasn't necessarily the most dangerous looming obstacle the reforms posed for the party.

That was Biden's fifth principle. In his letter outlining his recom-mendations for the primaries, Biden called for the calendar to be reset every four years. In agreeing to do this, the party baked in potential fights down the road.

The infighting that may occur during the 2024 race is likely to be just a small preview of what will come down the line. There has already been acrimony over the calendar with a powerful incumbent and a primary that is not expected to be competitive. Imagine what could happen if a more crowded field of candidates fights over the calendar. The reforms guarantee that, every four years, the stage will be set for serious battles and candidates scrambling to gain advantages from the schedules.

The calendar decisions each cycle, by necessity, will occur in obscure party committee meetings well before anyone casts a vote. Thanks to modern laws, you won't find anyone lighting a cigarette in those meetings, but they could represent a return of the smoke-filled room. After all of his efforts to heal the divisions within the party, Biden created a new venue for major internecine fights going forward.

Perhaps the clearest winners from the calendar makeover were South Carolina and the man who was pivotal in delivering the state to Biden: Jim Clyburn. At the end of the DNC meeting in Philadelphia, the last word went to "Big Jim," who delivered final remarks from the dais. His stamp on the new process was clear.

On his way out of the venue, we asked Clyburn whether he had talked with Biden about moving his home state to first position.

"Not for one second. Never. I don't know where people get that idea," Clyburn insisted.

However, as he was walking away, Clyburn paused, turned around, and seemed to admit he had indeed made a request on behalf of his state.

"I just wanted to be in the window," he said with a wry smile.

Chapter 16

AFTERBURN

THE PROGRESSIVE SURGE THAT IGNITED IN 2016 OFFERED A CHAL-
lenge to the Democratic party and posed practical questions. Will
it last, or is it a flash in the pan? Who will lead the insurgents as they try
to reach the next level and enact their transformative vision for American politics?

Bernie Sanders—the man who struck the match—does not have a
clear answer. A pair of phone conversations with him showed the questions that remain for the movement he inspired may be even more fundamental than worrying about its future.

"You use the word 'the left.' I'm not quite sure what that means,"
Sanders said in one of our interviews for this book.

Sanders knew the progressive movement he helped galvanize isn't
necessarily a unified force. He had no clear heir, and the leaders that
have emerged in the space have demonstrated vastly different priorities.

While progressives may not be entirely on the same page, in the
nearly ten years since Sanders launched his first presidential campaign, they have unquestionably become a force. The work Joe Biden,

a mainstream Democratic president, has done to cater to progressives suggests they will have an ongoing, important role in the party. And, from taking down local machines, to pressing for reforms in the primary process, and pushing through their legislative priorities in a hostile Congress, it's also evident they have already had immense impact. These gains, however fragile they may be, and the efforts of Biden, Barack Obama, and others to build an alliance with progressives within the Democratic Party, are a profound tribute to the political significance of the movement Bernie Sanders shaped.

While Sanders was reluctant to characterize the larger left, he knew what he wanted his own movement to be. For Sanders, progressive politics should focus on economics and policy rather than identity.

"The struggle for America is the need to bring together the working-class, low-income people in this country who form the vast majority of our people. It is not identity politics. Alright? It is not seeing that a Black woman goes to the moon. That's fine. It is to make sure that Black kids in America—they have the opportunity to get a college education, they get health care as a human right, they get jobs that pay them, and everybody else, a living wage," Sanders said, adding, "Our job is to bring people together around an agenda that works for all workers."

By explicitly rejecting "identity politics" in favor of socialist economics, Sanders chose a side in a debate that raged among progressives as they strived to build a winning coalition amid a series of new movements like MeToo, Black Lives Matter, and the push for transgender rights. Sanders also dialed in on the central rift within the Democratic Party and the question that bedeviled the Democratic Socialists of America in their electoral work: whether to operate within the Democratic Party or outside of it.

In his three Senate races, Sanders ran as a Democrat in the primary, won the nomination, and then declined it before running as an independent. During his 2016 presidential campaign, he briefly enrolled as a Democrat to participate in the New Hampshire primary before promptly un-enrolling. Sanders's contortions frustrated many mainline Democrats who viewed him as an invading force.

While Sanders was not exactly a Democrat, he clearly was invested in the party's future and saw it as the best vessel for progressives' ambitions. Indeed, pulling the party leftward was the overriding goal of his presidential bids.

"Obviously, what my presidential campaign was about was taking on the entire Democratic establishment," Sanders said to us. "You know, we had almost no support. . . . When I ran the first time, I had one senator supporting me. Second time, I think one senator, a few members of the House. So, we were taking on the political establishment, taking on the economic establishment of the country, taking on the media establishment. . . . We took them all on, but that is not only the right thing to do in my view for the Democratic Party, it's good politics as well."

In conversation, Sanders revealed why he's so focused on changing the party's establishment. To Sanders, the failure of Democratic leadership to connect with the working class was a major part of the country's shift to the right in the Trump era.

"The idea that working-class people are increasingly voting for these right-wing Republicans—corporately owned Republicans—is extremely painful to me," Sanders explained. "It just speaks to the degree that people perceive—and with some degree to be truthful—that the Democratic Party has become a coastal party, run by elitists and not a party dedicated to needs of working families."

These comments alluded to the personal struggles at the root of Sanders's political project. But forging a personal connection wasn't necessarily a strength for Sanders either. He had long disdained personality-driven discourse as "political gossip." He had a deep aversion to sharing his own story.

While rallies with hour-long speeches railing against economic inequality were a core feature of his campaigns, Sanders's advisers struggled to get him to tie experiences from his own life to the conversation. As Sanders prepared to run for president a second time in 2020, Mark Longabaugh, one of the top consultants from his 2016 campaign, drafted a plan. It was informed by mistakes from Sanders's first run and encouraged the candidate to make a more personal appeal.

Among the staff the document became known as the "Human Bernie Memo." It outlined a plan for Sanders to "highlight biographical elements" by announcing his campaign in Brooklyn.

"The symbolism of announcing where Bernie Sanders was born allows us to contrast a son of working class, immigrant parents with a man (Trump) raised in Queens who inherited a fortune and was raised in privilege," the memo said. In a nod to the energy of the new generation of progressives, Sanders's team hoped to have Alexandria Ocasio-Cortez by his side from the very beginning of the race (although the memo misspelled her name "Octavio-Cortez").

Longabaugh ultimately did not join Sanders's 2020 team. However, Sanders seemed to have taken the memo to heart and went on to share more on the trail about his personal life. Sanders kicked off his second campaign with a speech at his first alma mater, Brooklyn College. In those remarks he alluded to how his upbringing shaped him.

"My experience as a child, living in a family that struggled economically, powerfully influenced my life and my values," Sanders said. "I know where I came from, and that is something I will never forget."

That was about as close as Sanders ever got to telling the story that many of those closest to him knew had inspired his political mission. His parents were both Jewish. Sanders's father was an immigrant from

Poland and his mother was the daughter of Russian émigrés. Both of them died when he was a young man.

Watching his mother suffer from an illness drove Sanders's obsession with health care. That central tragedy of his youth also prompted Sanders to leave Brooklyn for Vermont.

In his interviews for this book, Sanders explained how his personal story crystallized into his ideological project.

"I come from a working-class family and, throughout my political life, being the mayor, congressman, senator, presidential candidate, what I've always felt my mission was, was to stand with the working class of this country and take on the oligarchy which has so much economic and political power," Sanders said.

For Sanders, turning the Democratic Party into an organization that represented working people would be the culmination of his life's work. And yet, even as he had become one of the most prominent members of that party and exerted an undeniable influence over it, in conversation, Sanders admitted he wasn't sure his mission would succeed. His cynicism was rooted in an acknowledgment of the institutional inertia of the Big Dem establishment.

"I think the Democratic Party today—right now—is in a pivotal moment and it has to make a very fundamental decision. In a sense, it's what our campaign . . . the presidential campaign, was about," Sanders explained. "The decision is, do you become a party which stands for the working class of the country, which involves the working class in the decision-making, which creates a grassroots movement, or . . . do you remain a corporately controlled party beholden to your wealthy campaign contributors and to the corporate media as well. And that's really the struggle that we're in right now."

Despite his withering assessment of the party, Sanders had a positive relationship with its leader at the time, President Joe Biden. As he expanded upon his own conception of "the left," Sanders indicated it actually included the Biden agenda.

"It means demanding the wealthy start paying their fair share of taxes. . . . It means a lot of what was in the American Rescue Plan on an emergency basis and what's in Build Back Better, which means dealing with the basic needs of our people in terms of, you know, in my view, Medicare for All, guaranteeing health care to all people as a right," Sanders said. "It means making public colleges and universities tuition-free, forgiving student debt. It means creating millions of jobs, building the affordable housing that we need. . . . Transforming our energy system away from fossil fuel to save the planet, home health care, that agenda."

With Biden's efforts to court progressives, the good feelings were mutual. Sanders even came close to joining the administration.

During Biden's first years in office, a wave of unionization was making headlines and hitting some of the country's biggest companies including Amazon and Starbucks. Sanders, who made backing labor a core part of his presidential campaign, was in the thick of it. He met with workers at union shops and held rallies for their strikes and drives.

Sanders claimed Biden reached out to him about joining the cabinet as secretary of labor. It was a story the White House did not refute and perhaps the most dramatic example of Biden's efforts to make overtures to the Democratic Party's progressive wing.

Sanders, through an inadvertent slip of the tongue, seemed almost wistful that he had been unable to take the job.

"I wanted to be—you know, gave thought to—becoming labor secretary," Sanders said, catching himself mid-sentence.

He went on to explain what got in the way: the battles over Biden's legislative agenda and the slight Senate majority Democrats won in 2020 made it imperative for him to stay in his Senate seat. At the time,

Vermont had a Republican governor who would have been able to pick Sanders's replacement.

"You know what, I would've been appointed if we hadn't ended up winning those two seats in Georgia . . . where the balance of the Senate hung," Sanders said with a raspy chuckle. "So, clearly, I had to stay in the Senate."

It's easy to see why Sanders would be particularly interested in the Labor Department. The resurgent union movement made him think the tide was turning back to "New Deal" politics, mid-century progressivism, and the unifying focus on workers' economic interests that he yearned for. Yet, as he described that dynamic, it was impossible not to notice that he seemed to be subtly comparing Biden to the only president who might be described as an icon of the left: Franklin Delano Roosevelt.

"I think we are seeing the beginning of what we saw in the 1930s. The conditions are different, but I think in the 1930s, during the Depression, you know, with the support of President Roosevelt, you saw a huge increase in labor union membership," said Sanders. "So I am not . . . unconfident that we may see the same thing in the coming years."

Sanders's comments provided vivid proof of how, under Biden, the Democratic Party was teetering between a new coalition with progressives and the infighting of the past. Just as Sanders was positioning Biden as a progressive leader who was playing the Roosevelt role and bringing the country in a new direction, he turned back to his deep skepticism about the Democratic Party establishment.

"I think people are tired of the growth of inequality, the growth of oligarchy, and they're prepared to stand up, and fight back, and move toward trade unions," Sanders explained. "I think that is just a major, major step forward for the country. If the Democratic Party is smart—which I don't know that it will be—it could be a real political advantage."

Sanders continually pointed to the fact his vision of the left, with its focus on transformative economic policies, was "enormously popular." He was not wrong on that front. When we spoke, polls showed that about 70 percent of Americans supported a public health care system. While the "Medicare for All" brand was somewhat more polarizing, it was supported by a majority of the country too. Student debt forgiveness was even more popular.

That appeal was, in Sanders's view, key to Democrats' hopes of stronger victories in the future. It also was, in no small part, attributable to his work. However, even as Sanders believed the country would be eager to accept his platform, he conceded progressives will have to navigate between transformational change and achieving incremental victories—particularly with the GOP back on the rise.

"Unfortunately, given the fact that we now have Republicans controlling the House . . . we're not going to be able to do what needs to be done," Sanders said. "So if we do the best that we can do right now, on one hand, on the other hand, we continue to raise consciousness about the real solutions facing the crises in the country today."

And Republicans weren't the only ones standing in the way of the progressive agenda. Sanders also criticized "conservative corporate Democrats in the Senate," alluding no doubt to the radical centrists, namely, West Virginia's Joe Manchin and Arizona's Kyrsten Sinema.

While he was concerned about continuing to grow the progressive footprint in Washington, Sanders recognized it has exploded since his first presidential campaign.

"I'm very proud of the fact we have elected more strong progressives for the House of Representatives than in modern American history," he said. "The House is now far more progressive, for example, than it was when I was elected there in 1991."

Securing those gains weighed on Sanders's mind.

"Well, I'll tell you what worries me very much is that there are now Super PACs raising a whole lot of money to defeat progressives in the House and elsewhere," he explained. "I tried to have the DNC outlaw Super PAC money in Democratic primaries, but without success."

Sanders believed progressives' battle with the "corporate Democrats" in the establishment was far from over. "I think we have gotten them very, very nervous," he said, adding, "I think they're going to do their best to try to defeat us."

Though he was reluctant to talk in personal, emotional terms, Sanders dropped his guard somewhat in discussing the threat the establishment might pose to the new progressives in Congress who he helped inspire.

"I have played a role in many of those campaigns and will do my best to make sure that they get reelected," said Sanders. "They're going to be facing a lot of money . . . and we will stand with them."

Bringing up "the Squad" prompted an uncharacteristically intimate moment from Sanders.

"I am very fond personally of the new progressives who are in the House, the Squad and the additions that we have seen in recent years. I really am," Sanders said, adding, "On a personal level and a policy level, I think they are a breath of fresh air for America. I think they are giving hope to their generation and to the American people, so I feel emotionally and politically very close to them."

Yet, when it came to talking about his own part in the progressive story, Sanders retreated to his insistence that politics should not be personal. "I don't wanna talk about legacy. Okay?" he said gruffly during one of our conversations. "You got any other questions?"

After a brief pause, Sanders allowed himself to contemplate the future. His concerns weren't about the judgment of history. He acknowledged that's beyond his control, and moreover trying to tip those scales is contrary to his nature. What Sanders wanted to leave to the world was a message and a model for politics.

"It is what it is, and people make their determination," Sanders said of his legacy. "What's important for everybody in the progressive movement is to educate, to organize, to stand up to enormously powerful, public forces, and to create the kind of nation we know that we can become."

ACKNOWLEDGMENTS

THIS BOOK REFLECTS THE WORK—AND THE PATIENCE—OF MORE people than we can name and thank in these lines.

Hunter is grateful to his wife, Gloria Walker, who has been a kind partner and crucial adviser. He also knows this book and so much more would not have been possible without the love of his moms, sister, brother-in-law, suegros, cuñados, and Bertha.

Luppe is thankful for his fiancée, Polly Mosendz, his parents and sisters, and Polly's mother and grandmother, and for the oceans of wisdom, kindness, and support they've given him.

We are both indebted to each other's loved ones, without whom we know our writing partnership could not have been possible.

This project was guided by many skillful hands. First and foremost, Molly Atlas, our brilliant, indefatigable, and steadfast agent. We relied on Molly from the first word of the manuscript to the last. Molly enthusiastically embraced our idea for this project, helped us to refine it, and ensured it ended up in the right hands. Our insightful editor, Tom Mayer, opened the door for two first-time authors, gave us much needed direction, and helped us steer our project to its distant shore with elegance and grace. Moreover, Tom's whole team at W. W. Norton impressed us again and again with their talent and professionalism. We want to offer particular thanks to Lauren Abbate, Nneoma Amadiobi, Steve Colca, Jessica Friedman, Laura Goldin, Matthew Hoch, William Avery Hudson, Yana Lande, Johana Ramos-Boyer, Don Rifkin, Rachel Salzman, and Sarahmay Wilkinson.

In addition, Hunter would like to thank Josh Marshall, David Kurtz, and the team at Talking Points Memo, who gave vital support in the final months of this project. He is also deeply appreciative of the friends who provided advice, contacts, and support along the way, including Alexander Chee, Chris Hayes, Richard Rushfield, Dolita Cathcart, Yariv Chen, Michael B. Kelley, Lisa Belkin, Danny Bloomfield, Colin Campbell, and his mentor, the late Gordy Weil. Luppe would particularly like to thank Sarah Binder, whose in-depth work on the filibuster informs much of the beginning of Chapter 11; he also wants to acknowledge his good fortune in being able to rely on Brian Beutler, Teddy Goff, Caitlyn Jacobs, and Jeremy Jacobs, dear friends who possess the best political minds he knows. We both would also like to express deep gratitude to Kevin Kruse for being one of our first readers.

We have elsewhere acknowledged the hundreds of people we spoke to, named and unnamed, quoted and unquoted, but it goes without saying that we could not have begun to write this book without their willingness to commit their time, get on the phone, and answer probing questions—an act of real generosity that often goes unacknowledged. Our sources and subjects trusted us with their stories, and we are profoundly grateful for every moment of their time.

SOURCES AND
FURTHER READING

As we explained up front, the material in this book is primarily drawn from our own original reporting including hundreds of hours of interviews specifically for this book. We also drew from time spent on the campaign trail during the 2016, 2020, and 2022 elections, in the press pool of the Biden White House, and covering other key in-person events, including union rallies, town halls, election days, and the 2023 Democratic National Committee winter meetings.

To supplement our own reporting, we also relied on primary sources including original video broadcasts of key events and contemporaneous reporting from major media outlets. Our work also drew from archival materials and books.

The following list includes some of our key source material for readers who might be interested in revisiting some of our work or learning more about this topic. Each source is approximately arranged based on order of appearance in a given chapter. We are very grateful to the sources and subjects who shared their stories with us and to the reporters and researchers who helped inform our work.

PROLOGUE

Somanader, Tanya. "In Memory of Beau Biden: 'Quite Simply, The Finest Man Any of Us Have Ever Known.'" Obama White House. National Archives. May 30, 2015.

Baker, Peter, and Helene Cooper. "Clinton Is Said to Accept Secretary of State Position." *New York Times*, November 21, 2008.

Walker, Hunter. "Biden Shocked His Own Team with His 2016 Announcement," Yahoo News, October 22, 2015.

Siddiqui, Sabrina, Lauren Gambino, and Dan Roberts. "DNC Apologizes to Bernie Sanders Amid Convention Chaos in Wake of Email Leak." *The Guardian*, July 25, 2016.

Enten, Harry. "Registered Voters Who Stayed Home Probably Cost Clinton the Election." FiveThirtyEight, January 5, 2017.

CHAPTER 1—KALORAMA

Cooper, Rebecca. "Is Jeff Bezos Buying Again in Kalorama?" *Washington Business Journal*, January 8, 2020.

Gamerekian, Barbara. "She Who Has Seen the Wheel Come Full Circle." *New York Times*, April 21, 1987.

"Ambassador Esther Coopersmith's 90th Birthday Party in Washington, DC," YouTube video. Posted by Janet Donovan. January 18, 2020.

Assessing Russian Activities and Intentions in Recent US Elections, official government ed. Washington, DC: Office of the Director of National Intelligence, January 6, 2017.

"Joe Biden Says He's Running in 2020—Then Corrects Himself." BBC News, March 17, 2019.

Thompson, Krissah, Kathy Orton, and Emily Heil. "The Obamas Just Bought Their Rental Home in Washington." *Washington Post*, May 31, 2017.

Milliot, Jim, and Rachel Deahl. "The Obamas' Book Deals Spark $65 Million Mystery." *Publishers Weekly*, March 3, 2017.

Keyes, Charley, Dana Bash, and Chris Lawrence. "Pentagon: Letting Openly Gay Troops Serve Won't Hurt Military." CNN, December 10, 2010.

Nilsen, Ella. "A Pro-Gun Democrat Could Win in Trump Country. Where Does That Leave Gun Control Activism?" Vox, March 12, 2018.

Herndon, Astead W. "Conor Lamb, House Moderate, on Biden's Win, 'the Squad' and the Future of the Democratic Party." *New York Times*, November 8, 2020.

CHAPTER 2—JUSTICE DEMOCRATS

"Bernie Sanders News Conference." C-SPAN, April 30, 2015.

"DNC Database Press Conference | Jeff Weaver." YouTube video. Posted by Bernie Sanders. December 18, 2015. https://www.youtube.com/watch?v=R7m-nnl7LSQ.

"Sanders Steps Up Feud with Democratic Establishment." Reuters, May 23, 2016.

Stahl, Jeremy. "Bernie Called Out the Clintons for 'Racist' Language, and Hillary Didn't Even Bat an Eye." *Slate*, April 14, 2016.

"Election 2016: Exit Polls." *New York Times*, November 8, 2016.

"Form 1: Statement of Organization." Federal Election Commission. FEC-1058293, April 5, 2016. Available online at: https://docquery.fec.gov/cgi-bin/forms/C00613810/1058293/.

"Political Group 'Brand New Congress' Modeled After Bernie Sanders," YouTube video, posted by MSNBC, May 19, 2016. https://www.youtube.com/watch?v=rvGtVu8gmtg.

"Form 2: Statement of Candidacy." Federal Election Commission. Image#

201705109053514055, May 10, 2017. Available online at: https://docquery.fec.gov/pdf/055/201705109053514055/201705109053514055.pdf.

"Form 2: Statement of Candidacy." Federal Election Commission. Image# 201705159053754545, May 15, 2017. Available online at: https://docquery.fec.gov/pdf/545/201705159053754545/201705159053754545.pdf.

CHAPTER 3—THE PEOPLE'S REPUBLIC OF QUEENS

Dao, James. "Manton Plans to Retire from Congress at End of Year." *New York Times*, July 22, 1998.

Duhalde, David. "DSA, YDS Membership Grew Fast, Still Growing." Democratic Socialists of America, November 8, 2016.

Krieg, Gregory. "Democratic Socialists Are Taking Themselves Seriously. Should Democrats?" CNN, August 8, 2017.

"100% Authentic—Civet Select—Kopi Luwak: Taste the World's Most Exotic Cup of Coffee" Archived by the Internet Archive February 3, 2018. Accessed April 15, 2023. Available online at: http://web.archive.org/web/20180203092802/http://civetselect.com/.

"Alexandria Ocasio-Cortez Stuns Rep. Joe Crowley in NYC Democratic Primary." Spectrum News NY 1, June 26, 2018.

CHAPTER 4—PULLING TEETH

Tilford, Julia. "The 'Bernie Would've Won' Meme: What Is It, Where Did It Come From and Is It True?" Mic, December 22, 2016.

Norvell, Kim. "Elizabeth Warren Finds New Strength among Bernie Sanders' Key Constituencies, Iowa Poll Says." *Des Moines Register*, September 21, 2019.

Theodros, Abby. "Las Vegas Restaurant Owner Speaks on Bernie's Heart Issue." FOX5 Las Vegas, October 2, 2019. Video available online at: https://www.facebook.com/FOX5Vegas/videos/las-vegas-restaurant-owner-speaks-on-bernies-heart-issue/392101741471056/.

Walker, Hunter. "At an Iowa Rally, Progressive Voters Already Talk about an Ocasio-Cortez Presidency." Yahoo News, November 11, 2019.

CHAPTER 5—FOR THE PEOPLE

Harris, Kamala. *The Truths We Hold: An American Journey*. New York: Penguin Press, 2019.

The Honorable Ronald V. Dellums, U.S. Representative of California (1971–1988), Oral History Interview, Final Edited Transcript, official government ed. Washington, DC: Office of the Historian, US House of Representatives, 2012.

Dellums, Ronald V., and H. Lee Halterman. *Lying Down with the Lions: A Public Life from the Streets of Oakland to the Halls of Power*. Boston: Beacon Press, 2000. Quoted in T. R. Goldman, "Ronald Dellums, Who Entered Congress a Firebrand and Left a Statesman, Dies at 82," *Washington Post*, July 30, 2018.

Martin, Jonathan, Astead W. Herndon, and Alexander Burns. "How Kamala Harris's Campaign Unraveled." *New York Times*, November 29, 2019.

Kamala Harris for District Attorney, "Police Reform & Effectiveness," 2003. Archived by the Internet Archive December 31, 2004. Accessed April 15, 2023. Available online at: https://web.archive.org/web/20031230025823/http://www.kamalaharris.org/about/issues/policereformandeffectiveness/.

Serby, Benjamin. "New York's Last Socialist Congressperson." *Jacobin*. December 20, 2018.

San Francisco District Attorney Kamala Harris, "Smart on Crime," 2008. Archived by the Internet Archive January 21, 2008.

Sewell, Abby. "Two Occupy L.A. Protesters Arrested at Foreclosure Event." *L.A. Now (Los Angeles Times)*, February 9, 2012.

Minugh, Kim. "Occupy Marchers Decry Major Banks." *Sacramento Bee*. December 7, 2011.

CHAPTER 6—WAR ROOM

Debs, Eugene V. "How I Became a Socialist." *The Comrade*, April 1902. Available at https://wwnorton.com/college/history/foner2/contents/common/documents/ch18_1902_3_transcript.htm.

Krieg, Gregory, Ryan Nobles, and Annie Grayer. "How Bernie Sanders Became the Democratic Primary's Early Front-Runner" CNN, February 18, 2020.

"Senator Bernie Sanders Presidential Campaign Announcement." C-SPAN, March 2, 2019.

Kottasová, Ivana, and Saskya Vandoorne. "Iowa Democrats Are Getting Ready to Caucus … in the Caucasus." CNN, February 2, 2020.

"AP Decides Not to Declare Iowa Caucus Winner after Recount." Associated Press, February 27, 2020.

CHAPTER 7—REGIME CHANGE

Siddiqui, Sabrina, Lauren Gambino, and Dan Roberts. "DNC Apologizes to Bernie Sanders Amid Convention Chaos in Wake of Email Leak." *The Guardian*, July 25, 2016.

Jackson, David. "Democrats Face a Crucial Test in the South Carolina Primary: Can They Energize the African-American Vote?" *USA Today*, February 29, 2020.

Rogers, Katie, Glenn Thrush. "Anita Dunn and Bob Bauer: The Couple at the Center of Biden's Inner Circle," *New York Times*, February 15, 2023.

Walker, Hunter. "Biden Shocked His Own Team with his 2016 Announcement," Yahoo News, October 22, 2015.

Walker, Hunter. "Latinos, Sanders's Secret Weapon in Nevada, Could Make Him Unstoppable on Super Tuesday," Yahoo News, February 22, 2020.

Stern, Ken. " 'Swing Voters Draw the Line at Socialists': New Polling Suggests Key Voters Are Skeptical on Bernie, Love Bloomberg." *Vanity Fair*. February 3, 2020.

Goldenberg, Sally, Christopher Cadelago, "$375,000 Salaries, Furnished Housing and a Lot of Sushi: Inside Bloomberg's Spending Spree." Politico. January 31, 2020.

CHAPTER 8—COUP DE GRÂCE

John Lewis: Good Trouble. Directed by Dawn Porter. Atlanta, GA: CNN Films, 2020. Streaming.

"Representative Jim Clyburn Fish Fry." C-SPAN, June 21, 2019.

"Caucus Leader Backs Gephardt." Associated Press, December 11, 2003.

Walker, Hunter. "Powerful Rep. Jim Clyburn Explains Why He Chose Clinton." Yahoo News, February 23, 2016.

Arnholz, Jack. "South Carolinians 'Leery about that Title Socialist': Rep. James Clyburn" ABC News, February 23, 2020.

Spangler, Todd. "Joe Biden Holds 24-Point Lead vs. Bernie Sanders in Michigan Primary, Free Press Poll Says." *Detroit Free Press*, March 9, 2020.

Leibovich, Mark. "Dearest Colleague." *Washington Post*, January 23, 2004.

CHAPTER 9—THE INSIDE-OUTSIDE GAME

Thompson, A. C. "Inside the Secret Border Patrol Facebook Group Where Agents Joke About Migrant Deaths and Post Sexist Memes." ProPublica, July 1, 2019.

Ruiz, Michelle. "AOC's Next Four Years." *Vanity Fair*, October 28, 2020.

Walker, Hunter. "The U.S. Is 'Headed to Fascism,' Says Ocasio-Cortez after Tour of Detention Facilities at Southern Border" Yahoo News, July 2, 2019.

Dowd, Maureen. "It's Nancy Pelosi's Parade." *New York Times*, July 6, 2019.

Killough, Ashley, and Claire Foran. "Congresswomen 'Squad' Respond to Trump's Attacks: The US 'Belongs to Everyone.'" CNN, July 15, 2019.

Collinson, Stephen. "Progressive Lawmakers Stand Firm against Trump's Repeated Racist Attacks." CNN, July 16, 2019.

"The Squad" Interview: Gayle King's Full Conversation with AOC, Omar, Pressley & Tlaib." YouTube video. Posted by CBS Mornings. July 17, 2019.

Otterman, Sharon. "'The D.O.J. Has Failed Us': Eric Garner's Family Assails Prosecutors." *New York Times*, July 16, 2019.

CHAPTER 10—THE BRIDGE

Joe Biden—Official Campaign Page. "Biden-Sanders Unity Task Force Recommendations." JoeBiden.com. July 8, 2020.

Forgey, Quint. "Biden, Sanders Name Leaders of Their 'Unity Task Forces'—Including AOC." Politico. May 13, 2020.

Leibovich, Mark. "The Ascension of Ron Klain." *New York Times*, July 18, 2021.

Goba, Kadia. "Blue Dog Democrats Urge Biden to Focus on Bipartisan Priorities." Axios, December 30, 2020.

Sanders, Bernie, and John Nichols. *It's OK to Be Angry About Capitalism*. New York: Crown, 2023.

Trudo, Hanna. "Progressives Alarmed over Biden's New Chief of Staff." *The Hill*, February 1, 2023.

CHAPTER 11—FILIBUSTER

Binder, Sarah A., and Steven S. Smith. *Politics or Principle: Filibustering in the United States Senate*. Washington, DC: Brookings Institution Press, 1996.

Everett, Burgess. "McConnell Seeks to Protect Filibuster in Talks with Schumer." Politico, January 19, 2021.

"Fighting the Filibuster." *Whereas: Stories from the People's House* (blog). United States House of Representatives. June 11, 2020. Accessed April 15, 2023.

"Indicted Vice President Bids Senate Farewell: March 2, 1805." Art & History, United States Senate. Accessed April 15, 2023.

Byrd, Robert C., Mary Sharon Hall, and Wendy Wolff. *The Senate, 1789–1989: Classic Speeches, 1830–1993*. Washington, DC: US Government Printing Office, 1988.

Adams, John Quincy. *Memoirs of John Quincy Adams: Comprising Portions of his Diary from 1795 to 1848*. Philadelphia: J. B. Lippincott & Co., 1874.

Sammon, Alexander. "Clintonism's Zombie: Making Sense of Josh Gottheimer's Attempts to Sabotage the Democratic Agenda." *The American Prospect*, August 18, 2021.

Solender, Andrew, and Sarah Mucha. "Progressives 'Bamboozled' by Biden Meeting." Axios, October 28, 2021.

Kennedy, Joseph, Kenna Richards, and Douglas Soule. "Does Joe Manchin Have a $700,000 luxury yacht?" PolitiFact, September 28, 2018.

The Child Tax Credit: Temporary Expansion for 2021 Under the American Rescue Plan Act of 2021, official government ed. Washington, DC: Congressional Research Service, 2021.

Parolina, Zachary, Sophie Collyera, Megan A. Currana, and Christopher Wimera. "Monthly Poverty Rates among Children after the Expansion of the Child Tax Credit." *Poverty and Social Policy Brief* 5, no. 4 (2021).

CHAPTER 12—EMPIRE STATE

McFadden, Robert D. "Mario Biaggi, 97, Popular Bronx Congressman Who Went to Prison, Dies." *New York Times*, June 25, 2015.

Pantuso, Phillip. "State Assembly Speaker Sheldon Silver Arrested on Corruption Charges." *Brooklyn Magazine*, January 22, 2015.

"Sheldon Silver, Top New York Lawmaker Sentenced for Corruption, Dies Aged 77." *The Guardian*, January 24, 2022.

Campanile, Carl. "Silver Crony Alice Cancel Wins His State Assembly Seat." *New York Post*, April 20, 2016.

Goodnough, Abby. "Unions and Local Groups Join to Form a New Political Party." *New York Times*, July 7, 1998.

Meyerson, Harold. "Dan Cantor's Machine." *The American Prospect*, January 6, 2014.

Balz, Dan. "Cuomo Rejects Bid for President in '92." *Washington Post*, December 21, 1991.

Hammond, Bill, and Ian Kingsbury. "COVID-Positive Admissions Were Correlated with Higher Death Rates in New York Nursing Homes." *Empire Center for Public Policy*, February 18, 2021.

Villanueve, Marina. "Cuomo Administration 'Froze' over Nursing Home Data Requests." Associated Press, February 12, 2021.

Hogan, Bernadette, Carl Campanile, and Bruce Golding. "Cuomo Aide Melissa DeRosa Admits They Hid Nursing Home Data So Feds Wouldn't Find Out." *New York Post*, February 11, 2021.

Hogan, Gwynne, and Christopher Robbins. "Cuomo Unleashes Tirade on Queens Lawmaker and Threatens to 'Destroy' Him after Nursing Home Deaths Criticism." Gothamist, February 17, 2021.

CHAPTER 13—THUNDERDOME

Cillizza, Chris. "How Big Will the Republican Wave Be This Fall?" CNN, April 7, 2022.

Goldmacher, Shane. "New York Loses House Seat After Coming Up 89 People Short on Census." *New York Times*, April 26, 2021.

Rakich, Nathaniel. "New York's Proposed Congressional Map Is Heavily Biased Toward Democrats. Will It Pass?" FiveThirtyEight, January 31, 2022.

Mahoney, Bill. "Final New York Maps Released and Lead to Midnight Shuffle of Congressional Delegation." Politico, May 21, 2022.

Mutnick, Ally. "Ocasio-Cortez Calls on Maloney to Resign DCCC Chairmanship if He Primaries Colleague." Politico, May 19, 2022.

Schnitzer, Kyle, and Sam Raskin. "Rep. Mondaire Jones Blasted as 'Carpetbagger' by New Brooklyn Neighbors." *New York Post*, July 4, 2022.

Konig, Joseph. "Rep. Mondaire Jones Won't Rule Out Another Run for Congress." Spectrum News NY 1, December 20, 2022.

CHAPTER 14—THE NEXT EPISODE

"52% of Americans Disapprove of the President." Reuters, March 8, 2023.

Sherer, Michael. "No Labels Group Raises Alarms with Third-Party Presidential Preparations." *Washington Post*, April 2, 2023.

Snyder, Tanya, and Lauren Gardner. "FAA Meltdown Is Buttigieg's Next Political Headache." Politico, January 11, 2023.

Elbein, Saul. "Buttigieg Gets Hit from Right, Left in East Palestine Crisis." *The Hill*, February 28, 2023.

Sullivan, Kate. "CNN Poll: 75% of Democratic Voters Want Someone Other than Biden in 2024." CNN, July 27, 2022.

CHAPTER 15—SOFT LAUNCH

Weaver, Warren Jr. "Democratic Reform Commission Asks Full Party Participation for Youths From 18 to 20." *New York Times*, September 25, 1969.

Mailer, Norman. *Miami and the Siege of Chicago: An Informal History of the Republican and Democratic Conventions of 1968.* Cleveland: World Publishing Co., 1968.

Splaine, James R. "The Story of the 1975 Law Requiring The New Hampshire Presidential Primary to be First in the Nation." New Hampshire Department of State. 2021. Accessed April 15, 2023.

"The Guardian." *Stranglehold*. New Hampshire Public Radio. Podcast audio. September 11, 2019.

Apple, R. W. "Iowa's Weighty Caucuses: Significance by Accident." *New York Times*, January 25, 1988.

Ulmer, Clare. "Why Is Iowa First? A Brief History of the State's Caucuses." *Des Moines Register*, August 30, 2019.

Shakir, Faiz. "Biden Is Putting South Carolina First. I Won't Vote for That." *New York Times*, December 5, 2022.

Dewitt, Ethan. "DNC Delivers Blow to New Hampshire, Iowa with Overhaul of Primary Calendar." *New Hampshire Bulletin*, February 4, 2023.

Seelye, Katharine Q., and Jeff Zeleny. "Democrats Approve Deal on Michigan and Florida." *New York Times*, June 1, 2008.

CHAPTER 16—AFTERBURN

Palumbo-Liu, David. "Progressives Should Not Cave to Anemic Liberals in the 'Identity Politics' Debate." Vox, December 7, 2016.

Dovere, Edward-Isaac. "Sanders to Run as a Democrat—but Not Accept Nomination." Politico, May 21, 2018.

Walker, Hunter. "Bernie Sanders on What He Learned from Baseball, Brooklyn and His Family's Immigrant Roots." Yahoo News, September 9, 2019.

Sommer, Allison Kaplan. "Bernie Sanders Is—Finally—Willing to Talk About Being Jewish." *Haaretz*, September 10, 2019.